The Handbook of Human Resource Planning

Other HRM books from Blackwell Business

The Equal Opportunities Handbook
Helen Collins

Total Quality and Human Resources
Barrie Dale and Cary Cooper

The Handbook of Human Resource Planning
Gordon McBeath

Developments in the Management of Human Resources
John Storey

Women's Career Development
Barbara White, Charles Cox and Cary Cooper

Human Resource Management in Action Series

Series editor: Brian Towers

Successful Training Practice
Alan Anderson

Managing Performance Appraisal Systems
Gordon Anderson

European Employee Relations
Jeff Bridgford and John Stirling

Practical Employment Law
Paul Lewis

The Successful Management of Redundancy
Paul Lewis

Managing the Team
Mick Marchington

The Japanization of British Industry
Nick Oliver and Barry Wilkinson

Strategy and the Human Resource
Ken Starkey and Alan McKinlay

Handbook of Human Resource Management
Edited by Brian Towers

The Handbook of Human Resource Planning

GORDON McBEATH

Copyright © Gordon McBeath, 1992

The right of Gordon McBeath to be identified as author of this work has been asserted in accordance with the Copyright, Designs and Patents Act 1988

First published 1992
Reprinted 1994

Blackwell Publishers
108 Cowley Road
Oxford OX4 1JF
UK

238 Main Street
Massachusetts 02142
USA

British Library Cataloguing in Publication Data

A CIP catalogue record for this book is available from the British Library.

Library of Congress Cataloging-in-Publication Data

McBeath, Gordon.
The handbook of Human Resource planning/Gordon McBeath.
p. cm.
Includes bibliographical references and index.
ISBN 0-631-18686-7 (pbk.)
Manpower planning – Handbooks, manuals, etc. I. Title.
HF5549.5.M3M39 1992
658.3′01 – dc20 92-13157 CIP

Typeset in 11 on 13 pt Plantin
by Best-set Typesetter Ltd., Hong Kong
Printed in Great Britain by Athenæum Press Ltd, Newcastle upon Tyne
This book is printed on acid-free paper

Contents

List of Figures and Tables

List of Examples

Preface

The first round of interest in manpower planning coincided with the bite of automation on manning standards across the manufacturing sides of manpower-intensive organizations, and the current resurgence may be related primarily to the progressive impact of office automation. However, many other influences are affecting both management requirements and supply, ranging from changing organization structures and attitudes to work, information accessibility, business globalization, demographic changes, etc. As these varied influences alter our future manpower needs, in specifications as well as numbers, the need to identify our future needs and to ensure continuous supply has never been more critical.

There was a time when manpower was simply a cost, but now it is recognized as an investment. Across the world, the phrase 'people are our most important resource' has moved from being a traditional statement in the annual report to being accepted as something we really mean. In fact, statements by chairmen that 'our people are our only unique resource, our only competitive edge' mean that people management is suddenly very important indeed.

The greatest attention to people management may be at the top, but what we term organization and management development are simply the top end of manpower planning which should take place at every level. The difference is that, at management levels, we deal in single positions and individuals, whereas much of the rest of manpower planning concerns larger numbers and groups of people. It does not matter whether the company is large or small. Neither is it different if the organization is administrative or public service rather than commercial. Full and effective utilization of people is to be encouraged and planned.

As organizations continue to evolve, it is likely that our manpower planning will focus increasingly on the people at every level, while the management of the career flows within an organization, and associated remuneration practices, will become more complex. The role of electronic databases will become more important as aids to handling the increasing volume of relevant data, and to facilitate faster responses to changing business needs.

Acknowledgements

I would like to express my thanks to Nick Bolton and Nick Fenton of Business Advisers Limited for their permission to use a number of examples from *Executive TRACK* and *HR/View*, and for their interest and support in identifying appropriate examples to match my text.

Manpower planners are unlikely to cope with the complexity of the subject without sound, purpose-designed software to facilitate analysis. While there is a range of personnel software available, I have found the focus of *Executive TRACK* and *HR/View* on manpower planning, management development and succession planning issues to be excellent, and the high-quality support from Business Advisers has solved all our problems.

Gordon McBeath

Note to Readers

Throughout the book, the word manager is used for convenience as a universal term to cover any individual with a supervisory, managerial or directing role, plus senior specialists, without regard to position title.

Similarly, the male pronoun used throughout is for convenience only, and all such references should be taken to apply equally to women.

The examples in this book are fictional creations designed to illustrate principles and practices. In general, they are based on a number of events in more than one company, and, in all cases, names and characters have been invented.

1
People: Your Only Competitive Edge

When we consider our competitive advantage, people are probably the only unique resource we have. In a recent private international survey of major companies' practices, there seemed to be almost universal agreement that competitive advantage resides with the quality and skills of people, and that these can be turned into a formidable edge if they are given scope and freedom to contribute.

All employers have the same potential access to financial and other resources – technology, equipment, etc. All decisions related to the acquisition and use of these resources will be made by your managers. The quality of the managers making these decisions, and their freedom to do so as they see fit, has an immediate impact on the effectiveness of the business operation through the quality of the decisions they make.

Competitive edge is dependent solely on your people. For example, consider a company that produces a new product which has a distinct edge over the competition. Within three months, the competition will have comparable or better products in the market-place, at comparable or better prices, quality and delivery schedules. Its competitive edge does not lie in its technology or product, but in its people and what they can achieve.

A simplistic conclusion is that we must have the best people and, in different ways, that seems to be a widespread objective. But what is meant by the 'best people'? Even within a single industry, the best people for one company could be ineffective in another, because of the style and ways things are done. The term, best people needs to be qualified, then, to define the setting in which they can be expected to be effective.

Again, this is simplistic, because employing the people most likely to be effective in a company may not give the expected edge if the way the company operates places it at a disadvantage in relation to competitors. It is necessary to study how you motivate and utilize people, for it is the combination of good people being well motivated and empowered which generates real competitive edge. To plan your manpower requirements and supply without recognizing this critical factor will limit the quality of the end result. This is demonstrated by examples where manpower was a critical limiting factor.

People as a potential limiting factor

A large company sought an acquisition to enable it to establish a presence in a new target market. It found a company which fitted the requirements and negotiated the deal. There was a need to place two key managers in the company to be acquired, but the acquirer could not find those people from the existing management. The deal was aborted for want of two people and, five years later, the company still had not penetrated the target market.

There are many examples where great opportunities have been identified, but have not been exploited for want of a few people with key skills – and as many again where companies have gone ahead unwisely and suffered substantial losses because they did not have key skills which one or two people might have provided. So one of the important contributions of manpower planning is to identify these limitations.

Of course, it is not always the absence of skills which is the problem, but, rather, their utilization. Some high-tech companies suffer from shortages of technical graduates, but might be better off with only half their numbers. It is astonishing how highly able people can spend large proportions of their time on work which can be done well by people with less ability and training. And it is rewarding to restructure that work and see the rise in morale and contribution from people who are properly used.

This example is relevant at all levels. A works cafeteria with a high level of employee turnover (and of breakages) on washing and cleaning work brought in workers from a nearby home for people of low ability who were in care because they were unable to look after themselves. They were happy with the work, which was within their abilities, and they did not break things. Getting the person specification right pays off.

While some under utilization is due to wrongly specifying the people required, or to poorly designed jobs, the biggest limiting factor on personal contribution comes from poor management of people. We are, in theory at least, moving away from the era of 'I command/you obey' management. We continue to use the same titles, but a manager at any level up to chairman of the board now needs to be a leader, to encourage, to motivate, to guide – to enable individuals to use their skills and abilities as fully as possible.

The extent to which the use of these skills is limited by the behaviour of individual managers or inhibited by the management style of the company, is also a measure of the extent to which those people limit corporate potential. However, untying the complexities of these limitations within an established corporate culture is not easy.

Good people, whose freedom to contribute and whose personal development are restricted, tend not to stay, but to flow towards cultures which give them scope. Less able people may stay in organizations which are poorly managed, and there appears to be some correlation between the least competent people, poor managers, and incompetent and complacent organizations, which emphasizes the difficulty of raising quality.

Leading-edge companies unleash people potential

At the top end of the spectrum are organizations which understand people and how to get the best out of them by giving them scope. As side benefits, these people tend to be hard working, highly paid, and happiest with their work. And there will be far fewer people to cover a volume of business than would be necessary at the other end of the effectiveness scale.

When we talk about best people, it seems that we have to start with the competence of the chief executive to lead and inspire his people, to provide direction and purpose, to trust them and give them scope and to allow mistakes from which they learn.

Companies truly at the leading edge in any sector are those which are most advanced in this respect. They have understood how to unleash the potential of their people. Unleash is a carefully selected word, for the critical element is that their people are not restrained by the need to refer to higher authorities and obtain approval for everything they wish to do – or be discouraged from bothering to try – but, rather, they are encouraged to use their own judgement to make decisions based on a clear understanding of the communicated vision of the corporate future. These are people with clear thinking and innovative minds, and the courage to accept responsibility for their own decisions.

The result of this attitude or culture is a pace of informal decision taking which is formidable, and which outclasses more traditional opposition to give enormous advantage. While others plough through pedantic decision-making processes, the leading-edge companies have taken and implemented decisions and moved into positions of commercial advantage.

The manpower planner needs to recognize this situation as he attempts to position his organization. He may not be the key influence on cultural issues, but he does contribute in opinion forming and can highlight disadvantage, and the way to improve corporate effectiveness.

Vision and Capability

As business managers, we need a vision of the future. We know that it will be different and we are obliged to predict what changes will take place. As well as managing the business now, we have to be preparing for next year and beyond. We have to have a vision of what we expect to face, what we expect to do and, most of all, what we *want* to do in the longer term. Planning becomes part of the way of managing for most managers; it comes with recognition of the range and scale of change and its impact, and of the comfort provided by anticipation of events. The time taken is acknowledged as valuably spent, with a worthwhile pay-back. As an early part of the planning process, it is necessary to look at our vision of the company's place in the envisioned future, and to ensure that the scale of our thinking is adequate.

Where much business planning very properly sets out to optimize the use of available resources and match them with opportunities, it is evident that some long-term missions can appear completely out of step with the available resources and organization capability of the companies now. But 20 years is a long time and, in that time frame, resources can be built up systematically to achieve the ultimate vision. It is indeed visionary and demands enormous commitment from managers to transform a company's inappropriate resourcing and capability and build competitive advantage.

According to the CEO of one major company, 'A business mission has got to be stretching; it has got to take your breath away.' Once that vision is there, it must focus all the actions possible to develop small but cumulative competitive advantages. Achieving a competitive edge involves not only vision, but also a great deal of detailed preparation so that there are few or no surprises, events are anticipated correctly, there is preparation for likely change, and initiatives are ahead of the competition. This sort of anticipation involves open-minded and critical analysis of self and of all elements of the business environment, particularly of competitors, enabling strategies to develop which continually place the company at an advantage.

The biggest failure of planning may arise from an excessive focus on existing resources and competitiveness, and inability to identify the potential resourcefulness and future capability of one's own people and organization, or of competitors. Some of the most dramatic advances have been achieved by tiny teams rather than by the concerted efforts of a heavily resourced organization. It is very easy to underestimate resource potential but, if it presents a serious obstacle to the desired progress, then strategic alliances may provide a route into new areas.

Waterman (1988) wrote that 'Nothing creates momentum for change like crisis,' but crisis or chaos is not essential to getting the adrenalin running and creative thinking becoming productive. If planning is to work well, it may first need to shake free of today's problems and move on to tomorrow. This is most effective where corporate culture encourages openness and can draw out all information, ideas and contributions from every level; where people have the self-confidence to be open minded and analyse critically; where there are no sacred cows and no need for political caution. A further element of this culture is the attitude of facilitating the growth of people within the limits of their abilities and preferences, which generates an upward thrust of ambition and ideas.

Few companies achieve optimum use of their human resources and capability. Not every company even thinks in these terms but those which do strive to develop a culture which encourages the growth of business through the growth of people may produce a powerful combination.

The degree of commitment to using the total planning process as a way of managing is critical. Limited commitment can be dangerous, as in the company which assembled a seemingly attractive plan without looking seriously enough at competitors. Enthusiasm and drive will not necessarily produce the best result, unless allied to an efficient system which ensures that nothing gets overlooked.

A systematic approach implies acceptance of thoughtful analysis and forward planning as the logical basis for managing a business towards its goals. Much of the plan will be under review at any point in time. System and planning imply availability of an information base enabling fast, informed and considered decisions. Planning must amplify the weak signals warning of future change. The business environment is changing at a tremendous pace and many elements of that change have human resource implications. The timely readiness of a team to exploit a market opportunity can make all the difference between achieving dominant market leadership rather than an unprofitable, also-ran situation.

The achievable plan

The end product of this approach should be a clearly stated plan in which progress towards the long-term corporate vision is supported by shorter term detailed business objectives, which are supported in turn by statements of the anticipated business environment and the strategies (including, particularly, human resource strategies) which must be implemented to ensure successful achievement. The degree of adaptability of people, organization and culture may be key influences on what will be achievable.

The overall plan, and particularly the human resource elements, need to be under continuous reassessment as both the timing of requirements and readiness of people are reappraised. Corporate ambition may need to be tempered in the short term, but (hopefully) should not be inhibited seriously by the present capability of the organization as the achievable plan is assembled.

Capability assessment

Organization capability is the full potential of which the organization is capable if it can maximize the use of all its resources, particularly its human resources.

Most organizations fail to achieve their full potential because of a combination of factors, including, in particular, failing to utilize and motivate their people, and also by pursuing objectives for which they are not ideally resourced, by having unbalanced resources and through organizational structures and cultures not designed to achieve the objectives.

The only sound base from which to improve capability and to plan the future is a very clear statement of where we are *now*, because the company may not be strong enough to tackle future tasks until we have made sure that our current business operation is more efficient, or until we have taken action to bring aspects of the business performance up to acceptable standards. This requires a complete check-up; an assessment of the potential capability of the organization, its people, purpose and culture. We need to measure and make judgements of how effectively it is operating now, and of its potential capability.

A SWOT analysis (Strengths, Weaknesses, Opportunities, Threats) is probably the most valuable analysis which can be done as part of this study, provided it is done with proper thoroughness. I recall one company which did such an analysis but missed key indicators to imminent changes in competitor strategies, and was quite unprepared for developments. Yet the directors had been confident of their future having predicted a clear way ahead following their SWOT analysis.

There is a great temptation to be complacent when looking at strengths, and tendency to turn a blind eye to weaknesses which have not been too critical in the past, or are unchangeable. It is dangerous to start this analysis unless the participants can be open minded and self-critical; it is only when limitations are identified that any corrective action can begin.

The analysis of potential threats is critically important, but difficult to analyse comprehensively. It requires substantial knowledge and understanding of the activities of each significant competitor. The greatest threat comes from competitor initiatives which do not conform to your analysis pattern. Sensibly, the threats category should be overdone.

There may be a danger, as conclusions begin to be reached, of reacting too quickly. For example, there can be very sound reasons for differences in manning between two apparently identical companies, and indeed for many other differences, once superficial conclusions have been probed. In one example, comparisons between two large companies in the hand-held computer business showed that one was concentrating on very high volume, low cost models while the other aimed at state-of-the-art models for technology application. The organization structure and the management and staffing mix differed substantially between the two although initial assumptions were based on their apparent similarity. If the conclusion had been that there *were* close similarities of operation but variations in manning standards, the task would have been to find a means of using people better.

The purpose of the analyses has been to answer the question 'How well are we doing?' and to examine how capability may be improved by realigning the deployment of resources and altering the ways we behave. Any problems identified may be associated with a particular function, or across the board, but they are almost certain to have some roots in the human resource area and raise some key questions.

- Is the organization best structured to give the right focus and dedication to the problem issue?
- Is the corporate culture supportive of the behaviour necessary for most effective actions?
- Is the inventory of management (their individuals skills and strengths) adequate and appropriate to achieve objectives?

At this stage, human resource actions can be extracted and an overall human resource programme determined, highlighting timed targets as milestones. If this indicates some unmanageable peaks of activity, then the phasing of some programmes may need rescheduling. (There should be similar extracts covering each of the main functions or elements of the business, particularly if the scale of improvement on a tight schedule is substantial.) The form which the human resource action plans take, and typical headings, are covered in some detail in the next chapter.

The total improvement programme, the targets and the timetable need to be assessed to ensure that they are both realistic and achievable, and that the company is not simply fooling itself that, having identified problems, they will inevitably be overcome. It may be judged that the total programme involves more upheaval than can be managed within the preferred time-scale. By selecting priorities and deferring some less critical elements, a large programme to upgrade capability can be progressed.

Capability and the changing business environment

The conditions surrounding our organizations make up the business environment, and they are changing continuously. Little is certain beyond a three-month time horizon, let alone one of ten to 20 years, but managers are in the business of forecasting change over extended periods. Understanding the changes taking place or developing around us has to be one of the most important preoccupations of managers in the 1990s. In this process, there is an overriding need for objectivity, with no room for complacency or acceptance of chaos. Only an open-minded and critical analysis of what we think may be possible will open our eyes to all aspects of potential environmental change and the impact it is likely to have on our businesses.

The ideal way to manage change is to anticipate the forms of change which may occur and to plan how to respond to them, and perhaps to develop contingency plans for the possible but less likely considerations.

Anticipating future opportunities and difficulties is what business planning is all about, yet many planners fail to make sufficiently comprehensive studies of potential change, or to follow through to examine the implications. We must be concerned with all environmental changes which will affect the business and may have human resource implications, and with changes which may affect our requirements for and uses of human resources, both now and in the future. In a high proportion of business situations, the critical element in determining the achievability of a plan will be human resource factors in some form or other. It should, therefore, be of the greatest concern that many business objectives are at risk due to a lack of awareness of impending change, compounded by a lack of preparation of managers to cope with that change.

Managing is Change

Managerial activity, after having been relatively static in content and style historically, has begun to change in recent years. The pace of that change is increasing. It now seems evident that a complete and remarkable metamorphosis is occurring, brought about by a number of influences which, together, will substantially transform the activities and specification of the effective manager by the end of the 1990s.

This change is not theoretical – activity in response to all of the identified influences is well established, and new practices are already in use (although rarely across the board) in many companies. These companies vary from small to very large, and tend to be at the leading edge of management practice around the world. They believe that the actions they are taking give them additional competitive advantage.

These changes are likely to affect the role of every manager; what he does and the means of doing it; what he sees as his objectives; and his involvement in the total process of managing. It appears essential for companies to evaluate the effect of these influences and begin to update their management resourcing strategies, adjusting graduate and other recruitment specifications and the emphasis in management development and training to ensure that their managers are prepared for the future.

The scale of this potential change is so great that some managers can be expected to close their minds and reject it on the basis that nothing like it has happened before but the same has been said about every major business innovation. The current phase of development, based on the revolution in office computing, is going to sweep away the old style of managing. We are witnessing a change as stark as the butterfly emerging from its chrysalis.

Think-tank sessions identified the following list of influences expected to bring about change.

Business environment   Business is continuing to become more competitive and international, with new systems, changing corporate ambitions, greater complexity generally, more emphasis on markets being customer driven, and so on. These developments will demand managers with much wider knowledge of many matters, capable of coping with very large volumes of information and other inputs, drawing appropriate conclusions and taking decisions.

Product/manufacturing technology change   These developments will alter products and product life cycles, choice of materials, and manufacturing facilities. Some developments are providing the bases for new industries, or radical changes in existing ones. Environmental issues are changing the acceptability of some technology. Managers in all functions will need to be more technology minded, and aware of potential technological influences on their businesses.

Knowledge explosion   In every field of human endeavour we are learning more, so that the total volume of human knowledge is expanding exponentially, presenting managers with the task of being more selective while ensuring that key data are not overlooked.

Information technology   Existing developments in computer technology, software and telecommunications, which are already in the laboratory or in prototype, will result in massive evolution in the management of information.

Corporate databases will be developed which will provide potential access from all functions and levels and, by removing restrictions on data flow and access, take away one of the main justifications for historial, hierarchical organization structures.

Information management, through the development and use of corporate databases which are fully up to date and openly accessed, will also provide instant feedback on many aspects of performance, providing public awareness of individual and team performance. This will be a significant factor in changing management/subordinate relationships.

Social change The change in social attitudes over the last two or three decades has progressively weakened acceptance of the command/obedience mode of management. The rising concern for improved quality of life, greater independence and a wish to do things one's own way has gone some way to modify corporate cultures – if it is accepted that these reflect a consensus of managers' views within an organization.

It is possible for a small number of individuals to dominate a company and largely determine its culture by their behaviour, while a powerful but suppressed majority view may also exist and will come through in time. Social influences are a strong factor in the move led by younger managers towards more open and participative management styles and organization.

A range of other social issues will have some influence, including growth in the development of women managers, rejection by many younger managers of workaholic attitudes, and concerns for equal rights, minorities and green issues.

Organization The combination of changes in information management which open up access to a corporate database, and the changes in the acceptability of the old command/obedience mode of managing, combine to make hierarchical structures largely obsolete. The are being replaced by open and participative management styles in non-hierarchical organizations.

The structural form which is evolving is much flatter with broad spans of control, and some organizations have progressed further into cellular structures, where cells of specialists will work in knowledge-based clusters in flexible open-plan structures, with extensive use of temporary project teams. One can see these solutions emerging in a number of companies, in some specialist partnerships, and in some aspects of health care. In each situation there is a radical change in the way a manager functions and in the competences required.

Social trends encourage progress towards greater openness and involvement, and influence the culture of an organization, which represents the consensus view of management thinking on how things should be done, as well as giving an impetus towards these flatter or cellular structures. The effect of these changes in structure is to enable individuals to contribute more positively to the business and to optimize the development of people, thereby enhancing their contribution potential. Those organizations which are most success-ful in this will achieve significant competitive advantage.

Corporate core competences As we question which competences are required in a business to ensure managers are effective, the approach we take can be from two directions. To improve current effective-ness, identification of competences relevant in each business unit or department points the way to achieving immediate improvements. But the longer term view should question what competences will be necessary to achieve the corporate vision.

Corporate core competences are those which are essential if the corporation is to achieve its longer term goals. While these are ex-pressed as corporate competences, they can only exist in employees, so that a core need for a high level of competence in some developing aspect of technology, or around particular markets, means that the corporation must acquire the services of individuals who are highly proficient in those areas.

The overall competence of the management and professional teams must match the corporate competency requirements necessary to achieve competitive advantage and the forward vision.

Manpower Planning Within Business Planning

Manpower planning needs to be an integral part of the business planning process. It does not follow afterwards as a translation of business needs into management requirements, for the costs of man-power and the availability of key skills, etc., are essential elements in determining the viability and achievability of plans.

Within the business plan, the manpower contribution will define whether business plans are achievable in manpower terms, and determine how manpower requirements will be resourced. In turn, they will determine the recruitment, development, training, and redundancy strategies of human resource policies, and strongly influence many of the remuneration policies. It is necessary to determine requirements in sufficient detail for them to be planned for and satisfied.

In an era when the business environment is changing rapidly, planning processes are having to cope with a continual input of fresh data and modified scenarios. In turn, plans for the provision of required manpower need to be under the same pressure of continual reappraisal, and flexible enough for long-term resourcing plans to be modified to satisfy new requirements.

In reviewing the achievability of any business objective, the most serious potential limiting factor is the availability of people to make it happen. It may call for one individual, capable of managing a particular development or with the specialist knowledge to make it possible, or could involve a larger scale deficiency in a range of skills and abilities. One objective of manpower planning must be to minimize occasions when developments are aborted, or opportunities lost, due to staffing limitations.

There is also a control aspect of manpower planning. Few companies know what their manning costs should be, yet in a large organization annual manning costs may run at millions of pounds above what they should be. Just 50 people too many, with accommodation and equipment, can cost well in excess of £1 million a year.

What manning levels should be is not easy to determine, but logical solutions can be reached by continually querying the necessity of all work activity, trimming out the unnecessary duplication, and structuring full and resonably demanding jobs.

Numbers

The effect of carrying too many people is comparable with a man carrying too much weight (which is perhaps why excess personnel tend to be referred to as the fat). The effect is also comparable in that efficiency is impaired and the organization becomes sluggish.

Most organizations can shed 10 per cent of their staff easily. A few need to take out nearer 50 per cent, although in a controlled way. As the company's spending power begins to be absorbed in excessive manpower costs – wages, salaries, accommodation, equipment, and so on – then capital expenditure on essential new equipment and on new product development is reduced because money is not available. In this situation, profitability is affected at an early stage.

To avoid our organizations slipping into obesity, we should appraise the structure and manning continually against updated objectives so that we can ensure that both organization and manning remain purpose-designed and slim. If we put on fat, a fast return to the slim purpose-designed structure has to be a priority objective.

A large insurance company decided to move from wholly centralized management to a divisional structure, largely decentralizing the various functions. Newly appointed functional directors in the divisions built up their departments and in two years the administrative costs of the business had more than doubled. There was no real increase in the work readiness, and duplication and added complexity had got out of control. The response was a sharp return to more centralized services to remove duplication.

Yet this sort of response is not universal. A typical alternative is to hold previously budgeted remuneration levels so that the available money is thinly spread over the increased numbers. This is a step towards disaster because the impact is immediately felt on quality as the more able people are attracted away quickly and the lower pay levels on offer attract poorer quality replacements who are less able to initiate positive change.

Quality of people and organization

The quality of people that an organization can attract and retain is related only partly to pay criteria and far more to issues of job satisfaction, culture and utilization. It is unlikely that a high quality individual can be retained by high payment alone. If the management style inhibits his freedom to act, to do his job effectively in the ways he sees fit, then he is likely to move to an environment which matches his abilities and preferences, and will do so easily.

Levels of pay below the norms of the employment market will attract only the lower levels of ability in each job category. Low pay levels over any period of time have a long-term impact on the quality of the employees retained. Once the side effects have built up, this trend becomes extremely difficult to reverse. As evidence of this, some local government and public service organizations have shifted from low pay/high security packages, which were probably appropriate in their labour market, to high pay/high security schemes. However, they have seen little change in efficiency because of deeply entrenched work practices and overmanning which only massive behaviour change can remove.

People who command relatively lower salaries in the job market than other individuals doing what appears to be similar work are generally not underpaid since, if they were able to obtain higher paid posts, they would move. The differences are quality related. That is how the market works.

In general, the lower paid sector of any job category includes those who are less experienced, less competent and less able. Given that people's work covers a wide span of different speeds and levels of effectiveness, it is to be expected that the slower, less effective individuals will be of less value to an employer. As a result, a greater number are required to do the basic work. This justifies the apparently excessive numbers already employed and leads to increased fragmentation and production of work. Further, with less able people, most if not all of the creative and planning work begins to be neglected and becomes outdated. Non-standard events are less frequently foreseen and the managerial role drifts towards troubleshooting rather than planning.

Most serious is the impact on job satisfaction as jobs become increasingly fragmented when work is spread between the excessive numbers of lower grade people. This can result in duplication of work, continuation of obsolete activities, continued use of obsolete systems and so on. Any remaining able people feel increasing frustration as job satisfaction levels continue to decline. Absenteeism is likely to be high and in itself may increase manpower requirements by a further 15 per cent. Money becomes more significant as a pseudo-motivator, and pay levels begin to be pushed up, for misinterpreted market reasons, without any of the advantages that apply where a planned workforce is highly motivated and effective employees are also highly paid.

The cumulative effect can be a massive absence of efficiency and quality. There is an inability to compete in export markets, inadequacies in industrial relations and communication that lead to disputes and strikes, deliveries are more frequently late than not and manufacturing methods become increasingly inadequate.

Upgrading an organization which has run down is not easy. The drive for change can come only from the top and then probably only by bringing in an outsider. An able CEO can make a considerable impact, but change will be very difficult to achieve without changing many of the individual managers, probably more than half. Change in depth will require major communication and training to alter attitudes and change established views of 'the way we do things around here'.

Of course, people vary enormously and not everyone is comfortable in a fast-moving successful company, which is likely to be populated by competent and, therefore, confident people. Such people are inclined to tell you that they and their organizations are the best in their field, that they can hold their heads up anywhere knowing that they are really good, that their companies are competitive and that they have a competitive edge wherever they choose to go, and that they need never be ashamed of their performance because they will naturally have done their best. As individuals, they do not join less efficient organizations lightly.

Manpower Control

In any manpower planning activity, control needs some attention. There are two aspects of concern. Firstly, as manpower costs can represent a substantial proportion of corporate costs, related decisions have a fairly direct impact on the bottom line and justify some control mechanism. The second aspect concerns the need for some form of audit to ensure that planned manpower actions are followed through. This is particularly relevant for actions related to people's development, which are critical yet longer term. There is, after all, no point in devoting extensive management time to planning the development of people if no development takes place.

Manpower as a fixed investment

A decision to recruit a permanent employee is comparable with the acquisition of any other fixed asset. Manpower loss rates may be high, but no employer can count on losing only the people he wants to leave. The decision to bring in an additional person should always be taken on the assumption that the individual is with you to stay.

Consider the implications of a decision to recruit a 'fixed asset'. One additional production operator or clerk costs around £12,000 to £15,000 a year in wages or salaries, plus about £4,000 to £5,000 in benefit costs, not to mention accommodation and equipment. Over 20 years, and with inflation, expenditure resulting from this single decision will be over £500,000. For a managerial slot over a similar period, expenditure will exceed £1 million. The decision to recruit and therefore commit the organization to this expenditure is frequently taken too casually and at a low level.

As a contrast, consider the approval of capital expenditure of, say, £25,000 on a new machine. There will be considerable investigation into the need for the machine and the optimum specification, taking into account possible future use rather than just immediate requirements. Then there will be a written justification for the expenditure, which will include the following points:

- a financial justification, showing recovery of the investment within three years, (or forget it);
- how it will be financed – cash, hire purchase, hire;
- what level of utilization of the machine is expected;
- how flexible will its potential use be in future;
- the expected operating costs;
- any potential industrial relations problems; and
- the obsolescence potential and the possible write-off plans.

Very similar questions should properly be asked before every single recruitment, particularly as the commitment of expenditure is so substantial and as it becomes progressively more difficult for employers to lay off employees who are excess to requirements or have obsolete skills. It is a fundamental requirement that manpower planning should provide as many of these answers as the company deems practical. In five years' time we may well have moved on to consider recruitment with as much care as capital expenditure. Companies that get there first may once again be establishing their advantage over competitors.

Manpower costs in relation to income

In any organization where the cost of manning is a significant proportion of the income, and there can be few where this is not so, planning and controlling that expense is important. It can have a significant impact on profitability (or costs in the case of non-commercial enterprises). In manpower-intensive industries and services, employee costs may exceed 50 per cent of income. Even in capital-intensive industries, where this figure drops towards 10 per cent, marginal overmanning cuts into profits. In manpower-intensive units the financial impact of overmanning can be disastrous. It can, for example, reduce a business with the potential for fast and profitable growth to a loss-making static position, where capital is drained by excess manpower.

Getting manning levels right is evidently important, but we must find a balance between financial objectives, fulfilling the work requirements, and the personal ambitions of employees. This is an intricate equation, as we shall see in the course of this book.

The manpower function

It is the task of the manpower planners to determine and specify the optimum manning requirements and means of supply, now and in the forecastable future. This activity fits most naturally into the human resource function, yet it is sometimes separated on the grounds that manpower planning exists in a real business situation, requiring commercially orientated decisions that human resource managers tend not to like. Certainly some human resource managers prefer to see their job as clearing up rather than associating themselves with management decisions about people. Tough personnel decisions have to be based on a combination of personal and commercial arguments, with human resource professionals needing to understand the harsh realities of international economics if they wish to continue to be secure in their jobs.

2

Human Resource Strategies in the Business Plan

A business plan must be achievable. It should incorporate a series of planned actions, tactics and strategies which will ensure that all of the key objectives will be achieved within the defined time frames. A business plan which does not incorporate the means of achievement is incomplete and may be valueless. It should also incorporate sufficient flexibility and reserves to enable a response to unanticipated developments and at the same time keep the plan broadly on course to meet its primary objectives.

Whereas business planning may have a horizon of no more than two to three years, the corporate vision of its future should span at least ten years. These corporate ambitions are likely to indicate the broad path the company would like to follow, but, against the ideal, we must identify the internal and external influences and pressures which will either enable the track to be followed, or will obstruct and limit progress. Availability of key people, the organization's capability and cultural factors may register heavily. The growing strength of competitors may cast doubt on what is achievable. Or there may be a straightforward shortage of appropriate skills, which can be overcome by positive action. Alternatively, there may be opportunities outside the central area of corporate preference which provide new avenues for profitable development. If the enterprise has the management skills and the human resources to exploit such situations, then the planning system should ascertain whether corporate ambitions are flexible enough to take in the opportunity.

Planning includes a large element of planning the utilization of resources, particularly any critical and limited resources required to achieve specific business objectives or to enhance overall capability.

Management resources tend to be crucial and frequently represent the single critical factor which limits what the enterprise can or cannot do. Financial resources are essential but substantial additional finance is generally available to a well-run business and is not generally the limiting factor. Equipment, space, etc., can be covered under the general heading of finance (the ability to pay for them), although there are time considerations on availability of specialized space, equipment and materials to be taken into account. The other resource which does impose limitations on achievements is time, which must be managed but cannot be supplemented.

In any business plan, we need to draw out the key human resource actions required so that appropriately designed strategies are planned, developed and implemented in a way that enables business objectives to be achieved.

In assessing the optimum mix of business options while assembling a plan, the availability of necessary manpower resources will be the key determinant in its achievability, with availability of relevant management the most critical factor. Planning both the need for, and deployment of, managers and specialists is particularly difficult where the timing of possible scenarios is uncertain and the same set of people may be required for several different purposes, possibly at the same time. For key manpower resources (say on product development teams, or management teams), availability must be matched to demand and the management planning task may require us to smooth the work-load to match availability of people, to reschedule the peaks and troughs and handle sudden surges. The ultimate response to events will depend on the effectiveness with which these resources are managed.

Matching manpower demands to manpower availability for the favoured options is, therefore, a vital element of business and manpower planning activity. The ability to acquire additional resources in line with plans is an important factor. Additional management may take months or years to recruit or develop, and a first-class management group may take several years to assemble and settle into an effective team. This imposes very real limitations on business development.

At lower levels, human resource limitations may arise from a lack of skilled manpower for a wide variety of possible tasks; this may be overcome by recruitment or by training. Some programmes have required deskilling of work and restructuring of jobs to concentrate the use of the available short-supply skills, with other aspects of jobs being done in new ways. Automation is another way out of short supply, but it is capital intensive, requires an adequate volume of activity to be viable and is rarely as quick to implement as is needed. Developments in information technology may enable some administrative work to be done at a point remote from the area where skills are short.

The need to tie down key human resources for a long period may reduce the favour with which some projects are seen. Return on the investment in key corporate assets (management and specialist resources) has got to be as sound as in any other financial evaluation. It is appropriate to compare options, but accept that the quantitative financial answer may not be the final consideration. For example, any project or opportunity with potentially high visibility, or high profit potential, will come into a special category. A project which fits the direction the company wishes to pursue in the longer term is likely to be selected as an important element in the overall plan, even if it involves a higher than normally acceptable risk and will be a heavy user of resources. Such options place a strain on any plan, but may be essential as the means of growing the future corporate core competences required.

Achievable business objectives

The accepted business plan and objectives consist of the selected options covering the immediate years and progression towards the envisioned future. A plan is not complete unless the means of implementation are clear, most importantly in regard to the availability of people to carry it through. There will be a range of critical steps, each of which is essential to the success of the overall plan. How these are to be carried out needs to be known and should be supported by a series of strategies which, if properly implemented, should produce a high probability of business success.

Human resource strategies

Many action plans will be multifunctional, but it is the human resource elements which are of concern here and which are invariably the most critical. For example, consider a new marketing venture which needs to be resourced. The manpower requirements are defined, but cannot be met wholly from inside, so some recruitment is required. The skills needed to analyse the market more closely and establish tactics must be provided by a combination of recruitment and some specialized training, designed and run in-house. Action programmes to cover these needs may assume the use of marketing consultants until new staff are appointed. It can be assumed that the level of staff retention will be high because the jobs should be interesting and challenging but, to ensure success, remuneration will need to be appropriate and management style positive. Action in this area cannot be taken in isolation, and complete human resource policies may require revision.

In another example, the plan might depend on a significant increase in graduate recruitment. If the company starts off with a limited base of university contacts and faces a rising national demand for the relevant graduates combined with a decline in numbers of new graduates, this requirement will be tough to meet. In such a situation a clear and determined programme will be essential achieving the desired result, and a contingency plan will be desirable to cover partial non-achievement.

In a further example, a company with its top management close to retirement and facing rapid environmental change may decide to bring through the next generation of managers quickly, yet properly prepared to deal with the changes.

As each business grows and becomes more complex, it is an important responsibility for every manager to plan his human resource requirements systematically and carefully to ensure effective manning and continuity. The repercussions of missing the significance of some key element of environmental change have been noted. Failing to plan for change and acquire adequate appropriate talent can jeopardize the achievement of objectives and future growth; and over-enthusiasm to maintain tight controls over manning levels and costs can be equally damaging. A proper balance must be maintained.

The line manager does not have the time to work from first principles every time he puts together a plan, so here is a checklist of changes in the business which may have human resource implications:

- expansion of existing business activities;
- addition of new capacity (new plants, equipment, facilities, etc);
- new ventures, acquisitions or divestitures;
- new products or services;
- new technologies or applications;
- new systems or changed information technology;
- changes in operating methods or productivity improvements;
- impact of projected inflation rates;

- new, pending or strengthened national or local government-legislation or regulations;
- adequacy of organization structure; and
- adequacy of management.

The implications of these factors may affect the achievability of the business plan through:

- shortage of any skill category in labour market;
- areas of technical incompetency;
- competitive recruiting activities;
- imbalances in age distribtion in any category;
- inadequate or excessive turnover;
- individual or group performance problems;
- career advance of able people blocked;
- employee mix does not match needs;
- equal employment opportunities being achieved;
- adequate supply of potential general managers;
- adequate supply of appropriate managerial skills; and
- sufficient breadth and depth of experience among existing managers.

The actions which need to be taken have to be elucidated. It is invariably worth while to write down an assessment of each problem and task, and the action which is planned to overcome them. This does not need to be elaborate but, if written out clearly, you confirm that you have a logical response and have a basis for assessing whether the plan has been carried through on schedule and is effective. The potential range of areas for action is considerable, including:

- modify culture to improve response to objectives;
- development and training initiatives;
- improve communications;
- recruiting programmes;
- modify recruiting/selection;
- organization/position changes and implementation;
- improve appraisals and counselling;
- remuneration policy changes;
- job evaluation;
- new specializations to be resourced;
- career counselling;
- retraining of people with obsolete skills;
- terminations;
- accelerate career advancement (general or on a selected basis);
- reassignments/lateral moves;
- accelerate management development;

- establish mentoring;
- cross-function/division moves;
- change staffing levels;
- implement new systems or procedures;
- modify job requirements; and
- reassignment of work in restructuring.

Where action in any of these areas is identified as being essential to successful business development, the objectives and the strategy for achieving the objectives need to be clearly stated and implementation monitored. In particular, it is likely that all aspects of personnel development will be driven by essential strategies arising from business objectives.

Manpower planning objectives in the business plan

Within most businesses, there will be a top-down philosophy of management development which may read something like, 'Ensure the provision of effective management level staffing, in purpose-designed organizations, to provide the management and leadership which will enable the enterprise to meet its business objectives.' This will have originated in the corporate objectives and/or the culture. In the business plan itself, it is those management development specifics which require actions that give management development programmes their legitimacy. And the concepts which apply to management development are likely to extend to manpower planning at large.

There is likely to be a range of manpower requirements, perhaps on the lines of some of the following paragraphs, the first of which is written as within a plan, the others noting a range of situations which call for strong manpower planning actions.

- 'Successors will be required to fill the listed management positions over the next two to five years, and for the estimated additional number of positions each year to cover unplanned promotions and transfers, terminations and unplanned additional posts. Short-lists of adequate quality will be required in advance so that any decisions to look outside can be taken sufficiently early to ensure vacancies are filled when required. A detailed action plan will be required, but the development actions to prepare internal candidates for all these opportunities should be shown to be deeply rooted, flexible and effective. Adequate early warning must be provided for all requirements which must be met by external resourcing.'

● Strengthening the marketing function may be essential to some business strategies. Timing will influence how far this can concentrate on the development of existing personnel but the programme is likely to include a requirement to recruit externally to fill a number of identified management and specialist positions within a designated time-scale, as well as to develop existing people. This might involve using consultants to help create and implement specialized training programmes to take the levels of knowledge of specified people up to new defined standards and even to provide operational support as these new skills begin to be exercised. Precise objectives will determine the needs.

● Planned and substantial management information systems developments may require a range of specialist and management recruitment, plus specialized training ranging from management briefings through how to operate a desk-top terminal (and utilize the available data and analysis facilities), to highly technical systems and language training.

● Proper communication of new technology applications will require articulate non-technical briefings for other managers to ensure widespread appreciation of potential change, threats and opportunities. Locating and training individuals to do this effectively is always difficult. Or there may be developments in legislation which can have a critical effect on the business and where a plain-speaking legal person is required to communicate the requirements and implications.

● Graduate recruitment is a permanent task, but the demographic effect on the availability of relevant graduates and the form of competition are constantly changing. As most companies require fairly steady but increasing intakes to cover current or future manning requirements, strategies for attracting and retaining sufficient individuals of appropriate calibre and with the right skills need to be continually reviewed and updated as necessary. The flows of people up through the organization and the ability to resource future management requirements may be directly affected by failures to recruit at the bottom end.

The justification for management planning is that it should safeguard the organization by ensuring that the required management resources are available in the future, with the appropriate skills, in the numbers and quality, necessary to enable business objectives to be achieved. Both the manpower planning and the management development processes are integral parts of the management process, and their elements contribute to increasing organization capability and gaining competitive advantage. Human resource strategies should be developed with that purpose in mind.

3
Manpower Planning: The Process

The purpose of manpower planning is to provide continuity of efficient manning for the total business and optimum use of manpower resources, although that optimum utilization of people is heavily influenced by organization and corporate culture.

Manpower resources include the intellectual property of the company and the possessors of its core competences, potentially the most easily lost or misused properties, and the most in need of thoughtful planning. As manpower planning is concerned with manning in the business, it cannot be a stand-alone activity, but must exist as a part of the planning process for the business itself. As I have noted earlier, the lack of suitable manpower can place severe restrictions on the ability of a business to achieve its objectives, which highlights both the importance of realistic manpower planning and the need for it to be fully integrated with the overall business planning process.

Like any other process, manpower planning has numerous elements and the process will not work efficiently unless the full range is used and properly integrated. The same applies to business planning, within which manpower planning should be viewed as a subset of elements in the overall system.

The manpower plan itself falls into two parts – the determination of the manpower required to run the business at a series of points in time into the future, and the means of supplying those requirements. For the planning to work well, I believe it is important to examine the full demand and supply position so that optimum solutions can be evolved. This is not limited to central or specialist activities, but should involve all line managers fully in the review of options.

The review process, which brings needs and supply together, is frequently given insufficient time and attention. This may be because, once all data are brought together, the result can seem complex and difficult to grasp, but any reduction in complexity is achieved only by ignoring some of the data and taking a limited view, which could reduce the potential for achieving the most effective resourcing.

The purpose of the comprehensive periodic review is to consider all of the needs across the business and to match these with the career preferences and development of the people so that a complete pattern of decisions can be devised for the resourcing actions anticipated over the months ahead. This review provides abase of preliminary decisions for all following actions regarding people. There may be sound reasons for a subsequent change of decision, but then the options and alternatives which were considered in the review provide a starting point for the fresh assessment. If some new requirement emerges, the considerations noted in the original review should help define the updated options quickly, and the implications of alternative actions. Should the scale of unplanned change be extensive, a fresh review might be initiated, at least locally.

In the review process itself, the management task is to balance the many competing and sometimes conflicting elements. Some examples might be:

- conflicting demands for available research and development resources at peaks of activity, with an excess supply available during troughs;
- inbalance of skills emerging as technology alters the product range; and
- uncertain timing of developments, which affects the timing of deployments.

These reviews cannot anticipate situations which develop at short notice, but should take into account the need for flexibility to cope with the manpower implications of events such as intended future acquisitions, new business opportunities not allowed for in plans or retention actions needed to avoid the loss of key individuals which might damage established plans.

The review process may be viewed as the master programme which integrates resourcing activities with business planning at an operational level to ensure that organization structures and the preparation of manpower resources are matched with the manpower requirements necessary to achieve business objectives and respond to a changing and possibly hostile environment. In parallel, the process should optimize the utilization and growth of the human resources available. The emphasis in most reviews may be on the short-term (one to two year) actions, but there must be a longer term (three to five or five to ten year) perspective – particularly for management continuity, which is a special section of the same process – as the lead time for supply can require this notice.

Meaningful manpower plans are only possible if the review process brings together all of the relevant information at regular intervals and uses these data to re-examine, at every level, the relevance of present and planned future organizations and the competences which will be required against those available. Outputs from each review should include: detailed decisions on future organization changes and anticipated manpower deployments for a period through to two to three months after the next scheduled review; outline decisions on longer term organization changes, deployments and culture change plans; plus confirmation that business requirements can be adequately resourced (or not).

All manpower supply plans and actions should stem from this process and should incorporate provision for continuous reappraisal to identify fresh problems, to respond to new or changed needs, and then to implement actions or monitor progress towards action. This is essentially the means of driving the process of effective resourcing within the business and involves management at every level in a network of associated decisions and action.

Preliminaries to review

Reviews require sound preparatory work and comprehensive personnel records which give accurate and objective data on all employees. We cannot make judgements on the supply of particular skills unless we have sufficient data on the skills possessed by existing employees. Building up full records requires both an effective system and determination to ensure the data are complete, up-to-date and accurate. Also, the information must be in a form that facilitates easy access during a review.

Personnel records can be seen simply as raw data and their contribution to reviews may come more from analyses of the overall inventory of personnel. Any flaws in that inventory, identified before the review begins, provide part of the review agenda. For example, heavy loss rates for a key employee group can be analysed carefully in advance, so that part of the action agreed in the review addresses the identified problem. Or, a progressively worsening distortion of the age profile of a category may need to be tackled.

Analyses of the manpower inventory and of flows can establish whether problems are developing which are likely to affect required manning levels, and should play a key part in preparing the agendas for reviews. Equally, as other agenda items emerge, analyses may offer potential solutions.

Manning standards and utilization

The whole manpower planning process depends enormously on the base of manning standards. This will start with what exists and what should be, and take in all of those factors which will change current standards, including by how much and when. Without some measures of this sort, meaningful planning is very difficult. Many organizations start with what exists now and refine the position as they identify the separate forecastable categories, the bases for assessing standards and the rates of change.

Manager, supervisor and employee involvement and interest is needed to determine standards of all sorts; the first-hand measures they have of the utilization of people are key factors in planning forward needs and subsequent implementation and control.

Ideally, manning standards should be developed from analysis of essential work requirements, with some form of productivity measurement wherever possible. Measurement is by no means restricted to direct manufacturing operations – it can also be applied to many office or support functions. Where local attitudes or management style make straightforward measurement difficult, existing data in the hands of supervisors and managers can provide useful standards which will encourage supervisors to improve their own human resources utilization, thereby improving manpower productivity.

Wherever this type of analysis is carried out, opportunities should be sought to restructure and enrich jobs and to match people's abilities to job demand, thereby raising the level of job satisfaction. With this comes lower manpower loss rates, lower absenteeism and tighter manning standards generally.

For all this, existing standards have an inertia which we must try to overcome. If we aim to improve the use of people in partnership with subordinate supervisors and managers, we may find the secret of radical improvement in overall manning quality as well as numbers. This is an area for experimentation to determine what works in your environment.

Manpower requirement planning

Manpower requirement planning follows on from the establishment of the main assumptions in the business plan. Once we know the level of sales volumes and mix, the manufacturing schedules required, the research and development programmes, etc., we are well on the way to establishing the matching manpower requirements. The plans should include built-in assumptions about the organization structures to be used, and their effects on the levels of manpower required.

Plans should be set out with schedules of associated manpower requirements, giving precise categories, skills and levels for every function. This detail will be necessary as a starting point when the questions of supply planning are tackled. Where appropriate, requirement plans should be based on manning standards associated with work demand factors to facilitate modification as volumes or systems change.

Manpower information systems

Modern management depends on having comprehensive data on which to make decisions. For any system, specification of required inputs and outputs is essential. In building up the manpower database, full coverage of traditional personnel records is required, and it is increasingly possible to cover sophisticated elements, such as competences required for effective performance of a job, and the competences possessed by individuals. Data on absenteeism and overtime are also part of the system.

Manpower inventory and analysis

Who are our employees; what skills do they have; how good are they; how are they developing? These are just some of the many questions to which we need answers. Much of the analysis should come from the information system, but the current inventory is altering all the time with recruitment and losses, promotions and transfers. Assessing the rate and form of change in the inventory is vital to questions of manpower supply because, what we cannot provide from within, we must seek out from other sources.

Data on appraisal of performance, assessment of future potential and the use of psychological tests are all part of the information we use to get the answers we need.

Flows

Analyses of the patterns or flows of people through parts of the organization are invaluable to the manpower planner; flows provide the major part of our supplies data and identifying changes in flow patterns can point to possible difficulties, such as when an existing flow pattern becomes insufficient to meet a changing demand.

Flows tell us about the availability of people who are ready to advance to their next career stages and also provide information such as the average rates at which individuals progress through jobs, and how those rates vary for different types of people in different functions.

Manpower supply planning

This is the crunch point where we bring together all the data we have on our future requirements, and on our present manpower stock and the ways we expect it to change. From these analyses, we see the future manpower supply set against the developing inventory, detailed by function, category, skill and level. These show our future recruitment needs, highlight needs to increase the promotion rates of some categories by intensive training and development, show retraining and redeployment needs and identify excess staff who are likely to become redundant.

In all of these areas, we need action programmes to ensure that we meet our recognized needs. We must be sure that the actions required are taken and are successful. Otherwise, basic assumptions on the provision of human resources within the business plan may be adversely affected so that business objectives are endangered.

Manpower control and audit

The philosophy throughout this book is one of planning ahead, but this requires basic controls and audits. The logic of controls on every aspect of manning should be evident. We are dealing with an expensive resource that can be easily misused or underutilized. Controls should be low key, yet quietly ensure that we continually try to use those resources in the best ways possible, and do not casually add additional and non-essential resources. Controls are exercised on current actions and decisions.

Subsequently, we audit results to be sure that intentions have been achieved and that decisions have not been overlooked or ignored. This happens far more than we expect where there is little or no audit. In the whole area of management development in particular, and across the spectrum of planning following the review process, ensuring that plans are followed through is essential. If this is not done, there is little benefit from the considerable use of valuable time involved.

Management manpower planning

Above a certain level, manpower planning ceases to be a matter of numbers by category, and becomes linked to individual positions and individual incumbents. For the top slice of the company, we are dealing with a combination of business development, organization development and individual career development. It must be handled with considerable care, by unbiased and imaginative executives; it must also take into account the employees' viewpoints and preferences, and involve them fully if it is to be a workable plan.

Corporate culture

How a company is managed, its organization structure, its manning standards and thinking on 'how we do things around here' are all determined within a corporate culture. Any significant change in efficiency is almost certainly going to be culture related, but culture is both difficult and slow to change.

If the business demands a change of pace or efficiency, or a different way of doing things, it is not going to come about solely from planning changes in manpower standards or utilization. There will be a need for some radical action to change what people accept as norms for many aspects of their work behaviour, which may well result in a severe disturbance in current manpower and organization. We will examine aspects of culture and manning standards elsewhere in the book.

Periodic full reviews

The way reviews are carried out is likely to vary enormously from one enterprise to the next, but the principles should be more uniform. The most critical of these is involvement. All of management should participate, with the lowest levels contributing their parts first and progressive reviews forming a reverse cascade up through the organization structure, finishing with a review of the overall manpower plan and the management continuity position at the top.

At the bottom end, each manager should discuss requirements and deployments with his direct subordinates. Then he can prepare for the review with his boss. A reasonable target time per level might be three weeks, if planned early into business diaries. As reviews progress up the structure, they should concentrate on the contiguous two or three levels in the organization, progressively dropping off the lower levels as the reviews progress upwards. However, issues thought to be of concern at higher levels will be carried forward, such as skills shortages which may have an impact on the business.

The supporting paperwork will vary, with much being prepared as working notes by the participating managers, but it is sensible to assemble and retain some basic record of the discussions and agreements to enable progress to be monitored later, or as the starting point for fresh consideration if an unforeseen development occurs. There might be sections in the notes for:

- business and environmental changes;
- organization and manning reviews; and
- human resource action plans.

The first section should record the business situation and assumptions on which the review was based. The notes might include a brief appraisal of actual business progress against the business plan, and changes in the environment which differ from the assumptions in the associated environmental scenario, followed by updated views and an evaluation of the implications for human resource management.

The organization and manning plans section should concentrate on: the immediate organization structure, including any fresh thinking on its evolution; the filling of all senior positions at each review level, both currently and in the future, including preparatory development; and reviews of manning specifications, standards and levels, and how they may change. It will be useful if all the main assumptions made in the plan are recorded, so that any need for change has a firm base on which to build.

The third section, covering human resource action plans, is a smaller scale replica of the human resource action plans detailed in chapter 2, and will include reference to major human resource strategies associated with the achievability of business objectives.

There should be notes on progress against the milestones in current action plans, plus details of any new plans triggered by new business or environmental developments, and the associated human resource implications.

A final section in the notes might cover implementation action, with details of plans to prepare individuals for fresh assignments, implementation of training plans, and a whole host of action points, covering individuals or groups, designed to ensure timely resourcing.

Frequency

The frequency of this process should be determined by need. One company in a rapidly changing high-technology sector runs through it at quarterly intervals with strong line management support for what they see as sensible discipline which keeps their organization and manpower utilization finely tuned. In less dynamic industries, a major annual review plus a less formal, but ongoing, midyear update may be sufficient.

The drive to carry through the review process must come from the top and from the line, who must recognize its value to themselves and to the business or they will not spend the time doing it! The human resource function may need to provide some of the drive plus some strong supporting back-up. Reviews compete for management time and must demonstrate their contribution to business development and profitability. Local management is generally supportive if the process is working properly and they can see value for their efforts but, even then, resistance to allocating sufficient time may arise as a result of operational pressures.

Essential actions triggered by these reviews, such as manpower movement between divisions, may be difficult to arrange without the involvement of higher management. Usually, these moves need to capitalize on knowledge of the immediate business and be local to those business areas the individuals concerned know well. Movement should generally be within functional disciplines, so that the fast learning is limited to the new business area.

Application to individual decisions

The periodic in-depth manpower review establishes a scenario or framework of preliminary decisions. Following this, there will be many day-to-day actions to take before gaining a final overview and implementing the decisions. For example, a chain of individual moves and appointments may be planned to follow a retirement. These should be under scrutiny as the implementation time approaches and they would normally be implemented in a straightforward fashions. However, one of the links in a chain may fail. Someone may resign, performance may falter, or other events may change the situation, causing the plan to be reshaped.

If circumstances change, the obvious starting point for fresh consideration should be the notes from the previous review supporting the original intention, which may record the options and contingencies considered. It is logical to go over this ground in detail, starting from the original review. It should not be acceptable to take a fresh ad hoc decision which is quite unrelated to the careful and wider ranging considerations which took place in the review process.

Actions involving changes from plans should require the discipline of reference back to the comprehensive discussion. For example, a decision to send someone on a training course should fit into his longer term development plans; secondments to meet an emergency are unlikely to have been planned far ahead, but should match a need to broaden experience; a change to a career plan may have been proposed on the basis of one incident, but should be viewed against the full assessment and track record; and so on.

Perhaps the most serious unscheduled actions occur when a key person resigns, or when an unplanned business opportunity requires an immediate appointment. (The review process may have covered these possibilities and noted contingency actions but, more often, the necessary response will upset the plan.) One such appointment was followed by a chain of seven other changes down the line, severely disturbing an entire plan. If that happens, a fresh examination of that sector of the business becomes a necessity. Indeed, any event which triggers a significant volume of unscheduled deployment changes should be followed by a full review to assess the degree of weakness caused and the actions which can be taken to reinforce the reserves of management.

4

Manpower Information Systems

Manpower information systems can range from basic personnel records through to sophisticated networks of subsystems with precise purposes. Today, most of these will be computer systems and their value in meeting your requirements may be restricted by the off-the-peg system chosen, or the instructions given to your systems engineer. A recent exhibition of manpower systems included some sixty offerings. Selection of one to meet your needs will require an investment of time.

In a climate of rapid environmental change and increasing awareness that the only real competitive advantage is to be found in the quality of our people and how well we use them, an effective manpower information system is an essential aid. It is also essential for any manpower planning activity.

Required outputs

An analysis of intended uses and required outputs is a useful starting point in designing what the system needs to be able to do and assessing the adequacy of your existing system. The general objective will be to ensure that the system can provide the necessary information, in a form that can be integrated with any other business data, which means that it has got to be comprehensive, up to date, accurate, and probably not stand-alone. Beyond that, the objectives become specific to applications.

With most database systems, there are facilities to pull out any of the data and present them in whatever form is required, but this sort of friendliness does vary. Applications should, therefore, be detailed. An analysis of the elements (modules) offered in proprietary systems, which we can presume have responded to market demands, show that the main thrust is to provide facilities for basic personnel administration, with strong links to payroll and pensions administration. Behind these come applications to recruitment administration and training administration, and to attendance, absence and time-keeping. A very wide range of other applications is possible and many packages give particular attention to a selection – for example, to job evaluation, salary administration and reviews, and bonus, all as a suite of software.

The outputs required from such suites can be listed, and then the precise formats determined so that these can be programmed. Using the same example, the outputs might be:

- salary listing for salary review purposes;
- salary review analyses and summaries;
- salary drift/wage drift, by grades, plants, etc.;
- compa-ratios – movements in average salaries by grade;
- performance rating analyses;
- grading – distribution by grade within departments, divisions, etc.;
- salary distribution – salary scatter within grade salary ranges, by occupation group, or area, or division, etc.

Required inputs

A surprising number of personnel departments still retain those large green folders containing all of the paperwork associated with each employee, although it may now have a printout of his current computerized record. When a new employee joins an organization, he or she normally completes an application form, which provides the basic data for opening an electronic record. It is the electronic record which is updated and which is always used, with fresh data added on job and remuneration changes, training courses attended, and changes of dependants, addresses, etc. From time to time, a printout of the current record is sent to employees to enable them to confirm that all is correct. This initiative invariably flushes out a collection of acquired qualifications and domestic changes but it should not flag errors in job titles, salaries or other internal data, which should be fully up to date at all times.

The data elements in a complete manpower information system are likely to include the following information. (There may be other elements specific to a country, industry or company.)

1 Identification:
Surname and forenames
Maiden name
Works or computer reference number specific to the individual

2 Other personal information:
Address (including postal code) and telephone number
Next of Kin
Date of Birth
Sex
Marital Status
Nationality and work permit detail, if relevant
Race – for analysis of race-relations practice
Registered disabled person – if relevant
Trade union membership number
Relative within company

3 Organization/locations:
Company or division within group
Location
Department
Cost centre reference number

4 Occupation history:
Prior to joining company
● Employers
● Positions held
● Dates
Date of joining:
● Details of broken service if relevant
● Recruiting source
● Status of employment: full-time, part-time, temporary or contract
● Positions held within company:
  – dates appointed
  – job titles and departments
  – job grades
  – occupation codes

5 Salaries and benefits:
Salary history
● Basic salary or wage
● Dates and amounts of changes
● Reasons for changes
● Planned next change – amount and date
Hours
● Normal hours

- Overtime paid/not paid
- Shift work

Bonus

- Supplementary payments, etc.
- Bonus scheme eligibility
- Amount, timing and criteria

Benefits eligibility/awarded

- Holiday entitlement
- Company car
- Medical insurance
- Company loan, etc.

Pension scheme membership

- Scheme
- Data joined
- Normal retirement date
- Life assurance cover, etc.
- Link to pensions administration system

6 *Performance and potential assessment*:
   - Most recent performance data
   - Most recent data covering potential
   - Psychological test score, results and dates

7 *Qualifications*:
   - Level (GCSE/A level/degree/doctorate)
   - Field
   - Specialist/professional
   - Apprenticeship, etc.

8 *Training received*:
   - Training courses attended
     - internal/external
     - level of course
     - duration
     - dates
   - Training planned

9 *Competences*:
   - Competences required in present job
   - Personal competences
   - Competency requirements
   - Language skills

10 *Development plans*:
   - Career moves possible
   - Planned next move (if relevant)

- position
- occupation code
- job Grade
- timing

11 Succession plans:
- Entries in succession plans

12 Medical history (confidential – restricted access):

13 Absenteeism:

14 Overtime/shift work/part-time work:

Depending on the system in use, some of this information may need to be coded to facilitate analysis. This is an easy enough task when the range of choice is limited, but increasingly difficult as the complexity of data increases. Academic qualifications can be covered through a series of steps or decimalizing the breakdown. Elements such as current job and, even more so, past experience, offer an enormous range of choice and coding difficulty. In some systems, this entails the creation of one or more separate files which subsequently need to be linked to the main file for some analyses.

Job coding (or job information)

Job information is difficult to use unless it can be translated into some form which computer logic finds easy to handle for analytical purposes. The best way of doing this is to use a numerical coding system, in which each job has a unique number, and the numbers form a logical pattern.

Such a coding system can, and often is, defined by the company itself to cover its own range of jobs. That approach may not be adequate if it is desired to make comparisons with information and statistics published externally. In this situation it may be better to consider using one of a number of standard classifications of occupations, as commonly used by government agencies.

The Department of Employment's system known as Classification of Occupations and Directory of Occupational Titles (CODOT) has, since its design in 1972, provided a comprehensive, even complex, system of classification to cover all occupations found in Great Britain. This system lists about 3800 separately identified occupations, each of which is defined so as to cover five basic components, namely:

1 A short statement of the occupation's essential characteristics;
2 The main tasks normally carried out;
3 Common specializations and additional tasks;
4 Additional factors that are important when considering employment in the occupation;
5 Other alternative titles for the occupation.

The 3800 occupations are grouped at three levels, namely:

1 378 Unit groups of occupations which share similar tasks;
2 73 Minor groups, combining Unit groups which are related in terms of work performed;
3 18 Major groups, combining Minor groups into comprehensible main headings.

A decimal system of code numbering is used. The following example illustrates this:

Major Group	II	Professional and Related Occupations
Minor Group	04	Personnel and Management Services Specialist Occupations
Unit Group	041	Personnel Management and Industrial Relations Specialist Occupations
Occupation	041.10	Personnel Officer

Two other standard classification systems that have been in general use are the Classification of Occupations (CO80), as developed in 1980 by the Office of Population Censuses and Surveys, and the International Standard Classification of Occupations (ISCO), as developed by the International Labour Office and dating from 1968.

Whilst these three systems of classification (CODOT, CO80 and ISCO) have certain similarities, the government departments that made full use of them, both in Britain and in the European Community, have sought to harmonize occupational and other statistics to international standards. The result of this has been a major revision of ISCO (ISCO 88) which came into general use in most European countries during 1990/91. In Britain, a major revision of both CODOT and CO80 has produced a new British standard known as Standard Occupational Classification (SOC). This appeared in 1990 and is available from HMSO in three volumes. It is closely compatible with the European standard ISCO 88.

Those companies that are considering introducing a standard classification system to their own job structures would do well to look at SOC. It would make for easier comparison with future British and European Community statistics.

SOC retains certain features of its 'parents'. The 3,800 occupations defined by CODOT are now analysed into 371 Unit Groups, 77 Minor Groups and 9 Major Groups. The decimal notation is retained but only to three levels instead of the four levels used by CODOT. As a result, the classifications do not provide the same level of detail as CODOT and may, therefore, be more manageable for companies to use themselves. An example of the less complex nature of SOC is the Personnel Officer referred to above. This is classified by SOC as:

Major Group	3	Associate Professional and Technical Occupations
Minor Group	36	Business and Financial Associate Professionals
Unit Group	363	Personnel and Industrial Relation Officers

It would be possible, if you so wished, to introduce your own fourth digit to differentiate between Personnel Officers and Industrial Relations Officers. This method of coding also means that it is not possible to have more than nine sub-categories of each group. As a result, the digit '9' is retained as a 'bucket' at each level of classification for groups that are 'not elsewhere classified'.

SOC may be less comprehensive than CODOT in the coding structure it provides. It does, however, provide a consistent and sensible approach to the classifications at each level, based on two key criteria – (1) skill levels and (2) the nature of work activities.

> **Skill Levels** – where appropriate the classification takes into consideration either the level of formal qualification required for an individual to be recognized as fully competent in the occupation, or the period of training/experience required to do the job competently.
> **Nature of Work Activities** – the classification considers any or all of a number of aspects of the work, including the materials handled, the type of tools and equipment used, etc.

What is generally not considered by the classification at each level is the status of the person doing the job. So, for example, the jobs of trainee clerk, clerk and office supervisor all appear under the same classification code. There are, however, some specific exceptions to this in the classification of managerial levels.

The definitions at the Unit Group level comprise:

A brief statement of the job content;
Typical entry routes and associated qualifications;
Tasks;
Related job titles.

Job information

It is important that job information used for analysis should be properly maintained and up to date. Usually, this requirement is tied in with job analysis and grading for remuneration purposes, highly motivating when keeping things up to date. Without job information, recruitment would be virtually impossible, training would have no target, salary administration would have no basis, organization structure and manpower planning would have no solidarity.

Job information refers to the essential data on the job which identify it and set it apart from other jobs. The information we require will concern its duties and tasks, the associated authority and the potential effect of action taken, responsibilities for assets and personnel, plus the specific objectives or standards to be achieved and the resources and time allocated for the purpose. The ideal incumbent will also be specified.

It is not particularly difficult, within any company, to find out what jobs people are holding. It is known who is called chief engineer and who is called a billing clerk and so on, but job titles do not tell the whole story. For example, the managing director of a small organization may operate his own production machines and type his own letters, while a technical assistant known to the author had considerable responsibilities for a costly research and development programme.

Proper job information is, therefore, essential. It has wide ranging applications, including job grading, salary administration and recruitment, and will often have associated relevance in the training and personnel development fields, or for organization planning.

Job families

Any form of job coding or job evaluation is likely to make use of the way in which jobs tend to cluster into families, i.e. families of associated jobs such as chemical engineers, or cost accountants.

In job evaluation, it is not difficult to judge the relative values within a series of accounting jobs, or within a group of development engineering jobs, but it is rather more difficult to tackle the evaluation of an accountant in relation to a design engineer. Some job evaluation processes totally avoid the question of comparing jobs in one family with those in another, limiting their results to series of job family-based but, otherwise unrelated, structures.

Equally, within job families, movement between jobs is relatively straightforward, because job holders have related skills, while transfers between families are more difficult. Within a job family, the knowledge and skills requred are closely related – common scales of education and training exist – so that the flow of people between jobs is predictable.

The relevance of job families here is that they provide the parameters for many career flow structures, and also that they define limitations on manpower supply, particularly for categories in short supply.

Taking flow structures first, flows are likely to be reasonably free within a job family. Accountants are able to move to more senior accounting jobs as they acquire experience, but would face some difficulty moving into a different stream. Even within accounting, they would have difficulty in moving from the mainstream to one of the subfamilies of specialisms such as those in the treasury or corporate tax office. Appointments in each subfamily are likely to be filled by other specialists from the same subfamily but possibly from a different company. The flow follows family lines.

When a shortage occurs – usually as demand rises – it would be useful to examine a nationwide flow chart, which operates in the same way as an in-company pattern. There is an attempt to pull through a larger volume of people at particular levels than the input flow and development activity can generate, and the flow fails to respond.

The response to the recent shortage of corporate lawyers has been a great increase in the intake at the bottom end, speeded up development, many promotions made too early and exceptional pay for younger people. The activity is so specialized that it is not practical to draw in people with different training and experience, the only source being from the ranks. This possibly has resulted in larger numbers choosing to study law at university.

It will be a number of years before the situation balances out. It is possible that, at an interim stage, the heavy wave of fresh people will result in an oversupply at middle levels, leading to reductions in intake at the bottom.

Analyses of various categories show the same pattern – national shortage is followed by a surge of supply at university entrance and company intake levels, and a subsequent reaction against oversupply which clogs career flows. Chemical engineering is another good example from the past. One finds trained chemical engineers in a great variety of different careers, having been frustrated in their initial ambitions through being part of an excess supply.

In examining the structures of career flows, a knowledge of job families is relevant, together with an understanding of supplementary skills necessary to facilitate movement across boundaries. For example, there is frequently a flow from research and development into sales and marketing, and to manufacturing; this flow is aided by product knowledge. These flows can be assisted by specific training designed to provide the additional skills relevant to planned future transfers.

Competences

A number of organizations have developed the practice of building up a profile of required competences for each job, particularly at more senior levels. If the same competency profiling is applied to all existing personnel, there is a basis for matching people to jobs for short-listing candidates. The *Executive TRACK* system offers this facility, leaving open the selection of competences to be used as there appears to be an infinite variation judging from individual company lists. As discussed elsewhere in the book, the identification of competences needs to be based on the priorities in the business concerned, on corporate culture, and on the actual use of terms within the company, to ensure that the words used are meaningful to the users. They do not need to convey anything to outsiders.

The value of this process for analysis depends on the relevance and accuracy of the selection and definition of competences; of the identification of competency requirements in individual jobs; and of the assessments of the strength of competences in individuals. In my view, much of the work done so far has lacked precision, although the quality of analysis is improving steadily, so that this will be a valuable aid by the mid-1990s.

Lack of precision appears to result from attempting to define universal management competences. This can be overcome by shifting the focus to specific groups of jobs, possibly in one job family, but perhaps best by concentrating on a functional unit of organization. Within a department which has a specific commercial purpose, the success criteria guide analysts to the specific areas of competence which are critical. These are not universally required of every person, but need to exist in balanced quantities for overall team efficiency. When the same competences are sought within the team staff

**Example Calculation for the
Candidate Search Report**

Competency Dimensions	Ratings for John Bailey	Minus	Group Marketing Director	Equals	Net Score	Running Total
Motivation	3 *******	-	5 ***********	=	-2	-2
Interpersonal Skills	2 ****	-	4 *********	=	-2	(-2 - 2) = -4
Written Communication	3 *******	-	3 ******	=	0	(-4 + 0) = -4
Verbal Communication	4 *********	-	4 *********	=	0	(-4 + 0) = -4
Leadership	4 *********	-	4 *********	=	0	(-4 + 0) = -4
Delegation	3 *******	-	3 ******	=	0	(-4 + 0) = -4
Control	3 *******	-	2 ****	=	+1	(-4 + 1) = -3
	↑ Individual Competency		↑ Competency Requirements for the Job			↑ Final Score

Example 4.1(a)   Comparison of one candidate against competency specification of a vacancy – prepared using *Executive TRACK*

Candidate Search Report

Name/ Position	Grade	Perf	Pot	Score	Next Planned Position	Date
PHILIP HOBBS MARKETING DIRECTOR - GROUP	28	3	28	5	RETIREMENT	Nov 92
CHARLES WHITE MARKETING DIRECTOR - INTERNATIONAL	26	2	28	2	MARKETING DIRECTOR - GROUP	Jul 92
JOHN BAILEY MARKETING DIRECTOR - INFORMATION SYSTEMS	26	1	28	-3	MD ANY DIVISION INTERNATIONAL ASSIGNMENT	Oct 92 Jan 95
JOAN DANIELS NATIONAL SALES MANAGER - INTERNATIONAL	25	1	27	-7	MARKETING DIRECTOR - INFORMATION SYSTEMS	Oct 92

Example 4.1(b) Comparison of competency matches – prepared using *Executive TRACK*

itself, it becomes possible to identify the competences requiring strengthening, which in turn will upgrade departmental effectiveness.

Executive TRACK has the capability to store competency information relating both to the attributes of individuals and the requirements of positions. The information can be generated from a variety of sources, such as assessment centres, psychometric tests, performance appraisals and skills audits. Once held within a database, the competency data can, for example, be used to identify training and development needs or to perform candidate searches.

In example 4.1, competency profiles are used to help identify a short list of international candidates – managers who may be suitable for a specified position – and to generate a best-fit score of their attributes in comparison with job requirements. It is possible to use fairly complex mathematical techniques to generate a score. This may involve weighting the individual calculations, or identifying critical and non-critical factors, or both. However, this example uses the simplest method, which is a straightforward running total of the differences between the position requirement scores and the individual competency scores.

The first part of the example (a) shows a comparison of the ratings of one of the candidates with the ratings required in the job, using the competency specifications for that job. An overall weighted score is developed, which is compared with the scores of other candidates in the second part of the example (b).

It is important to note that one would never make a candidate selection decision based on this information alone. As well as other, more objective information which can be used to identify suitable staff, the final decision will almost always be based on traditional methods. The value of using competency profiles is principally to narrow down the range of candidates (assuming that a wide range of candidates is available) and to focus attention on the relative merits of each one.

Manpower models

A large number of off-the-peg software packages are available for various aspects of manpower planning. Some of them perform narrow, specific functions and some assemble substantial data banks for major analyses associated with business options.

The most useful form of model for most manpower planners is one which can respond to 'what if?' questions, or which will enable a

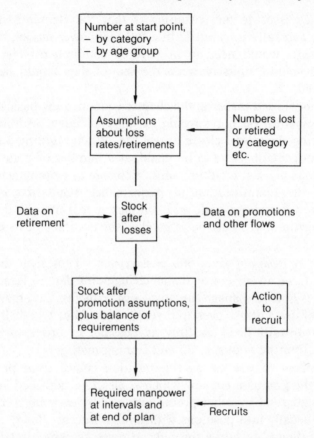

Figure 4.1 Simplified model of data and assumptions necessary to meet requirements

series of assumptions to be balanced in relation to each other to provide a desirable end result.

As with any computer application, the machine will do only what it is told. Therefore, the purpose of a model needs to be determined, and the calculations which it is to make must be programmed precisely. Even a complex programme is basically straightforward provided that the workings of the manpower situation are understood and the flows within it have been quantified. If the patterns can be written down, they can certainly be programmed. Figure 4.1 shows this in greatly simplified form. Every company organizes its people planning process according to its needs, and some use only parts of a total system. It was noted earlier that some of the standard packages address only limited aspects, and the market for such software demonstrates that interest is restricted in some areas.

The key issue in any planning is that the elements should be complete and fully integrated. In a full manpower model, the essential elements would need to be covered comprehensively, and the time and volume links between the sets of data would need to be interlocked.

The model used earlier in the chapter contained the basic elements, and for practical purposes would be quite adequate. Additional elements bring the model closer to real life. When building a statistical model, judgements have to be made, at a number of points, on the implications of, say, a culture shift, a change in employment legislation, or the quantification of performance standards. For some purposes, a very large-scale and complex model may be developed, but its accuracy will only be as good as the accuracy of its elements.

Example: A model of flows into management Typical of the sort of problem faced in an era of major change and flatter, leaner organizations, is how to manage the process of reducing, say, management manpower by a third over five years. Naturally, we shall want to continue upward flows as fully as possible in order to minimize reaction from the younger, up and coming managers.

The inflow to the manager population comes from promotions through the graduate stream, which is clearly established and needs to be safeguarded by other promotions and by external recruitment, which is usually into positions with limited internal flows.

The outflows are losses through retirements, which total about 3 per cent a year, a few transfers to other businesses in the group and a few early retirements, which are usually on health grounds.

All these flow data can be incorporated into a simple model and parameters for varying the pattern can be tried. A series of decisions and actions may be planned and tested, such as the set of five shown in this example:

1 Over a five year period, trimming the graduate intake will have little impact at management level, so leave it alone. Also, ensure that the flow of this source into management is not changed.
2 Promotion from other internal sources is to be tightly controlled, and the volume trimmed by one third for the first three years.
3 External recruitment direct into management is to be halved for the first year and then allowed to return progressively to the current level by year six.
4 Natural wastage is assumed to drop by one quarter in year one, as it tends to during tough times, and then to revert progressively to current levels in year five.

5 The retirement pattern is to be changed, as it is the major factor in achieving the required reduction. Early retirement is to be encouraged from the 50- and over age group, with a target of 20 per cent of the relevant population during year one, plus 15 per cent of the relevant population in each of the next three years.

The impact of a strategy along these lines can be calculated quickly, with subsequent modication of the assumptions until it appears achievable and likely to meet the target levels. Communication of this strategy may well be somewhat restricted, but it provides key guidelines to all key managers and HR people for achieving the change.

Example: Modelling the impact of major change   A large insurance company is substantially updating its total information management and decentralizing. Installing new equipment and preparing new systems is absorbing two years of a five-year programme, at the end of which its 10,000 plus workforce will have been reduced in number by a least one quarter.

Its manpower planning pointed to a strategy of minimizing involuntary redundancies. During the initial two years, the total number of managers will have to be increased, but the company has abandoned any permanent recruitment which is not critical to long-term flows and engaged many people on fixed-term contracts. This will allow the manpower planners to a substantial portion of the required outflow after the new systems come on stream.

Additionally, the planners have been able to identify skills which will be in less demand, plus new skills in which the company lacks sufficient volume, and are gradually retraining many people in parallel with their current work. This will facilitate many planned transfers, particularly during year three, from the excess stock of people with obsolete skills.

Obviously, the company's manpower model has been evolved to respond progressively to more specific and sometimes complex issues, and it was the speculations on the impact of various options which enabled it to develop and test possible strategies. From an initial analysis of total numbers on a level by level basis, the data from each major function and organizational unit were quickly separated and were set against the vision of the future organization. This flagged the major discontinuities as points for action.

One of the major discontinuities was geographical, with part of the information processing function and some large sections of administration transferring to local offices. Allied to skill changes, there were large-scale questions of the feasibility of relocating people, many of whom would need retraining. Many of the employees had partners in other local companies and willingness to relocate seemed severely restricted, so assumptions were made accordingly, leaving the minimizing of enforced redundancy as the only option, but allied to low turnover.

These examples appear to say more about the principles of modelling than rather drier descriptions of the models themselves. If you have a detailed understanding of the established flows in the area under scrutiny, it is likely that a straightforward model will enable you to study the manpower implications of change.

Example: Modelling the impact of demographic change   If a company is used to a substantial intake of school leavers, or of graduates, and anticipates that the numbers they will be able to attract will decline, what will be the effect?

One outcome is visible in the large retail chains, which have supplemented a declining school leaver intake by recruiting early retirees from other industries. While this gives an immediate remedy (and an unexpected bonus of better attendance levels from the older folk), the input to flows into more senior positions will be changed.

Similarly, some large recruiters of graduates have shifted from a standard entry age of 22 to 23 to take in many women returners and older graduates. However, all their career progression planning is based on the fast learning and progression of young graduates within quite tightly designed parameters, and some speak of real confusion about how to deal with this new intake. For example, many of these people have very different life-style objectives and ambitions, and this reduces the size of the pool of individuals striving for advancement.

A model which quantifies the change and builds up assumptions about the likely development of the new stream will enable strategies to be developed to cope with the change. For example, one company has modified its recruiting specification for young graduates to ensure a higher proportion are likely to become managers, while the specification of the older intake will take most of them into non-managerial specialist positions. This reflects the preferences of the first two years of older intake.

A different level of problem may be seen from the demographic impact on intake into the nursing profession. Here, the numbers of eligible people required to maintain levels are so high that it is inevitable that the supply of suitably qualified recruits will shrink. In such a situation, a manpower model needs to look at the utilization of trained people, and see how changes in the structure of jobs can reduce the demand for fully trained people, with a view to supplementing this reduction with increases in much less qualified people to do basic jobs. In turn, this increases lower level intake, some of whom may qualify more slowly for the higher level, providing a fresh source flow.

Example: A model for wastage analysis Another area where a model can prove valuable is where there is a change in the level of wastage. For example, if established flows assume a wastage of 7 per cent a year from, say, young accountants, but this has risen by a cumulative 2 per cent in each of the last three years, with the loss rate building up within the under 30s, a model should be able to demonstrate the damage to date and implications for the future.

The wastage model itself may not reveal the cause of the problem, which may well be largely external, but it may help to pin-point the problem and to point to some possible solutions, or factors which will partially alleviate the problem.

Personnel software

A number of database systems are available to assist managers in the planning and administration of human resources. The most popular ones tend to be PC based since they provide the user with greater independence, control and flexibility than has previously been possible using corporate mainframe systems.

A recent exhibition called Computers in Personnel, sponsored by the Institute of Management Studies, included 58 exhibitors. The bulk of the systems on offer were basic packages associated with personnel, payroll and pensions administration, and absence control. Others had particular applications to the administration of large volume recruitment.

Relatively few packages have sufficient scope to be relevant here. One that does and is now, perhaps, the most widely used is *Executive TRACK*. It is supplied in the UK by Business Advisers Limited. *Executive TRACK* is primarily designed to enable human resource managers to store, organize, analyse and present the information required for management development, career, succession and manpower planning. It was one of the first packaged systems to become generally available for these applications and has since been adopted by over one thousand companies world-wide. *Executive TRACK*'s developers have successfully refined the system over the years, based on the practical experience and input of many of the world's leading companies.

The ability to analyse the inventory in almost any conceivable way is made possible by such a system, and these analyses provide vital data for projecting future manpower availability, an essential ingredient in manpower supply planning.

Business Advisers Limited also develops and supplies the *HR/ View* statistical report generator which has been used to prepare many of the tables in this book. *HR/View* effectively combines an ad hoc reporter and a spreadsheet in one package which manpower planners can use to produce statistical reports from employee and job information held in *Executive TRACK* databases, or link to business planning data. A further package, *Corporate CHARTER*, enables information to be prepared in the form of organization and succession charts (such as in example 16.1).

Centre-file's *Personnel Partner* systems can be used for recruitment and training administration, succession planning, job evaluation, etc. So too can the *Compel* system, CSI's *Resource* system, Info Support's *Professional Personnel*, and APT's *Midas* system. Unibit's *Peodesy* is useful for handling succession planning and competency analyses. IMS has a specific manpower planning package called *Sussex*.

5

Manpower Inventory and Analysis

Manpower supply to meet requirements can come from two sources, namely internal and external. The preferred source is internal, but we need to know in detail the extent to which we can meet our requirements from the people already employed. If the full requirement cannot be met from internal sources, external recruitment will be necessary. If we have people in certain categories who will become surplus to requirements, then time for retraining, redeployment or redundancy is needed.

To complete an assessment of our existing manpower resources in relation to our planned requirements, we need to take a careful inventory of our stock in considerable detail. Subsequently we shall need to analyse the changes taking place within; rates of progression through the structure on promotion, and the rates of loss.

The Basic Inventory

Basic personnel records are a mine of information. The basic inventory represents the first stage in accessing the content of that mine. It involves detailed analysis of the current 'stock' of employees, and analysis of recent past trends as a contribution to projecting the future evolution of the stock.

Analysing the manpower inventory involves a large number of related analyses which explore the mix within the various main headings.

Head count

The most simple question is How many employees do we have? The first thing we find is that this simple question gets answered in different ways in different organizations. The obvious answer might seem to be the total number of people on the payroll, but that is only one answer for someone will observe that many people work part-time and should be counted as halves. The effective full-time (EFT) head count is less than the sum of names on the payroll. Ah, yes, but the hours worked by part-timers vary considerably, so would it not be more accurate to express each individual as a proportion of normal hours in order to get a true EFT? And so it can go on.

For complete logic, all categories, including shift workers with regular long hours, need similar treatment. In a process plant with seven-day continuous shift working, the basic week averages out at 56 hours per man. A negotiated change to a 40-hour week required a significant increase in manpower for an unchanged volume of work. For a year afterwards, the divisional director had to explain this each time the manpower figures were discussed, yet there had been no change in the EFT manpower.

Overtime hours can be evaluated in a similar way. A demand for a 10 per cent cut in the number of jobs may be offset by discontinuing the 10 per cent level of regular overtime working – at least in theory. Good overtime control is important as overtime hours carry premium payments so that the manpower cost is higher than normal time rates.

If we can resolve the initial question of how to measure head count with some internal rules, the most immediate application of the result is a comparison with budgeted head count, hopefully calculated on the same basis, and the examination of trends from recent months.

Company-wide figures have limited value. It is necessary to get inside them to see the pictures for the separate parts of the organization. Analysis needs to go down to department level and even smaller units. Then we want to know something of the make up of the numbers – initially divided between full or part time, direct or indirect, male or female, and so on. Example 5.1 is an extract from a departmental analysis. This represents the simplest level of manpower stocktaking. It is fairly limited in value, but triggers further analysis. This inventory can progress into a range of 'how many?' questions. For example:

- Employment – How many people are employed as salesmen, etc?
- Qualifications – How many employees have arts degrees, etc?
- Training – How many have attended particular courses, etc?
- Age distribution – How many employees are aged between 55 and 60?

Manpower Analysis for Marketing Division at June 1991

Department	Total	Executive Grades		Monthly Staff		Weekly Staff		
		Male	Female	Male	Female	Male	Female	Female P/T
Marketing Director	2	1			1			
Marketing Services	11		1	1	2	3	2	2
Market Research	14	1	1		2	2	1	7
Competitor Analysis	5	1		2	1		1	
Field Sales	12	1		6	2	1	2	
Export	6	1		4			1	

Example 5.1 Extract from a monthly head count analysis of a marketing division – prepared using *HR/View* with data held in *Executive TRACK* management development planning system

The question may also ask for these people to be identified. Much of this aspect of checking the inventory is straightforward, although many questions involve more than one factor, which we will examine subsequently.

Employment

How do we employ the people summarized on the company manpower report? A simple form of analysis is of very limited value here. In any organization, the variation between types of work undertaken involves the use of a substantial number of job-type categories for any meaningful breakdown. In a large company, some systematic basis for a detailed analysis is necessary, because a straightforward list of, say, 12 salesmen, five progress chasers, 17 export billing typists, one production manager, and so on, filling several pages, would be extremely confusing. Some form of job family grouping is required at an interim stage.

All jobs can be fitted into the pattern of job families. These families link together jobs requiring similar training, experience and skills, so that individuals are better able to move to another post in the same family than to one in a different family requiring an unrelated range of skills. Job family groups include: marketing, personnel, production operations, production engineering, clerical, secretarial, and so on.

Each main family breaks down into series of subgroups, each distinct in itself, but unmistakably part of the major family. For example, in the personnel family, subdivisions would include recruitment posts, training posts, industrial relations posts, and a further breakdown, for instance into different types of training posts, is still possible before we reach individual jobs. A straightforward decimalized coding system is generally used for analysis purposes in large organizations, and is often linked to computerized personnel records. This approach is easily adaptable to companies of any size.

By probing into the organization, data will show the numbers employed in the finance function in relation to budget. If required, we can list the individual positions in descending grade order, or summarize manpower by common titles, by grade levels, by subfunction, etc. The same sort of breakdown can be extracted easily for each functional category, so that an immediate review of utilization can be done, or a review of current manpower against budget can be made.

Inventory of Qualifications (abstract)

Qualifications	Total	Graduate Level				Other	
		Post-Grad	1st/2nd Hons	Other	Profess-ional	HNC	ONC
Arts Graduates							
Economics & Political Science	9	2	4	3			
Languages:							
French	4		2	2			
German	1		1				
Russian	3		2	1			
Other	3	1		2			
Sociology, etc.	1			1			
Others (Classics, History, etc.)	6	1	1	4			
Technical Qualifications							
Mechanical Engineering	36	-	2	2	7	17	8
Electrical Engineering	37	1	1	1	9	13	11
Mech. & Elect. Engineering	5	-	1	-	1	1	2
Production Engineering							

Example 5.2 Extract from a qualifications inventory – prepared using HR/View with data held in *Executive TRACK* management development planning system

Incidentally, if a review is being made against budget, it will only be comprehensive if it incorporates statements covering all known transactions which are in progress – the resignations which have not been effected, agreed transfers in and out, and current recruitment initiatives, particularly new recruits who have yet to start. These employment commitments may alter the apparent position substantially.

When we come to more complex analysis, we shall need to use a measure of job level, and job grade is probably the most convenient form, particularly within a function, although it is rarely of any great value in isolation.

Qualifications

Any collection of people is likely to contain a cross-section of skills and abilities which we would want to analyse as part of the inventory. The first and easiest analysis is of formal qualifications, as shown in example 5.2.

The basic data on the numbers or proportions of graduates will tell us very little in itself. Degree subjects, degree class and university all add value to the inventory but beg further details such as the age distribution and location in the organization.

Data on qualifications should not concentrate on graduates alone, but should cover the academic achievements of the entire workforce and include all professional and other certified achievements.

Training

Much internal training does not lead on to examination and certification, although there are a number of new moves to enable internal courses to add credits towards DMSs or MBAs.

Even without this, employers rate internal training as important and purposeful, and are likely to require an inventory of people who have completed certain courses. For example, in some companies employees have to complete a corporate pre-management course before they can be appointed to any managerial post and one international group uses this method at five distinct levels. An inventory of qualifying candidates will be necessary when vacancies occur, or would be an important element in a selection specification.

Experience

An inventory of the experience available in the company would be valuable, but the sheer complexity of assembling a meaningful summary makes this almost impossible. The problem is that the range of possible experience is vast and this is compounded by the levels and duration of experience within each area, and the mix.

Within a full personnel record, the career history of employees, showing job titles and indications of level such as remuneration or grade, provides a reasonable indication of the range of experience of a particular individual. Accessing this data depends on the capability of the software to identify combinations of keywords or titles or, alternatively, on the extent to which experience can be summarized in some form of coding.

Coding an employee's experience can be immensely time consuming, but a great deal can be covered simply by flagging the major functions and subfunctions performed by the individual. This may enable a long list of candidates to be drawn up and their full records scanned. In terms of basic inventory, details about people in a function can be supplemented with data showing the extent to which those individuals have experience in other functions, an increasing requirement in the 1990s.

Competences

Many companies have been putting a great deal of effort into defining the competences required for managerial jobs. So far, much of this work has been troubled by semantics, as the language used in one organization (or part of an organization) is marginally different from that used elsewhere, and may be understood differently. There is also the problem that the competences in one business may be different from those required in similar posts in another industry, where the business issues and priorities are different.

Of course, we cannot duck the issue of defining competency. At a recent one-day conference on the subject, one delegate quoted the six conflicting definitions used by speakers in the course of the day, and asked, 'What is a competency?' Perhaps the best response would be to say that competences are the required strengths listed in the specification drawn up to define the ideal candidate for a post. But today there are further definitions. For example, some organizations have identified the general competences they want to help establish culture change.

In spite of these difficulties, a number of large organizations have established a language and sets of corporate competences which they find of value. Naturally, these are being built into the corporate personnel database against each job, along with a matching set of each incumbent's competences, to enable any shortcomings to be identified for attention.

In my experience, the competency analyses which are of greatest value are those which identify the competences required within a small management group with a clear mission and the required balance of those competences. This is followed by matching the balance of competences within the group of managers, exploiting individual strengths and covering individual weakness, and leads to efficiency improvements for the group, where as efforts to overcome an inherent limitation in one individual do not.

Returning to the issue of some inventory of required and actual competences, this can be prepared from the information available within an organization. This may result in a substantial variation in the choice of headings between organizations, but this is not important as long as the words are meaningful to the users.

Languages

The evolution of the European market and the general globalization of business have resulted in a substantial increase in the demand for foreign languages and this will be an important element in any inventory. As a general guide, for each language, we need to know who can speak the language and who can read/write it, at 0 level standard, degree level/fluent, or business level.

The inventory may need to identify the linguists in the sales and marketing function as a primary need, backed up with a summary of the total range of languages available. For example, at a business negotiation in, say, Russian, it can be valuable to have one or two inconspicuous Russian speakers around. (One company dressed up two of its graduates as a commissionaire and tea lady.) In negotiations, a second view on translations of what is said can prove valuable.

Another area where languages can be important is research and development, particularly in multinational companies where joint international teams must be functional. Some international companies will only recruit graduates if they are fluent in a second language, and demand some overseas working. Again, the inventory of linguists

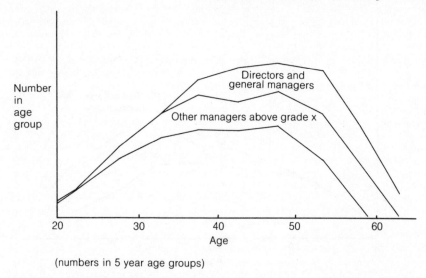

Figure 5.1 Managerial age structure – numbers in five-year age groups

is likely to be relevant. The human resource function in multi-national companies is also finding linguistic ability essential.

Age distribution

Actuaries are very fond of analyses of age distribution for pension and life assurance funding appraisals, but analyses which show the overall age distribution of a company, unit or function, plus the scatter by types of people or by departments, has much wider applications.

Study of such analyses can highlight the areas with age distribution problems. These may arise whenever there is a clustering of any staff category into one age group, meaning many people could reach promotional readiness, or retirement age, in a short period, imposing a strain both on succession planning and continuing effective operation.

Figure 5.1 shows the age distribution in a company in a declining industry where recruitment and retention of younger people has long been poor, and where the age distribution has become heavily weighted to the older end. It will take a further 15 years for the main body of long-serving people to have retired, and the business implications of that fact may need to be digested.

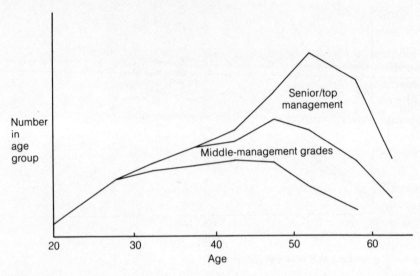

Figure 5.2 Ageing management population

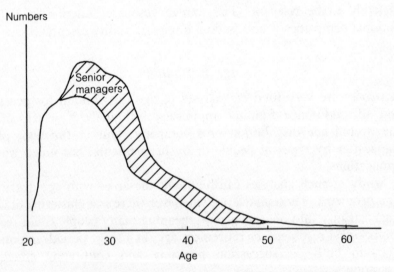

Figure 5.3 Management age distribution in a fast-growing young organization

Figure 5.2 shows a similar position, with the analysis limited to the management grades only. Once again it is evident that the older managers in place will dominate thinking for some time, and some drastic action would be required to open the way for younger blood.

Of course, having a younger management group is not without its problems. Figure 5.3 is drawn from a company created less than 20 years ago, which has grown rapidly, drawing in young managers. Because its business is maturing and growth is slowing, and the age wave of senior managers will take more than 10 years to begin retiring, there are serious implications for the company in terms of the limited prospects for its bright younger people. Likewise, age clustering at the younger level can mean restricted promotion prospects, frustration and excessive loss of able staff.

A study undertaken by one of the largest British organizations revealed that its overall age distribution differed from the national age distribution. Analysis revealed that the company's peaks were related to the intake of many younger people at times of rapid expansion. The board of the company felt that an improved age scatter was desirable, and that this might be achieved by tending to favour during recruitment those people born during the company's off-peak periods. However, operationally this proved unrealistic.

This type of corrective action needs to be restricted to areas where definite problems arise, rather than attempt to create an ideal distribution which has little positive advantage. If a problem exists or is expected to develop due to age distribution, then it must be planned out of existence. For example, a major paper company went through a ten-year phase of recruiting virtually no graduates. This only became a really serious problem five years later when the absence of serious candidates for middle management, and ultimately top management, became evident. Recruiting to fill the gap was possible, but proved difficult in their culture. The company certainly understood the more serious message, that you cannot have gaps in a recruiting pattern which sustain essential flows.

When increasing numbers of younger people reach high managerial positions at early stages, the age distribution within management may point to future difficulties. For example, if the directors of a company are all between the ages of 35 and 40, then other staff in their 30s, 40s and 50s are likely to feel heavily restricted in their prospects for further promotion. Few situations are as clear cut as this, of course, but an analysis of the age distribution for each level of management may bring to light less obvious difficulties which can be given serious thought before they grow into problems.

Grade, rather than management level, provides a basis for finer analysis against age. Alternatively, salary may be substituted for grade. Gaps in the pattern may indicate potential succession problems (as in the paper company mentioned), or clusters on the age versus salary graphs may indicate potential problems which require further investigation. Alternatively, the study may confirm an acceptable picture of relationships which present no apparent problems.

Combination of factors

The discussion of analysis of age distribution above shows that, as analysis of the inventory progresses, separate headings are rarely informative in isolation, and it is combinations of factors which demonstrate strengths or problems in our manpower.

The distribution of our stock by age gives only the baldest of data, and it is the age distribution within segments of the population which may flag concerns, as we saw above. An ageing population in research and development may suggest experience is a strength, but could highlight the likelihood of a lack in up-to-date knowledge of fast moving technology, and limitations in the proportion of people for promotion.

A common analysis is age distribution by grade or salary. Figure 5.4 shows such an analysis in pictorial form, highlighting the relative

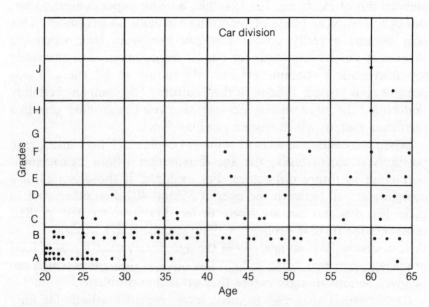

Figure 5.4 Age and grade distribution – note the lack of younger men in the middle grades indicates potential succession problems

lack of younger people in the middle grades of the organization. A particular application is to examine the relationships between salaries and grades of young high fliers against the population at large. There will not be a perfect relationship, because some highly paid younger people will be specialists whose skills are in great demand and command high market values, but whose potential may not be outstanding. The analysis may identify individuals of high potential who are not being progressed fast enough (in remuneration or grade terms) or individuals who are highly placed and whose further potential needs to be reviewed.

Distribution of the graduate population is worth analysing. Is there a reasonable distribution across functions, for example, or is, say, sales and marketing poorly endowed? The age/salary or age/grade distribution of graduates is usually interesting. One analysis revealed a couple of Oxbridge graduates in their 50s employed in jobs at the graduate entry level, and both with long service. They were not ambitious people, which might explain why they were overlooked years before, but they were obviously intelligent and could have progressed further. Instead, both had developed substantial outside interests, having accepted rejection by the company. Distribution of technical graduates by age and grade is an important element in the flow analyses examined in chapter 10 because, if the mix is wrong, the arteries of career development begin to clog up with people who are not progressing and surgery may be required.

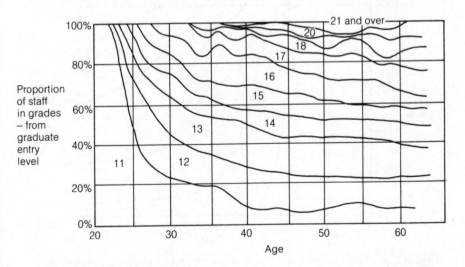

Figure 5.5 Age/grade analysis

Figure 5.5 shows a different form of age/grade analysis, indicating the proportion of people from each age group within each grade, and showing the pace of progression through a structure in relation to age. Unless you have a large population, preparing these charts can be difficult, requiring some smoothing out of rough patterns.

If the dividing lines are for broader categories than individual grades, as is the case in the study of managers in figure 5.6, the general career opportunities for graduates can be seen. It is worth noting that the development of parallel career streams, with many graduates likely to achieve high level specialist positions, makes this graph potentially confusing, but the company in question had adopted the common practice of using the title manager for people managing significant specialist areas, even where no subordinates were involved.

Analysis of leavers

Analysing who is leaving is an important aid to managing manpower losses, and is addressed later. Much of this analysis involves looking at combinations of factors, such as in figure 5.7 which looks at the age and salary pattern of leavers against the rest of the population.

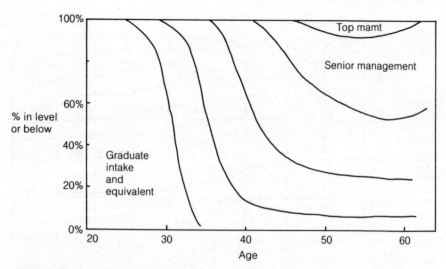

Figure 5.6 Management age distribution by levels, showing promotion flows

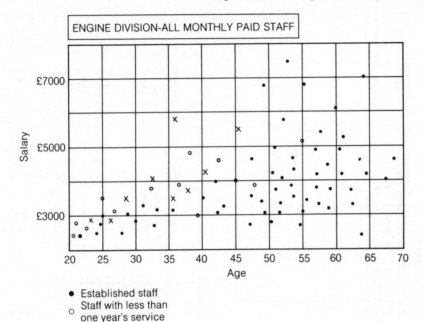

Figure 5.7 Age and salary distribution, showing loss analysis

This suggests that the division in question may be losing many of its better people.

Of course, we would want other basic data on leavers as well, perhaps along the lines shown in example 5.3, and further statistical analyses will supplement this information.

Perhaps one of the most useful analyses is of survival rates. If we recruit 50 graduates each year, we can make comparisons of the survival rates of these cohorts, and assess whether changes of policy have had some impact on encouraging people to stay with the company. The use of this analysis is covered in some detail in chapter 14.

Inventory of Performance Appraisal Data

Appraisal is well established as part of normal business life, although, looking at the great variety of appraisal methods and purposes, one sometimes wonders quite what is being achieved and quite what some managements think they are measuring. For selection purposes

Analysis of Staff Turnover (extracts)

I. Analysis by Category

Job Category	Average strength during year	Terminations in year		Termination % for previous year	Number transferred or promoted from category
		Number	% of average strength		
Female Staff:					
A. Secretarial					
(1) Secretaries	7	2	29	33	
(2) Shorthand Typists	12	7	58	55	
(3) Copy typists (inc. billing, etc.)	27	18	67	76	2
(4) Other	4	2	50	25	1

II. Analysis by Reasons for Leaving

Reason	Primary Reason		Primary + contributory	
	Number	Proportion of total	Number of mentions	Proportion of total
Male Staff:				
Salary and benefits	4	14%	21	18%
Promotion prospects	7	24%	15	13%
Under-employment	2	7%	9	8%
Generally dissatisfied	3	10%	14	12%
Domestic reasons	2	7%	3	2%

Example 5.3   Extracts from an analysis of staff turnover

we need to have a basis for feeding our manpower inventory with information on performance and potential.

Appraisal is concerned with how well the employee carries out his present job. The purpose of the appraisal should be to identify, in collaboration with the individual, how his performance might be improved. In this process, development and training needs are identified.

Additionally, appraisal has some application to, or influence on, remuneration. This purpose may be perceived to be in conflict with the primary purpose, as managers may be encouraged to produce favourable appraisals to achieve a desired remuneration advance, and feel that they can more easily override the development aspects.

In addition, we shall need an inventory of people's potential ability to do other work at the same level, or to work at a more senior level. This is covered later in this chapter.

The purpose of any performance appraisal plan is to provide a standard means of appraising how well the employee actually does the job for which he is employed. This must start from a clear understanding of the job itself, the specific immediate and future objectives and the time and resources allocated. This is not just an ideal state, but an absolute necessity which must be achieved if the appraisal is to be meaningful. The appraiser or rater must fully appreciate that he is appraising the individual's performance against the requirements of the job, and that any factors not associated with performance of the job are irrelevant.

It is also essential for the appraisal to be carried out by managers who have been trained to appreciate the difficulties of the task they undertake. Bias, attributable to lack of appreciation of these points, may produce silly results, such as high ratings for senior people and low ratings for junior people, which the manager could justify by quoting a straight comparison between one of his senior supervisors and one of his clerks, making the obvious statement that 'the supervisor is contributing much more than the clerk'. Such a rating obviously contains a combination of performance and job value, and is of no use until the two factors can be identified and examined separately.

To provide a sound basis for appraising performance, it is invaluable to have a set of personal objectives agreed between manager and subordinate at the beginning of the appraisal cycle. This may be modified somewhat in the light of unanticipated events, but gives a starting point for all of the informal performance discussions through the year, and for the rounding-up session when the year is complete. Questions of achievement or non-achievement are resolved against the agreed parameters and provide a basis for financial reward.

However, the more important aspect of appraisal is concerned with how results are achieved and how performance (and possibly potential) may be enhanced. Achievement of a key financial result might be matched by failures on a number of other less highlighted but nonetheless critical elements. Loss of key staff or failure to develop people are typical elements which may be played down within a system, but are vital to the business.

In looking at appraisal data, we need to be aware of what they are based on to ensure that they are relevant to the proposed application. There will be a greater need in future to get a measure of interpersonal skills and leadership abilities, and these factors within an appraisal scheme may be recorded separately from the overall conclusion.

I am more at ease with appraisals designed to encourage performance improvement. Unlike appraisals applied to remuneration, these do not need to be quantified or reduced to a score, but they are difficult to summarize in a database. I prefer a simple approach. I want to know if the jobholder is new in the post and still learning basics; is established, but has much scope for improvement; is established, but still has scope for small improvements; and is fully in control of all aspects of the job.

Taken with potential, the last category can help identify individuals in need of an early move to a fresh appointment. The middle two categories could be merged, but separating them is useful in identifying individuals who are well established, but still struggling to reach full effectiveness, and those who may have been overpromoted.

Inventory of Potential Ability Data

What other jobs could this person do now? What jobs should this employee be able to do in future, given proper training and the opportunity to develop experience? Answer these questions fully and accurately and you have an excellent start to the assessment of future potential.

A classic example of the difference between present performance and future potential occurred when a high-calibre graduate doing a stint in the personnel department was assigned to the personnel records section for two weeks to get to know the work. He picked up the entire operation in a couple of days and was given records clerical work to do. Bored, he made appalling blunders while his mind was on other things and was clearly useless as a records clerk. But his ability to run a complete personnel department within a year or so was undoubted, and subsequently proven.

The senior clerk in the same records section, who had his routine job completely under control, was given a small promotion, but had to be relieved of his new post a month later as it proved to be beyond him. Potential ability does not necessarily correlate with performance on present work. Both assessment and inventory of potential must acknowledge that all employees are likely to be changing but at greatly differing rates – some will be growing rapidly in capacity towards readiness to take bigger jobs.

An even more valuable list is that identifying people with potential who are on top of their present jobs and ready for a move, as these individuals are not only valuable to the company, but also to other employers. As a Personnel Director, the list of ready-nows lived on my desk for daily attention.

Worthy of a footnote are the people who disappear from potential lists. It is not surprising that when a person is moved into a challenging new job, his initial performance is not sparkling and he may need extra guidance. It is evident that such performance, taken in isolation, does not demonstrate further potential, and his name is deleted from the list. A couple of years later, it may reappear as he gets on top of the new job and his potential is recognized again. I do not like such people to disappear and try to ensure that they stay on the list, possibly marked, until they are taken off the list deliberately on the basis of a careful reassessment of longer term potential.

Analysis of Absenteeism

Absenteeism is relevant to manpower planning if it has a possible influence on future manpower requirements or supply. Of course, there is a need to record absence, and the reasons for it, and logical to analyse the severity and causes.

Control of absenteeism should fall wholly with line supervisors and managers, and they are also the source for much of the data which feed into absence records. It may be that there is no problem;

that the level of absence is tolerable and felt to be under control. Or, it may be that with absence running at above 15 per cent, we have had to increase manning levels to get the work done.

Our interest is likely to focus on any problem area. To be sure we have a full measure of the problem, we need data from which we can assess the frequency of absence for each individual, analyse the reasons given (or lack of justification), and also determine the frequency and extent of lateness (although this should be left entirely in the hands of the supervisor). These analyses identify the areas where absence tends to be high, and individuals with poor records, as a basis for action.

Individuals with poor records may be chronically sick – most larger companies have such cases for much of the time. Is enough being done to rehabilitate or redeploy these people? There will also be a list of probable malingerers. These people require the attention of the medical department, including visits to see if the treatment they are getting is adequate.

Some habitual absentees are likely to be from areas with particularly poor absence records, and which may also have unpleasant working conditions and repetitive unsatisfying jobs.

A few years ago a Government paper on absenteeism picked out the provision of maximum job satisfaction for all employees as the major corrective action open to employers faced with high absenteeism. But not all jobs can be made more satisfying. Some things can be done, and frequently small things have a surprising impact. Even tidying up and fresh paint tells employees that someone cares. Listening to employees may provide pointers, but remember that the things that really cause distress and which employees assume cannot be altered will probably not come to the surface readily.

Many companies have attempted to reduce absenteeism and failed. Any shift to a more open style of managing, or the initiation of a total quality programme, opens up communication and encourages many of the causes of absenteeism to surface, together with suggestions on how they can be resolved. Given the heavy cost of absenteeism, it is always worth seeking a solution rather than inflating manpower requirements.

Conclusions

Assessments of potential are likely to be reliable only for two or three years ahead and only for one career step beyond the present position.

An inventory of stored materials reflects a stock position which is reasonably stable (although some may deteriorate and other stock may become obsolete). An inventory of people, and particularly of performance appraisal and potential, is far more dynamic. Last year's data are of interest, but only the latest picture will provide the basis for current action and decisions. The latest information on an employee's weaknesses and strong points, motivation, ambitions and the limitations he accepts, together with an assessment of his response to new situations and general development, allow further potential to be judged afresh.

Which of our employees has potential for significant career advancement within a reasonable period? Appended to many staff appraisal forms is a short final section directed at the employee's overall suitability for other work. For all staff considered to have potential for advancement, there will be further question in another form. Below is a typical tail-end question from the performance rating system of a major engineering company. This short report breaks potential into five categories and is appended to the performance report

1 Unlikely to progress beyond current level.
2 Some potential ability evident, but form is unclear at this stage.
3 Potential ability to develop within present area of work.
4 Ready for higher level work within one year – see full report.
5 Ready for higher level work within one year, and evident capacity for substantial further progress – see full report.
(Detailed reports are to be prepared for all employees in categories 4 and 5.)

This is an opening gambit which leads on to a further questionnaire and useful data for inclusion in our inventory.

These questions can be assumed to weed out the real non-starters effectively, but overestimation of future potential is a widespread fault because most managers recognize that they are on uncertain ground and prefer to let them still go forward to be tested further. It is comparatively rare for any individual to be marked below his realistic level, although it is not unknown for a selfish manager to try to conceal the ability of a prized subordinate in an attempt to retain the individual. There is, therefore, no advantage in covering all staff by detailed questionnaires on potential.

Having short-listed those individuals considered to be able to progress beyond their present levels during the next five years, a standard approach is necessary to gain a more complete picture. The most common approach is to use assessment or development centres.

These can provide invaluable guidance for individual career development, but the data are too diverse to provide any basis for analysis and cannot be used directly in the inventory.

I find the most useful aid is a list of people with potential generated by the line managers and suitably amended to exclude individuals whose development centre conclusions support an absence of any significant potential.

6
Manning Standards, Culture and Utilization

Any forecast of manning requirements must involve assumptions about the work that will be required (and whether it is really necessary) and the amounts of that work which can be done by an employee or group of the relevant category. Relationships between volumes of work and the people required to do it provide the manning standards to be used for planning purposes.

There are many potential influences on these standards. The organization of work, the ways things are done, the attitudes of the workforce, and the suitability of people can all have a considerable impact on human efficiency and the numbers of people required. Hence, standards cannot be an absolute measure and the apparent levels will vary enormously. In many businesses, there is an ongoing pressure for greater efficiency and higher productivity, which tends to mean tighter manning standards so, before we look at the determination of standards, we should understand these various influences because they hold the key to improvement, yet are difficult to change. For example, these influences mean that it is necessary to look at the corporate culture and how effectively people are utilized and motivated when building up any picture of present and future manpower. If we wish to improve the utilization of manpower and manning standards, it is likely that cultural factors will provide the means.

The work to be done

Identification of the work to be done appears relatively straightforward. While this is the case for most direct production and similar activities, it is more difficult for jobs with greater discretionary elements or less quantifiable activities.

Measurement can also be straightforward. In direct production, a required volume of output can be divided into known work units and the number of standard hours required to complete the work is easily calculated. Assumptions can be made for minor changes in production methods and time standards, related to current experience. An alternative is to determine the optimum team size for a sequence of operations and agreed volume.

In administrative activities with highly variable work elements, it is still possible to measure the manpower required with some degree of accuracy, but the analysis required will take longer to pick up the full range of activities embodied in the job. For example, a job with a cycle time of one month would need to be studied, part-time, over the full cycle. Many accounting posts have such a cycle time, from the production of one set of monthly accounts to the next, but to cover every aspect of a job, the study would need to take into consideration the production of annual accounts.

The way in which work is done is also significant because analysis may show that large amounts of effort or time are wasted, perhaps due to poor job design or work planning, or simply for historical reasons. An example of good practice might be where the smooth flow of materials from one work point to the next enables each worker to get on with his primary tasks without fetching and carrying. Work planning should also ensure that individuals have sensible work-loads which do not result in excessive idle time.

Necessary work

Many departments are fully occupied or overloaded because a proportion of their time is spent on unnecessary work. In reviewing manning requirements, it is always worth asking 'Is all the work really necessary?' Almost always, there will be some activities which have ceased to be required, or are duplicated, or could be simplified. If some additional task is required, you can be sure it will be initiated, but, somehow, nobody looks around for what can be trimmed out – until a manpower analyst comes round.

Time spent on trimming back work requirements to the necessary minimum will improve manning standards. There can be no satisfaction for an employee in knowing that the work he or she is doing has no impact on anything or anybody and can be deposited immediately in the rubbish bin. It does not follow that there is immediate redundancy for the unfortunate employee. In all normal circumstances, natural wastage is likely to provide redeployment opportunities within a short time, with the knowledge that the new work is essential to the ongoing operation of the enterprise.

Study of the work to be done might use systems analyses to ensure that the most suitable systems and equipment are used, and that the whole is properly integrated with the overall management information systems. There is an increasing need to reappraise information systems to ensure that the more remote parts of these systems feed back relevant information on manpower utilization.

Variation in people

Manning standards can never be absolute because people vary too much. People are far from identical. Beyond the obvious differences of size and strength which seem to be readily accepted, intellectual differences are, proportionally, vastly greater.

In reality, there are enormous differences between individuals which mean enormous differences in their suitability for any type of work and in the performances achievable. Hopefully, the selection of people for any particular job will be based on a personal specification to ensure that employees can do the work required adequately, and that individuals who did not match the required basic abilities were excluded. Then some reasonable average level of performance can be determined.

Poor specification or poor selection can lead to a much wider spread of performance levels. However, efforts to raise quality by setting recruitment specifications at too high a level generally have an opposite impact because over-qualified people become bored and frustrated, and more inclined to making errors, to absenteeism and turnover.

Effective utilization of people begins with a proper understanding of the job itself and the skills and abilities required, so that the position can be defined, with an appropriate personal specification which matches the job demands. A professional standard of recruitment practice should ensure that the specification is observed. Given that approach, the range of individual performance variation should be limited. At the bottom end, inexperience will justify low achievement, but it is reasonable to expect a fast learning curve. As full competence is reached, variations may develop as some individuals show greater commitment and drive, but the range should not be so great that a standard cannot be determined.

Corporate Culture

Corporate culture evolves from a consensus of the views and behaviours of the people who make up the company, particularly the managers. Given that culture is about 'how we do things around here', it has a critical influence on the quality of people, on efficiency, and on the manning standards of the company. For this reason, we need to understand corporate culture and the form of its influence on manpower planning.

Corporate culture is about company values; what the company believes and how it behaves. The company, for this purpose, has its identity in the body of directors, managers and other employees, whose collective individual viewpoints make up the consensus. The company view should be provided primarily by the top leadership and be communicated through, and supported by, the management structure, so that a broad consensus agreement exists. This consensus is evident in many organizations but, in others, there is a disparity between the words of the leaders and their behaviour, so that the real culture is not the spoken but the perceived. In a large company, product and geographical differences may lead to distinct variations of culture in different units, which are logical and sound.

Corporate culture is credited with determining the potential success or failure of many an enterprise. If the business objectives and strategies of the company are strongly supported by the values and behaviour, or style, of the organization, the will to achieve desired objectives will be strong; but where those values and behaviour are not clear or not supportive, the probability of success will be substantially reduced. For example, if sales objectives (and thereby, profit objectives) are seen as being critically dependent on good customer service and product quality and the company is developing strategies to improve these, then any historical attitudes which brand customers as nuisances, or carelessness in manufacture, will require substantial and long-term corrective action to achieve the critical behavioural change. Meanwhile, the sales objectives will be seriously at risk and the overall achievability of the plan uncertain, solely due to cultural factors.

Culture is . . .

Most individuals who have had holidays abroad have been aware that the locals behave differently. They have different languages, dress differently, have houses which are different, eat different things cook in unfamiliar ways, and so on. It is likely that their behaviour and attitudes will be discernably different from our own, and perhaps that fundamental beliefs differ. We recognize that we come from a different culture. Within one country, there are many communities in which we may recognize cultural differences that are just as marked, and analyses of cultures within companies may show the same pattern.

As with many aspects of human resources management, discussions of what culture is are likely to result in argument and a feeling that, for many, it is a rather woolly concept. Culture (without the corporate) has been defined by the anthropologist, Kluckhohn, as: 'The set of habitual and traditional ways of thinking, feeling and reacting that are characteristic of the ways a particular society meets its problems.'

Moving to corporate cultures, we can perceive differences between, say, Marks and Spencer and British Home Stores, or between Allied Dunbar and a more traditional insurance company. In corporate terms, the word 'culture', argues Edgar Schein (1985), 'should be reserved for the basic assumptions and beliefs that are shared by members of an organization, that operate unconsciously, and that define in a basic taken-for-granted fashion an organization's view of itself and its environment.'

Culture shows itself in a collection of rules, overt and covert, in principles and values, all strongly rooted in tradition, which influence behaviour within the organization. It is the commitment to common objectives and values which runs through an organization.

Corporate cultures are clearly visible from the way people behave, their interactions internally and with outsiders (particularly customers), and the systems or rituals which they establish. There will be acceptable ways of getting things done, and resistance if the norms are challenged. There may be a declaration of values, associated for example with quality, or equal opportunity, etc. And there will be a feeling about how the enterprise is managed, so that a company needs to be seen to be acting correctly, even if this occasionally causes some pain.

Culture may be said to be 'owned' by the company at large, or the opinion formers within it. It is complex in a large organization in that any corporate culture is both an overlay and an amalgam of the cultures of many subgroups within the structure.

As culture is developed by people, and people are continually changing, culture too is in a constant state of evolution. Given also that the enterprise exists in a continually changing external environment, there are performance-related pressures on individual managers in the enterprise to adjust to environmental change which may involve some modification of thinking, attitudes and behaviour.

The behavioural norms which develop in a corporate culture have been said to be those which provide solutions to problems of survival and adaptation to the environment and integrate the internal systems and processes which support these solutions. Within this, the development of a consensus between all those involved is a key element in the formation and evolution of corporate cultures. People will function easily together only where there is a high level of consensus which leaves them free to concentrate on their primary roles.

This consensus will cover a range of aspects beginning with the need for a common language; a common interpretation of jargon or technical terms, without which outsiders would find it difficult to participate. Membership of a group, and the means of gaining acceptance are crucial, as are all other relationship rules related to direct and indirect authority and influence.

Slow to change

Once established, culture appears to be fairly static and gain intertia. People who join the organization become indoctrinated and may adapt some of their own thinking and standards to conform. To some degree, this may be essential if they are to get things done in their new environment. Anti-cultural behaviour can make it impossible to achieve anything. There may be some scope for the charismatic maverick to operate, but he will be tolerated rarely.

A long established culture matures and the background to it may be rich in stories. If the norm is of long service and a reasonably static business environment, then the patterns of thinking and behaviour may have become deeply entrenched. The style of leadership will be embodied in the culture which, in turn, will influence management development and the growth of the next generation of leaders. In this way, culture can come to control the thinking of an enterprise, dictating how things are done, the form of systems, the form of organization, the type of managers and influence the direction of the business objectives and operating standards. This dominance of thinking can become rigid and dictate what the enterprise judges to be effective management, as well as making it selective about what it hears of (or from) the outside world. This increases its vulnerability.

Culture and Effectiveness

Corporate culture can be highly supportive in enabling an enterprise to achieve its objectives. Certainly there are organizations which seem to have cultures which are completely right and to be progressing with great energy as a rusult. In contrast, one finds companies in business environments which offer great opportunities, yet they appear to be unable to exploit those opportunities. On closer examination, such companies appear preoccupied with internal problems and may be unaware of events which have opened new doors for them. The effect of the culture on corporate performance is crucial.

Margulies and Raia detailed the critical value areas as:

- Providing opportunities for people to function as human beings.
- Providing opportunities for individuals to develop their full potential.
- Creating environments within which work could be satisfying.
- Providing opportunities for people to influence work.
- Accepting the complexity of human beings.
- Increasing organization effectiveness.

These can be seen to be of primary importance in business issues, and are the fundamentals one looks for in statements of corporate beliefs. If these values are evident in company leadership/management philosophy and behaviour, then the culture of that organization is likely to be unambiguous and widely held.

The constraints which are culturally based appear to stem from the absence of leadership; lack of corporate values or consistency in behaviours; failure to communicate any clear vision of the future; or diminished drive. To illustrate the extent to which culture can influence manning standards and efficiency, it is worth looking at each end of the scale.

Low efficiency in the use of manpower is likely to be associated with poor leadership, which leaves subordinates unclear about what is expected of them and exposed to conflicting objectives, demands and behaviours. The cumulative result is the retention of less effective people who are less educated, less well trained, with less initiative and drive, and disinclined to accept responsibility or exert themselves. Generally, they are less well paid because the organizations which attract them have far too many people and cannot afford higher wage levels. Absenteeism is also significantly higher and may increase manpower requirements by a further 15 per cent.

The immediate impression one gains in a highly efficient company is not one of people rushing and working very hard but, rather, there is a clarity of purpose and style which enables people to work intelligently and get things done. Its people will be competent and inclined to tell you that they and their organization are the best in their field. They feel that their company is competitive and that it has an edge wherever it chooses to go. They will naturally have done their best because the environment enabled them to make a real contribution. These are natural achievers with initiative and flair. They are the highest paid in their categories and this is natural and justified.

Improving manpower utilization

The quality of our manpower and the quality of our leadership determine the level at which we can set company objectives and the probabilities of achieving those objectives. Their effectiveness can be reduced by poor organization, poor structuring of work and poor utilization of people. A central purpose of manpower planning and control is to improve utilization of the company manpower resources.

A theme for consideration is that we must aim to move beyond merely controling head count, by delegating responsibilities for manning standards to managers and supervisors. An extention of this may be to alter the control from head count to total remuneration, giving managers greater freedom to increase manpower quality by using fewer people at higher pay levels. Improving manning standards is improving use of the manpower resource.

Manning Standards

Having set the scene by examining the extraordinary strength of some of the potential influences on manning standards, we can get back to the practicalities of how they may be determined.

Work measurement

To what extent can we measure the work to be done, and determine the numbers and categories of manpower necessary to carry out that work? In the past, work study has been commonly used, particularly in manufacturing operations where large volumes of similar activities were carried out by large numbers of similar people. It is worth a brief look at some of this, as the principles are sill relevant.

Work study has been defined as the systematic investigation of all of the factors that affect the efficiency and economy of the situation being reviewed with the aim of effecting improvement. These practices could be applied to any regular operational work, even in the office, but could be applied only with difficulty to thinking activities.

It is necessary to observe, record, and measure the actions involved in the work studied. The analytical work therefore tends to be a full-time job for an individual (rather than a part-time job for a foreman or supervisor) able to observe and record every aspect of the work under study, with the agreement of all involved. The more sophisticated systems provide estimates for non-observable jobs, and various systems could be applied to cover most production, service and clerical work.

Work study has two main elements; method study and work measurement. In simple terms, method study will help to simplify each job (and perhaps to identify more economical means of getting the work done), while work measurement enables one to measure the time required to do the job.

The *ILO Manual of Work Study* quoted eight steps to be taken in any work study exercise:

1 Select the job or process to be studied.
2 Record from direct observation everything that happens, using the most suitable of the recording techniques available, so that the data will be in the most convenient form to be analysed.
3 Examine the recorded facts critically and challenge everything that is done, considering in turn: the purpose of the activity; the place where it is performed; the sequence in which it is done; the person who is doing it; the means by which it is done.
4 Develop the most economic method taking into account all of the circumstances (method study).

5 Measure the quantity of work involved in the method selected and calculate a standard for doing it (work measurement).
6 Define the new method and the related time so that it can always be identified.
7 Install the new method as agreed standard practice within the time allowed.
8 Maintain the new standard practice by proper procedures.

Method study covers the first four of these steps. Record everything that happens from direct observation means just that. In some situations, there may be a considerable amount of slack time or ineffective work due to lack of planning and other reasons. Some studies show effective working time can be as low as 25 per cent of the total. Work sampling will identify poor areas quickly.

Interrelationships between one activity and another, one worker and another, and between groups of works and machines possibly offer the greatest scope for productivity improvement, particularly when linked into effective work planning. Of particular relevance is the need to plan sequencing when an activity involves varied skills. Much of this analysis may be charted to help clarify exactly what is done and why it is done. The answers obtained should point to the means of developing the most economic method.

Establishing manning standards

Work measurement is concerned with determining how long it takes a qualified worker to carry out a specified job at a defined level of performance. The concept is applicable to the establishment of manning standards for most types of work in all functions.

Work measurement is not a single technique, but covers a range of approaches developed in companies and by consultants. It is a fairly specialized area, and will not be covered in detail here. However, it usually involves building up a picture of normal practice so that normal standards of output can be assessed to provide a basis for determining ongoing manning requirements. Because individual abilities do vary considerably, judgements may be required to determine a reasonable norm. In the process, a wide range of allowances may need to be incorporated to cover everything from visits to toilets to many sorts of interruption and work delay. In the end, there has to be a conclusion which is of value to the supervisor or manager.

A range of these analytical approaches has been designed specifically for clerical work by management consulting firms, mainly derived from time study, estimating and activity sampling. There is no difference in the purpose of these schemes, which is to measure the time taken to perform the work content of an activity for cost control and manning standards, and provide some groundwork for methods improvement. In each case, an assumption has to be made about the work pace because individuals vary enormously in their abilities to do work at particular speeds. It is possible to observe variations in the work rates of people over several weeks, with the objective of stabilizing utilization at the levels achieved in the better weeks.

Manning standards in indirect areas

One large company developed a highly participative programme with the following objectives:

- To re-establish proper manning standards covering all indirect categories.
- To install a simple reporting system which will give everybody, and particularly junior management, continuous information on the utilization of manpower.
- To use the system as a tool to increase the awareness of manpower utilization, to ensure that it reaches, and is maintained at, satisfactory levels.
- To provide information on current and future manning requirements.

The company set up a small project team to support the programme through the first year. With line mangement, they identified seven stages:

1 Introduction of the programme and its objectives to all involved.
2 Detailed analysis of the work to be done, systems in use, relevance of all actions involved.
3 Improvement of work flow and content, and identification of significant systems changes required, where appropriate.
4 The establishment of initial work standards and manning levels.
5 The installation of work movement and manpower utilization controls.
6 The training of management and supervisors in the use of the controls.
7 The subsequent maintenance of the system by the users.

Most of the project work concentrated on the last three stages and, after the information bases were established, everything was left to local managers, who used their data and developed them further. All felt better informed and more able to make positive comment on manning requirements for budgeting, several volunteering targets in excess of current achievement.

It is important to note that the initiative for much of the improvement came from a level of management previously excluded from real involvement in manpower planning and control, and to highlight the potential which this implies. This is typical of improvements generated through TQM programmes, which empower a wider range of people. The opportunity for involvement in decisions, plus recognition of the importance of making better use of people, appeared to be the critical factors which led to support.

Manpower/work ratio trends

Unless the organization is undergoing major change, existing manpower standards exert such a powerful influence on future standards that the ratio trend provides a sound forecast. The basic assumption being made is that the ratios of people to work required will remain roughly the same and that the trend of any change will remain relatively even. For example, the direct manpower required for set volumes of activity will approach a straight-line trend. In many situation, past actual levels provide the best 'manning standards' to be used to forecast future requirements.

Fundamentally, all manpower requirement forecasting is derived from analysis of the past. By using ratio-trend forecasting, we are accepting that current standards provide a base which may be a crude measure, but which will produce something more than generalized forecasts as we are using figures which have been tested in practice. Alternatively, ratio-trend forecasts provide a cross-check on more detailed forecasts which have been developed from analyses of requirements by category, indicating whether the results of that detailed analysis conform to previous general manning patterns or whether some substantially different pattern is emerging.

Ratio-trend forecasting relies on the inertia that results from acceptance of existing manpower ratios, and the problems of changing those standards. It accepts the logic of applying existing standards to planned work volumes to establish a start point for determining future needs, prior to any adjustments for changes in methods or standards taking place.

Ratio-trend operation uses the analysis of past staffing to build up a picture of the trends in ratios to show what has happened to date. The basic manpower inventory can provide a great deal of data for

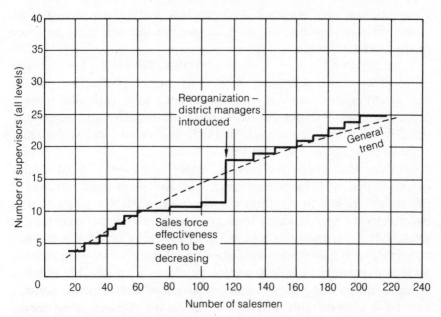

Figure 6.1 Ratio-trend graph: ratio of supervisors to field sales force

this purpose. In addition to assembling data on meaningful work/ manpower relationships, it is necessary to identify and record all of those events which may be expected to influence or change those standards. For example, there may be forthcoming changes in equipment and its use, as in a factory which is gradually being automated, or in an office where a new generation of data-processing equipment is to be introduced. Not all will result in sudden changes, of course, as many developments are gradual, producing a trend effect over several months or years.

For this reason, apart from the advantages of using visual aids, it is advisable to plot this data on a series of ratio-trend graphs, as these will highlight any changes, be they sudden or more gradual. Figures 6.1 to 6.4 show ratio-trend graphs, some of which are explained in detail below.

The key to effective ratio-trend operation is selecting meaningful ratios – it must be possible to link measurable amounts of activity to the manpower required to carry out that work. For example, in a sales and marketing department we might have manpower/work ratios for salesmen/sales targets, salesmen/supervision, salesmen/ branch administrative staff, and so on. The ratios selected must be clean because any influence by irrelevant factors would make the conclusions misleading. Figure 6.1 examines the ratio of supervisors to the field sales force.

Line and staff activities respond rather differently to this type of analysis. Line activities, with their direct productive nature, are ideally suited, so that production and sales activities present few difficulties. Relationships between work required and manpower directly employed are straightforward, and related ratios for close supporting staff are also relevant.

In pure staff areas, work is less easily measured. Ratios cannot be developed with long-term standards, and short-term ratio-based projections represent the limit one can go to with this method. It is more relevant to consider company objectives and the expectations from staff departments as a basis for determining manpower needs.

Service activities fall between the two categories. For example, the finance department's billing section produces a measurable number of work units, and the personnel department's recruitment activity may have a measurable output, but not so the research department. Its team of electronics engineers may have quadrupled over the past two years, and they may have produced some valuable results, but each result is a one-off and future objectives cannot be assessed in the same terms. Only an assessment by engineers of the work required can determine whether seven or 14 or 21 engineers will be needed next year. Or the question could well be reversed to ask: 'What can be achieved with the engineers we have?'

Returning to line operations, look at some figures for an office equipment company with a substantial service maintenance workforce. In this rather straightforward case, there is a direct relationship between numbers of machines covered by service contracts and numbers of engineers. Variation occurs in areas where machines are fewer and more scattered, requiring longer travelling/non-working time. Future variation may occur if additional types of machine are installed with different service requirements.

Figure 6.2 shows a trend line drawn through the ratios of machines to total numbers of engineers. Figure 6.3, showing similar data plotted on a logarithmic scale, brings out the variation that occurs between small and large areas. Almost any line operation can be examined in this way, and the relationships between manpower categories and measures of the work required illustrated. In the company servicing machines in figures 6.2 and 6.3, other relationships were used, such as between:

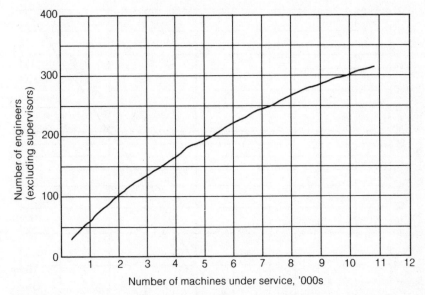

Figure 6.2 Ratio-trend graph: ratio of service engineers to machines in the field

- salesmen and machines sold;
- direct production employees and production volumes;
- administrative support staff and the size of the employee group supported (separate relationships for service, sales, production);
- overseas activities and home-based divisions; and
- overall manpower and total business volume (measured in financial and volume terms).

It was possible to note significant developments and the resultant changes in manpower standard trends on these charts. Projecting trend lines allows anticipated developments to be taken into account. A guide to optimum levels of manning can be determined for most situations and blended with other data. Forecasts of manning requirements for new product launches are also possible. As a short-term measure, it is sensible to relate the new situation back to the old and then adjust it for different market factors which are likely to alter the trend lines.

Work demand factors

In some of the examples quoted, there is a high correlation between total manpower required and one particular work demand factor, to

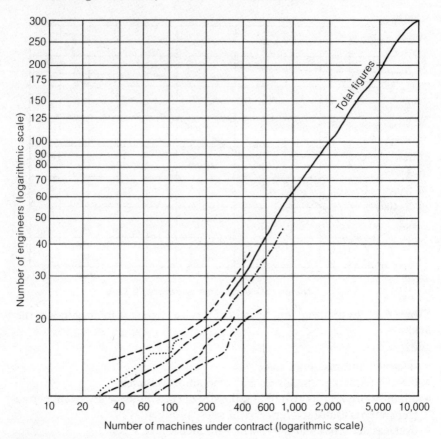

Figure 6.3   Ratio-trend graph: ratio of service engineers to machines in the field, by district – note that the variations of ratios are due partly to the length of time the district has been established (i.e. the numbers of older machines) and partly to the spread of the territory and the density of machines

the point where it is possible to read a manpower requirement figure off a graph against any planned volume. From this type of data, it is also possible to define the relationship between the variables in a simple formula which might be $y = a + bx$ where y is the manpower requirement, x the work demand factor and a and b are constants. If the formula is applied to a manufacturing situation, then a will define the fixed manpower level associated with support services, which changes to a minimal degree with volume change, and b is a factor connecting the units of work in the work demand factor to the variable manning requirement associated directly with volume change. Of course, *a* and *b* are not precise: for example, there is likely to be an additional variable, associated with higher productivity on higher volumes.

Such a formula will have been developed from operational data and, provided that volumes do not vary substantially from past levels, it should prove reasonably accurate. However, if volume is to be stepped up to, say, 30 per cent above previous experience, the formula can provide no more than a starting point number which must be reviewed in relation to changes in organization, equipment and skills.

Manpower is rarely dependent on one variable and you may like to proceed into more complex mathematical models. This is certainly possible, particularly as corporate databases increase in complexity and computer models of manning situations develop further. From practical experience of the accuracy possible in real-life situations, I believe that a single variable, or at the most two, can give the optimum working result, provided we take care to identify them properly. My personal choice is to allocate time and effort to identify meaningful work demand factors rather than engage in more complex models which give an appearance of science but poor forecasts.

Ratio trends are most suited to production line situations (see figure 6.4) and other manpower-intensive areas with relatively

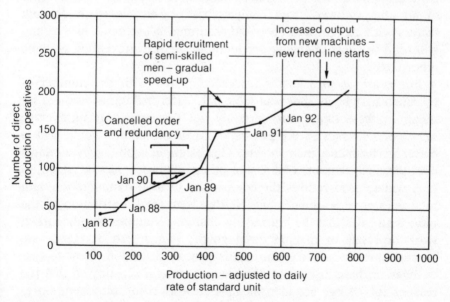

Figure 6.4   Ratio-trend graph: ratio of operatives to production

Table 6.1 Average sales per salesman

	Sales (£000s)	Number of Salesmen	Average sales (£000s)
Year 1 actual	1000	10	100
Year 2 actual	1200	12	100
Year 3 actual	1800	15	120
Year 4 forecast	2400	18	130
Year 5 forecast	3600	22	145

Annual figures not adjusted for inflation

standard work output, and can guide initial manning standards when new production lines are planned for, with manning levels based very simply on planned output, previous standards, and adjustments for new influences.

Other manpower ratios

Many simple ratios can be used from time to time to influence managements to accept or reject manpower forecasts. The simplest of all are produced from comparisons of sensible work demand factors with current and proposed manning. Movements in the ratio will tend to show changing productivity, or the intevention of some other factor.

For example, the level of sales compared with the number of salesmen may be as shown in table 6.1. After making allowances for inflation, these figures are certainly not spectacular, using average sales per salesman as the key ratio. Most companies would seek a better performance than shown. This example is obviously a simple one, to which data on a variety of other influences may be added.

A widely used ratio is the comparison of total remuneration with total sales or with added value. Neither is an ideal comparison, as the ratio with sales may be blurred by changing volumes of subcontract work or resale of manufactured goods, (which can be taken into account), while added value needs precise definition. Year-to-year changes in these key ratios deserve very careful scrutiny so that the reasons for change are identified. A steadily rising remuneration to sales ratio suggests the probability of a build-up of non-essential manpower which is almost certainly eroding the company's profit margins.

Covering the unmeasurable

Whatever approach is used to establish manning standards, some groups will be excluded as future manning requirements will have to be assessed on a judgement basis. All positions treated in this way should be listed, together with a brief note justifying the listing. These lists should be under continual scrutiny to ensure that no jobs slip through and exist unnecessarily. Included on the list will be:

Managerial positions specified within the company organization. Such posts are likely to be under continual review as organization structures are reviewed. They will extend down to middle management positions and possibly to most if not all supervisory positions.

Many of these positions will have secretaries. All forms of personal staff should be reviewed from time to time to ensure that they are a necessity or are accepted status appointments. Small, high level secretarial teams can produce great secretarial savings.

Specialist departments are frequently small, and cover a varied and changing work-load. These would include the central staff departments, whose objectives and manning should be evolving continually, and whose manning requirements will fluctuate. There is a need for continual monitoring and audit of influence, and of adapting to change.

Centralized services are not the same as central staffs (whose roles are more fluid). In general, I would expect the bulk of service work to be measurable.

Project and discretionary positions exist in most organisations. They are created to achieve specific objectives within defined time-scales. If management defines a need and accepts the cost implications, the ongoing task is to ensure that the justification for the position continues; and that on completion of the assignment, the positions are discontinued. Initial studies can usually achieve some immediate savings by identifying project and discretionary positions which have continued indefinitely after completion of their purpose, and further savings from jobs created to provide data to the first group of deleted positions. The process of listing, challenging and auditing provides the basis for determining discretionary needs, and subsequent control.

Modify standards as work content changes

The greatest difficulty in maintaining manning standards is that work, and how it is performed, are constantly changing. With the whole business environment evolving rapidly, there is a range of influences on what work is required and how it should be done, with the result that any manning standard can become obsolete quickly.

As with many aspects of planning ahead, there is need for a scenario of what is expected to happen, and what impact the expected changes are likely to have on manning requirements. Then, actual change can be monitored against forecasts, and manning standards and projections continually reviewed.

Even in areas not immediately affected by change, we should be somewhat uneasy with stability. There should be a continuous search for means of improving the utilization of manpower, or enhancing utilization through motivation. Given the high costs of manpower, this should always be a business priority.

Inertia of existing standards – attitudes to change

Very few manning requirements are examined against a blank background. Even if the organisation is new, there will normally be a pattern of industry, or regional, practice which immediately imposes some existing norm in the form of a history of stated work-load requiring a known number of people.

These past standards may have evolved from indifferent or inadequate use of financial and manning control mechanisms. Perhaps the only factors used to develop departmental budgets were the figures which applied in the previous year, with ad hoc judgements on necessary changes and pious hopes for an about-right result.

Without adequate challenge, manpower levels have often been allowed to ride too high. New machinery in the factory, for example, might have increased productivity, yet redundancy tended to be avoided. Useful employees were stockpiled against vague future needs, or excessive manning was negotiated by a union fearful of redundancy. Through these actions, and from employees' natural instincts to justify their employment, work was carefully shared, or fenced off into separate compartments for protection, unless manning requirements were rigorously examined.

Productivity improvement invariably requires a change in cultural attitudes and involves training in new skills at supervisory to middle management levels. In a construction company, I reported that productivity at site level was very low due to poor planning, site layout, materials handling and manpower utilization, and suggested that a general improvement of 20 per cent or more seemed completely feasible. The managing director concerned pulled a report from his desk, dated some years earlier, saying that he knew about these things, but what should he do. The things he had tried had produced no result.

The problem was tackled by training the contracts management in the various techniques and skills required. This was followed by training site agents and foremen on site in the routines they should follow to tighten their own working disciplines. By increasing their knowledge of how to plan and control every aspect of their work, and by helping them practically during the initial work, we reached the stage where they suddenly realized that life was less stressful and the contracts could be run more easily.

Back in his office, the managing director watched the performance figures begin to rise, and then go up far more than he had hoped, as planning and control became effective and spread into every aspect of the business over a two-year period.

Changing the existing pattern on the grounds of pure logic may be difficult for the employees affected to accept, yet change without their support is not practicable. So, any change in accepted standards must be on a basis acceptable both to employer and employees; and each must feel it is to their own advantage. There is no standard cost formula or balance to be achieved, but the new arrangements must seem reasonable to those affected. In obtaining agreement to changes, a number of factors are relevant, including:

- Management must understand and support the proposed changes, the reasons for them, and how they are to be achieved.
- Employees must be satisfied that they will be treated fairly, and that the end results will be acceptable to all those affected, both directly and indirectly.

Management support stems from analysis of the situation under review and clear communication of the proposal. If the purpose and objectives are understood and potential benefits appreciated, then positive management encouragement of change and improvement will result, and management's enthusiasm will be communicated naturally to subordinates who may be affected. A great deal of support can be achieved, assuming the proposal is sound, through the informal relationships that exist with managers or supervisors. Where employees have natural or elected leaders, a second level of support can be obtained. The key is acceptability of proposals.

7

Organization Planning

When Peter Drucker (1988) writes that 'The typical large business 20 years hence will have fewer than half the levels of management of its counterpart today, and no more than a third of the managers', we can be sure that the organization revolution we see around us has much further to go.

Organization provides the structure for getting work done in a co-ordinated way by a group of individuals. It defines the way in which the work necessary to achieve business objectives is divided into packages of similar activities and ultimately into job-sized units grouped under a manager. It enables a series of work groups engaged on separate parts of the whole task to work independently towards a common objective.

Live organizations are continually changing as they adapt to the evolving business environment, and adapt to make best use of the skills and abilities of the people who make up the organization. In the longer term, the organization should evolve to enable people to meet fresh business objectives in the most effective ways, and this evolution should be carefully considered and planned.

The organization plan can be considered as a translation of the business plan into the managerial strata of manpower requirements, which provides the framework for determining the detail of sup-porting manpower needs. Business planning sets out the future objectives of the entire enterprise against anticipated scenarios of environmental and cultural change, and incorporates statements of the major strategies including those required for human resource issues. Each strategy will need to be converted into what needs to be done for the strategy to be implemented, how it is to be made to happen, and how it can be managed. The volume and range of activities necessary to achieve the plan need to be determined and then allocated to logical groupings which can be managed within an overall structure.

It is necessary to plan the evolution and ensure that the structure remains purpose-built to achieve objectives and is slimmed down for optimum efficiency. An organization plan defines how anticipated change in the business is to be managed and shows how the planned sequence of adjustments to the organization will meet new objectives.

Organization planning is essentially a long-term activity concerned with developments over five or more years ahead and incorporates the preparations to move from the present structure towards the future ideal. In setting the pace of this evolution, the availability and readiness of suitable personnel will be of critical importance, so much so that people may be the only determining factor in the timing of the plan. This emphasizes the close relationship between organization planning and the various aspects of manpower planning. While organization planning is essentially long term, the process will also draw attention to more immediate organization problems and short-term actions.

The analytical process of reviewing organization requirements is basically identical to that of planning a new or revised shape and implementing decisions, no matter if the application is immediate or gradual. A difference arises only where urgency forces immediate action of an uncomfortable nature; planned change over a longer period might have been kinder to individuals and easier to digest. Resistance to such change may force slower action or some compromise which defers a proportion of the change. Implementation of organization change is examined separately at the end of this chapter.

The organization planning process falls into three stages:

1 Analysis of the purpose and form of the present organization, of its failings and of the new and potential future influences on it.
2 Determining logical organization structures which are theoretically capable of achieving the company's future objectives, but flexible enough to adapt to possible developments.
3 Implementing the agreed changes.

In practice, reappraisal may be proceeding under all three headings at one time and at various paces covering various parts of a company's operations.

Organization planning is ultimately concerned with the future organization and the implementation of organization change. Patten and Vaill (1976) suggest that there are seven issues to be addressed:

(1) The organization now; (2) Why change?; (3) Who is initiating change?; (4) Is there resistance to change?; (5) How is change to be achieved?; (6) How is change to be assessed?; and (7) What values apply?

For organization to develop, there must be a clear vision of forward business goals which the organization is designed to achieve. These overall objectives will be supported by an array of short- and long-term supporting strategies which can be translated into organization requirements designed to ensure that all necessary activity is managed and carried out, with due consideration of information systems, management style, leadership issues, motivation and teams. The structure should be developed for a series of points in time, linked to business projections, to define its evolution.

The detail of future organization, together with evolution from the present structure, may be established through analyses to determine the groupings best able to achieve the required goals. The analysis and discussion required is unlikely to be comprehensive unless top level interest and support is forthccoming, as the process may well challenge and change some part of the company's culture. Successful implementation will take account of existing personal power and be politically sensitive, and will exploit opportunities, such as those which occur when a post is vacated, to introduce elements of change.

Organization structures

There are historical or traditional patterns of organization, some of which can be traced back at least two thousand years, but these long-established hierarchical patterns are being influenced by changing attitudes to work and quality of life, by the ongoing information technology revolution which is removing some of the activities which take up much of the traditional middle manager's time, and by a range of other factors. It will, though, still be necessary for managers to get work done through people and to co-ordinate their efforts towards common objectives.

The starting point for much organizational change will often be the traditional organization structures, which have developed great complexity in the biggest companies and form the accepted norms. These have only recently begun to be change. The logic of these structures is based on the grouping of like activities, initially into main blocks and subsequently into job-sized work units. This process keeps associated activities together under managers who act as co-ordinators and controllers and provide a communications link. In this way, the pieces are linked into a whole through a series of co-ordinator/controller levels which rise through broader and broader spans of responsibility until the chief executive is reached. It is designed to direct and co-ordinate the efforts of many individuals to achieve the corporate goals. The result should be a structure capable of achieving the required overall objectives, yet consisting of a multitude of defined jobs with identified tasks and responsibilities. It is a constant managerial task to achieve optimum organizational groupings (and thereby optimum effectiveness and corporate capability) because, if related activities or responsibilities become separated organizationally, it is more difficult to promote harmonious operation.

The simplest form of organization structure is one in which there is one manager to whom all employees report. The next step occurs when the number of people is more than can be managed effectively by one individual and the first intermediate management levels appear. Growth requires a further increase in the number of levels and clarification of groupings of related activities. Around six to eight prime groupings have tended to emerge. These usually include technical and design, production, marketing (including sales), finance, personnel and legal, subject to inevitable variations. They may possibly also include distribution, research, quality, planning, etc., depending on the overall size and complexity of operation.

As a company grows, further groups of thinkers and planners, or specialist advisers, may be created alongside the mainstream of line operational positions. These staff support the directing group of the company, with delegated responsibilities for functional management, collecting and feeding up ideas and plans, auditing and analysing line operations, and encouraging improvements in their functional areas. This produces the organization form known as staff and line, which occurs in large decentralized companies where complex ranges of activities are divided into separate business entities covering distinct product groups or geographical areas, each being run by a subsidiary team of top executives and having substantial autonomy. Such decentralization is co-ordinated by a central board supported by a high-level staff advisory group whose role is to develop broad principles and policies. Another variant is the financial holding company, with a very small central board to co-ordinate only what is critical to the central team, which may allow a great diversity of systems and management in group companies.

Decentralization and delegation of authority go together in these structures, ideally with a matrix of strong line management balanced by competent staff professionals who are accepted as the chief executive's major means of evaluating performance in operating divisions.

Informal organization

In parallel with the formal structure runs the network of personal and informal relationships which grow up when a substantial number of people are in regular contact working towards common goals. This networking, or informal organization, of the company plays an important role in distributing ideas and information which helps to bind the whole structure and cut red tape by means of informal discussion to clear the lines. The place of informal relationships must be understood as part of corporate culture and its growth encouraged. Formal and informal structures are complementary.

Future organization

Organization patterns and shapes are changing. Over the next ten years, it will not only be necessary to adjust organization to address changing business objectives and environments and to respond to the increasing influence of information management technology, but also to respond to changes in attitudes to work, management styles and accepted organization concepts. Radical changes in environment demand radically different approaches to organization and to the roles of the managers within. There has been much research into future organizations and many of the concepts have already been adopted – particularly, but not solely, in young, high-tech companies – so allowing us to examine real practices which are providing competitive advantages rather than speculate about what might be. Key elements of change include:

- Substantial reductions in the number of middle management posts.
- The disappearance of co-ordinating managers as information systems make these roles unnecessary and all managers become computer literate.
- Much flatter organizations with much wider spans of control, conceived as teams or cells rather than hierarchies.
- More emphasis on specialists and higher levels of specialist knowledge, and a much greater emphasis on having rounded businessmen in all positions, who can appreciate the business implications of their specialist contributions.

- Emphasis on project management, with informal teams continually forming and reforming.

Peter Drucker, writing on organizations in the future, suggests that we can expect fewer levels of management in what will be knowledge-based organizations, composed largely of specialists who direct and discipline their own performance through organized feedback. Corporate objectives will be clearer and more widely communicated. These knowledge workers will resist the present day command and control organization model; an information-based organization provides for self-discipline and actions are visible through the systems.

The nature of tasks will change; for example, capital investment analysis will be transformed from opinion to diagnosis by rational weighting of alternative assumptions. Management jobs which only co-ordinate data collection and convey requirements will become obsolete as information is processed more effectively, and is more widely accessible. There will be many more specialists in operating units, but fewer centrally. The way work is done will be different, and largely self-directed, enabling large control spans.

Task-focused teams will be normal, assembling and disbanding as required to bring groups of specialists together to resolve issues. These can be seen already; for example, integrating research, development, manufacturing, and marketing to speed the pace of new product development. Teams or cells will replace hiera-chial structures, with clusters of teams around the central co-ordination function and non-hierarchial remuneration structures also.

Drucker uses the modern hospital to illustrate the new organization. The many different medical and paramedical teams are established in self-contained specialist areas (or cells) with their own knowledge, training and, even, language; each has a relevant head person who reports to the top. Many ad hoc multispecialist teams form to deal with single patients. There is little direct supervision of medical operations from the top, as the objectives of the organization are understood universally.

The working of a professional practice may be linked to a large cell, with each member conducting his or her own business, yet communicating and consulting with colleagues, and sharing services. The professional staff in a legal practice will link with client groups to form temporary project teams to tackle their various cases, for example. Internal specialist cells will work in much the same manner, and may include some external members employed on a retainer basis.

There will be 'unprecedented emphasis on people and talent as the organization's most precious resources, on the need to utilize human resources fully and on the need to draw out people's commitments, ' says Drucker.

Supporting this pattern is the recognition that business growth may depend more on the inventive capacity of individuals and small teams containing the corporate core competences than on the actions of top managers. It is from the resourcefulness and originality of small dedicated teams that fresh tactics develop which may lead to building new competitive advantage. There are many examples of extraordinary achievements by such teams whereas most larger organizations with heavy resources are unable to make the mental adjustment needed to achieve a breakthrough.

A good analogy is a large orchestra, which has a conductor (the CEO) and then a large number of specialists/instrumentalists. Effectively, the whole orchestra reports to one individual, but the degree of management control is negligible because they are all working to common objectives, a single score. Information responsibility is taken individually by each musician working from that score. 'Information responsibility' to others will be understood and acted by asking: 'Who depends on me for information, and on whom do I depend?'

The conclusions reached by a research team at Ashridge Management College were along similar lines. The Ashridge team took a ten-year horizon (as opposed to Drucker's twenty) and, therefore, foresaw a less radical organization change, but concluded that future organizations will form a different setting for the practice of management. The organization itself will be flatter, faster moving, market driven, more cost-conscious, fluid and complex. It will be decentralized, even fragmented, but the parts will be integrated by overall strategy and culture. (This is closely in line with the evolving Drucker model except that it anticipates less impact from information technology.) Horizontal relationships across organizations will become more important than vertical (directing) ones.

Given the inability of a deeply hierarchical organization to alter course rapidly, any business which requires fast response or innovative actions to seize initiative will need to be designed with the ability to assemble small high-powered teams for dedicated tasks, and must be resourced accordingly.

The Organization Plan

If the business environment changes very rapidly, the existing structure will have to cope for a while. Organization change can rarely be implemented rapidly or without careful preparation and briefings; any sudden change may take some months to settle into effective operation.

For the longer term, we may have a view of the organization ten or more years ahead, but most of the detailed planning will have no more than a three- to five-year horizon. Within this time frame, most of the major developments likely to affect the business and the organization should already be visible if the environment has been analysed carefully, although the precise timing of various developments may be far from certain. A forward organization plan may take shape while the timing of implementation may remain flexible. The degree of uncertainty in the timing naturally increases in longer term plans, their value being more in identifying likely future changes.

Studies of the existing organization and current organizational requirements are going on all the time. For example, it is probably rare for any management level vacancy to be filled without some analysis of the requirements of the job, now and in the short-term future, to ensure that the job and person specification used for the purposes of replacement are as up to date as possible.

Also, organizations are constantly changing in minor ways, with substantial change evolving by many lesser steps. One can be reasonably sure of finding something seriously wrong with a structure that has remained unchanged for five years, and pretty likely to find problems developing even after two years with a static structure.

We must know what the organization of each unit is designed to achieve and where it fits in with other units if we are to be constructive in our review. If there is any doubt about objectives or purpose, or if these have recently been changed, there is a reasonable prospect that any problem stems from this.

Organization analysis

As business objectives are updated, it is necessary to ensure that the organization continues to provide the most effective structure for achieving them. This involves examining the objectives of the various functions or departments to ensure that these too are designed to achieve their subsidiary objectives and that they represent a logical division of activities. We should ensure that there is comprehensive coverage of all things that need to be done and that duplication is avoided.

Any flaw identified in the existing organization may require immediate correction before determining longer term requirements. For example, splintered fragments of a function may be apparent, but if the subgrouping is around personalities, the study may require detailed job analysis to support a logical proposal.

Whether the analysis is for immediate action or for planning longer term changes, much the same sort of analytical approach is required. If a problem or need to change is identified, an analyst (who may be a seconded line manager), obtains data from managers at several levels and perhaps also from supporting staff, checking out conflicts or differences as he goes along. He then sits down quietly to determine a logical solution as a basis for negotiation. This task is not done quickly, especially where the span of the review is wide and the level in the organization being examined is high. Individual interpretations of actual roles may vary so the analyst must work with blurred lines, particularly in the newer flexible structures.

Out of the analysis may come a picture of segments of work which have broken away from their main group; blank areas which no-one covers properly; plus areas of duplicated activity and confused responsibility, perhaps between staff and line. This provides a basis for redrawing areas of responsibility to clarify which post is primarily responsible for each activity. At the end, all activities required should be properly covered, and none overlooked or duplicated. The work grouping in use should be effective; relationships between staff and line and with other departments should be clearly understood and acceptable, and the manpower requirements should be clear.

Before we leave analysis of current structures, a valuable contribution to any organization review is provided by a job grading schedule or, preferably, a stratified organization chart, in which all jobs in the organization are shown in a value relationship one to another as well as reporting relationship.

Where the relationship between supervisory and subordinate grades and salaries deviates from an acceptable pattern, difficulties may arise. A salary relationship between manager and subordinate of three to two is considered acceptable and where intervals between salary values of job grades are of the order of 20 per cent one would expect to find manager/subordinate differentials in steps of two or three grades. If the study shows an area with consistent one-grade intervals between jobs, it should be taken as a strong danger signal justifying further investigation. There is little doubt that the individuals personally involved in the structure would be very much aware of the problem and of the need for rationalizing reporting.

On the other hand, a department with four or more grades between the manager and his subordinates is equally unsound. The difference in work level involves the manager in a volume of work at too low a level while some of his subordinates will be stretched to do some work at a level far above their average level. This situation may result from a growth situation where the rising level of the job content and value of a senior job is recognized, but the effect on the supporting positions is overlooked. Creation of an intermediate level plus a re-allocation of responsibilities should provide a solution.

Some of the problems of rapid growth can be made clear by grade analysis. Where a division is growing very fast, the scale of the top jobs will also grow. While one hopes that the individuals in those jobs will grow too, this does not always happen. Then the job, as carried out by a limited individual, may remain static in content and contribution and inhibit the growth potential of the business. The inevitable result is recognition of the need for a more substantial post and a suitable incumbent to carry out the newly grown broader responsibilities.

On the fringe of any organization study are the local anomolies. The most obvious are the personal assistants, assistant managers or deputies, or one-over-one reporting relationships. Each of these may be a special arrangement designed to meet specific organizational situations and problems, but they should never be permitted to establish precedents or continue after the original purpose has been dealt with. Nor should they ever be accepted without strong justification. Any excess will disturb the smooth running of the organization and require remedial attention.

The end result of an organization study is likely to be a definition of a structure plus a set of job descriptions and objectives, plus associated employee specifications. These are ideal and ignore the people who actually fill the boxes. The ideal is rarely attained and we have to accept that any organization structure will be adapted to some extent to suit the people in and around it.

We all know examples of organizations built around or adapted to fit a particular person. This may be to arrange optimum use of a special individual, but any organization built around one person is obviously special. It is acceptable provided that it is effective and enables the particular talents of the central figure to be utilized to the full, but no general guidance on the type of organization structure to use can be given. More to the point is what happens when the spell is broken and the key man is no longer there. As he will not be replaceable, the organization built round the man will cease to be appropriate. Even the objectives of the unit may change.

In contrast with the effect on structure of one outstanding individual, a shortage of a particular type of skill may result in similar pressures. Within a computer applications department, for example, it may be necessary to structure the work to increase the training and development role of all experienced personnel to pass on experience to as wide a range of people as quickly as possible.

One must also watch for the odd organization that is too odd. A senior executive may wish to structure product development and manufacture together on product group lines and produce an acceptable structure. On the other hand, if he should propose to merge the human resource function with finance, expecting the personnel activity to be no more than administrative, his judgement would appear faulty.

Influences for organization change

The forward organizational plan is likely to start with a theoretical or ideal model which ignores the present structure and systems, and sets out ideal structures with logical future groupings of activities, functions and divisions of responsibilities, and optimum shapes for the co-ordination of effort and achievement of objectives by appropriately skilled groups of people or individuals. It will need to take account of all critical influences:

Information technology (IT) is having a considerable impact on how managerial and administrative work is done. It will dramatically change the content of many managerial jobs and is the largest factor enabling the development of flatter organizations: fewer managers, fewer levels, much wider spans of control and self-monitoring of progress and achievement which will remove that role from line supervision. Evaluation of the pace of this change in the organization is essential and may benefit from contributions by external consultants as the scale of potential change induced by IT seems rarely to be appreciated until it begins to bite. The telecommunications revolution, which will enable an increasing number of people to work from home or at distributed centres, will also have an influence on organization.

Changing attitudes to the work ethic and increased interest in quality of life may be a similar factor affecting managerial jobs. A popular view is that the length of the working week is going to decline for everyone except senior managers, a proportion of whom will need to remain workaholics. Yet many of the young graduates currently moving into industry and commerce are expressing concerns about their quality of life and may be unwilling to accept the commitment. Perhaps they will not be the ones who rise to the very top.

Empowerment and openness are associated influences. As both managers and subordinates are empowered, giving them greater freedom to use their initiatives, then much wider spans of co-ordination become possible and the manager becomes a leader rather than a director of people. The combination of IT, changing attitudes to work and empowerment emphasize the flattening of organizations and also encourage evolution towards cellular structures.

Quality, in a total business sense, has become a more significant issue in recent years. It may not feature specifically on an organization chart, but its influence will be felt on the way the organization works. Originally, the focus of quality was on the quality of manufactured output, but with the advent of quality circles this began to widen, to cover design quality and, subsequently, become all embracing. Now it covers the quality of customer relations, the quality of service, the quality of information systems, and so on; but in the quality organization, this shows through as quality orientation.

Mergers, acquisitions and divestments are a normal part of business with various organizational impacts. They can involve extremely complex organization issues, particularly where two units are being brought together, linking different cultures. Then it is not structural logic which should concern us, but the task of getting two groups of people with differing styles and beliefs to work together. Inevitably, significant change will be required from one or both parties and this will take time to prepare and implement. Mergers or acquisitions can fail simply due to cultural differences where there is a necessity to integrate the units quickly. Only the virtual destruction and replacement of one of the management groups will create a situation where integration is practical and even this may take two years or more, not to mention the devastating impact on the business. If cultures are different, there is likely to be great advantage in keeping the units separate, running in their established styles and even competing, and then gradually developing joint working and collaboration.

Interfaces are becoming more visible. New product development no longer involves independent initiatives by marketing, technical and manufacturing people, but is more likely to be handled by a flexible, multidiscipline team backed by all functions. The teams themselves will emerge from strategies defined in the business plans, indicating the thrust required. Project teams will be major element in the new organization, forming and changing in membership as tasks are tackled and as the detailed work requires different skills. The project leadership role will be extremely important, not only for the operation of the business, but also for providing generalist development opportunities for high ability people.

The management and motivation of professional and specialist people will be one of the big challenges for future managers. The combination of increased specialization by function, increased self-monitoring of work and progress, and wider spans of control will generally encourage a higher degree of self-reliance and independance. There may be a parallel in the management of commission-only sales people, which requires a very high degree of skill in personal relationships, close involvement in mutual objectives, and a supporting remuneration policy to keep the sales people focused on the objectives of the business. While the future professional may get on with his activities extremely well without supervision, the broad direction of his efforts and priorities in a changing world will need influencing. Linking remuneration with the contribution required may become more significant.

Similarly, the entrepreneurial talent in the organization will be unleashed by greater independence, but will need to accept occasional redirection towards changing business objectives rather than simply being left to exploit disconnected opportunities. The task for the entrepreneur may be to seek out and exploit opportunities which fit into the broad vision of the future business, and the task of his manager will be to encourage and support conforming actions.

Implementing change

The most detailed organization planning will focus on the immediate one- to three-year period, covering evolution through reasonably accurate business and environmental projections. For this period, it is likely to be practical to put together the fine detail of organization development, down to unit or even individual objectives, job descriptions and person specifications, on which management development plans and provisional appointments decisions can be based. Longer term organizational outlines should provide guidance on the competences and numbers of managers required within the progressively flatter organizational shapes.

The development in organization for the 12 months immediately ahead is vitally important and planning should be very accurate. Most of the major developments likely to have an impact on our organization requirements three to five years ahead should already be apparent so that our immediate organization plan can be expected to be related to that future vision.

Planning for a substantially changed situation expected three to five years hence involves all of the skills of organization planning. Over such a period, all current faults can be planned out of existence and all future requirements may be met by the use of normal organizational components designed for their specific purpose. If necessary the fine detail of the future organization can be filled in with job descriptions, forecast objectives and future employee specifications, so that the supply stage of long-term management manpower planning may be followed through.

In the long term, say ten years ahead, the fundamental changes to come may well have begun to emerge, but many other developments will be less visible. Further, the timing of various breakthroughs will be uncertain so that while the long-term organization plans can be developed, it is likely that the timing of their implementation will be the major uncertainty.

The manpower planning required to support future organization development is absolutely vital, for even where there is a period of several years in which to prepare the staffing for the ideal structure, the problems of assembling a group of precisely the right people at exactly the right time could achieve only momentary success, being quickly unbalanced by individual development and changing organization requirements.

Individuals, however, also provide an inertia against organization change which must be gradually circumvented to achieve each step in the evolutionary plan. The implementation phase of organization planning is concerned with phasing-in adjustments necessary to approach the ideal. While the objective might appear to be achievable by one catastrophic change, the effect on morale, productivity, security and stability may throw out the whole balance of the structure which would then require early further appraisal.

A logical organization structure, however carefully designed, is still a long way from being an effective operational structure. Planning inevitably involves a range of people and some will have functional loyalties, say to finance or production, and may place these loyalties ahead of the overall interests of the company. At the long-range planning stage, these difficulties are only in the background and there is plenty of time to identify and overcome disputed points, but when change is imminent we must face up to the reasons why proposals may not work – to the personality clashes, to the politics and to the resistance to change which arise whenever one attempts to change the organization.

It may appear to take a daunting amount of time to persuade all of the interested parties that it is their study, conforming to their requirements and in their interests, but this seems to be the only way to ensure successful implementation. Once they take credit for, and own, the design, no-one is going to stop them making the change they have planned. In this process some minor concessions may be necessary, but these may well produce an improved final result.

Analysing any difficulties to be overcome and identifying the individuals likely to be adversely affected helps to sell the proposals. I have found that individual discussions with the more senior people concerned enables much of a proposal to be negotiated confidentially, piece by piece, over a short period of time. A hard core of problems can be gradually isolated. Chances are, these were anticipated anyway and manoeuvres planned from an early stage to deal with them. They are likely to centre around what is to happen to individuals (which leads us into career planning) and the way forward is then focused on the handling of these people. If career side-tracking or demotion is involved, it may be proposed to dress up the move as a promotion, but it is preferable for the employee's manager to face him honestly, fully briefed and with the complete story of the move planned and of everything it will involve. There is never a long-term advantage in failing to face up to a personal situation of this sort. Failing to do so leads only to loss of respect and authority. The handling of this stage is subject to few other rules.

Where a planned future organization takes a radically different shape from the organization now, implementation should proceed by evolution which must be planned meticulously. Implementing change always requires great care, beginning with clear communication of facts, handled with due consideration for individuals who will be affected in any way. There needs to be an explanation and justification of the changes if they are to be understood and accepted, followed by real help and training to prepare and assist individuals whose jobs or responsibilities are being altered. Change cannot be considered to have been implemented until people are performing their new tasks.

A common element is a change in the priorities within a job, such as a sales and marketing director being required to delegate more of his selling involvement and concentrate on marketing strategy. Where these changes do not play to the individual's strengths, it may be necessary to arrange some intensive training or other development procedure, or to go back to the organization design to see how modification of supporting roles can achieve optimum use of individual strengths and still address key issues. The objective must be to develop a fully effective structure, backed by a detailed and timed (and possibly phased) plan to introduce the changes with minimum disturbance. This may be achieved by moving through an interim or transition organization if this reduces the degree of upset and allows people to make a partial adjustment in readiness for a further step.

The review process and management continuity planning play important roles here. Where there is major change, the application at quarterly intervals of the review process described in chapter 3 will plan and monitor the implementation in detail, with full participation by the managers in the area. Even if some are adversly affected by the changes, the effect of participation is sympathetic and supportive, and will achieve progress to efficiency much faster than a less participative approach.

Organization charts

An organization chart is a pictorial description or statement of an organization structure. Standard organization charts show the reporting relationships between all of the posts in the structure which are covered, perhaps restricted to the top two or three reporting levels. Occasionally, there is an advantage in using an everyman chart, showing the total staffing of a department, giving the number and types of all emplyees reporting to each supervisor. In companies which operate strict manpower control, these posts may be listed in full.

More sophisiticated, and in many ways more useful than the standard model, are stratified organization charts. In addition to showing the straightforward reporting relationships, the relative job value levels of all posts are also indicated. Vastly greater appreciation of a structure can be obtained from a stratified chart. It is invaluable for management development purposes because it clarifies possible lines for career advancement which may be less clear on ordinary charts. This is also discussed in chapter 16 on management succession, where an example is included.

Summary

The planning of future organizations has a great influence on future manpower requirements and must be based on analysis of how achievement of future business objectives is to be managed throughout the period of the plan. It involves identifying what is to be done at each phase of the business plan, drawing on the environment scenarios and the defined business and functional strategies, and recognizing the key influences on forward organization design to achieve optimum utilization of human resources. From these, the shapes of the operational and functional activity groupings and their tasks will emerge to provide a logical structure.

The end result should be a series of planned organizational forcasts which can be developed to show an evolution in the number, content and levels of management and other jobs; which identifies the requirements to be addressed for management continuity; and which provided a framework for the detailed planning of manpower requirements at every level.

8

Planning Manpower Requirements

Manpower planning is an integral part of business and organization planning. It involves detailed planning to establish the future manpower requirements at every level, by category, skills, etc., at a series of points in time, and subsequently planning the manpower supply to ensure the people required are available at the right times. This chapter is concerned with the first of these two stages. Only when we have a complete analysis of future manning needs will it be possible to make a comparison with the evolving manpower inventory and to plan to satisfy those requirements.

The quality of manpower requirement plans depends on the quality of the analysis and data on which it is based. A reasonable degree of accuracy will be essential in the core business projections and operation scenarios from which the manpower requirements are to be determined. This means that the business plan will need to include adequate detail about anticipated future business, the volumes of production and sales, and details of all other supporting activities. Not all business planning goes into such fine detail, but it is difficult to determine meaningful manning requirements without having a reliable base, and even more difficult to determine the prospective profitability and viability of the business without adequate manpower costs.

From this data a picture of the required manpower can be assembled, showing manning standards against planned volumes of various activities. Due allowance for improvements, system changes, product changes, etc., will be essential, because accuracy also depends on the quality of data on current manpower and its utilization, the skills available, recruiting and loss rates, rates of flow between jobs and levels and, even, data on the employment market for all of the categories and skills involved. If these data are of a reasonable quality, then the resultant manpower requirement plans will be as accurate as they can be against the business scenario and business plans on which they are based; and there will be a sound basis for calculating changes in those requirements, should the scenario modify.

From experience, where the data input are of a high quality, the factor most likely to be wrong in the basic assumptions will be the timing of anticipated future events, particularly those more than one year ahead. This should not be too serious as long as these events have been anticipated, and the manpower actions associated with them are understood. As the plan unfolds, changes in timing will become evident and the plan can be adjusted accordingly. Only in the event of unavoidably long lead times being overtaken by dramatic advances in timing will the plan have an element of failure.

The manpower requirement plan is a translation of other data within the business plan and is an integral part of it, so, if the two become separated at any stage, the manpower plan ceases to have a sound base and the achievability of the business plan is then jeopardised in terms of its most critical resource. For example, if the business and manpower plans assume a defined level of activity, but an amendment to the short-term business plan (or budget) alters the rate of incoming orders, thereby modifying the level of work necessary, it becomes essential for the short-term manpower plan to be amended in parallel, to increase or restrict recruitment as the case may be, or to initiate more drastic actions. All planning is business related, and the manpower planner must have his finger firmly on the pulse of the business.

As part of the essential base of the requirement plan, I like to have a comprehensive extract of relevant points from business plans and associated strategies and action plans. This would include:

- A full extract of the human resource implication sections of all elements in the plan.
- A full extract of all assumptions made, on which any manpower conclusions have been drawn, as a base point from which to assess corrective action following changes in assumptions.
- An extract of all other data relevant to manpower needs which may affect manning requirements. This might include planned capital expenditure or planned systems studies.
- All indications of the timing of changes.
- All strongly anticipated variables and the manpower flexing associated with contingency plans.

Manpower Requirement: Summary of Monthly Staff Required in each Position in a Rapidly Growing Unit

Month	Management	Technical staff		Production staff			Marketing staff		Services	
		Research	Product development	Product engineering	Product direct	Other	Marketing development	Sales	Finance	Personnel
Present	1	10	-	2	-	-	3	-	2	-
1						1				
2			1							
3				3					3	
4			4		1					
5			6		4					
6				5	6	2				
7					6					
8								1		1
9										
10										
11						2	3	1	3	
End of year	1	10	6	5	6	2	3	1	3	1
1			8	6	8	4		2	4	2
2					10			3	5	
3		>7		8	12	6				3
4			12		14			6	6	
5								9		
6				10	16	6				
7								12	7	
8										
9										
10										
11			15				3			
End of year	1	>5	15	10	16	6	3	12	7	3

Example 8.1 Manpower requirement analysis summarizing the staff required each month for each position in a rapidly growing unit – prepared using *HR/View* Spreadsheet with forecast data from the business plan

Manpower Requirement Forecasts (Extract from Working Sheet)

Job Category	Strength at 1.1.1992	Forecast strengths - 5-year forecast											Notes
		1992				1993				End 1994	End 1995	End 1996	
		End 1st qtr.	End 2nd qtr.	End 3rd qtr.	End 4th qtr.	End 1st qtr.	End 2nd qtr.	End 3rd qtr.	End 4th qtr.				
Applications engineering department:													
Manager	1	1	1	1	1	1	1	1	1	1	1	1	
Head - customer service	1	1	1	1	1	1	1	1	1	3	3	3	Regional breakdown 1994
Head - application research			1	1	1	1	1	1	1	1	1	1	Vacancy advertised
Head - applications library								1	1	1	1	1	Part of regionalisation plan
Senior engineer	7	7	8	8	9	9	9	10	10	15	15	15	F/C on work analysis
Applications engineer (a)	18	19	20	21	22	23	24	25	26	30	34	38	(a) Ratio-trend F/C (not used)
(b)	18	18	20	20	22	24	26	29	34	35	42	50	(b) F/C on work analysed
Research engineer				2	2	2	3	3	3	4	5	6	
Technical assistant (a)	20	21	22	23	24	25	26	27	28	32	36	40	(a) Ratio-trend (not used)
(b)	20	20	20	18	18	18	18	20	20	22	24	26	(b) Work analysed F/C used

Etc.

Example 8.2 Extract from a divisional manpower requirement forecast – prepared using *HR/View* Spreadsheet with forecast data from the business plan

In parallel, I would seek an analysis of current manpower and manning standards which is as detailed as possible.

Manpower requirement summary

The manpower requirement plans for the component parts of the organization should build up into a comprehensive summary, showing how many jobs of each type will exist. In practice, pure requirements-only examples are comparatively rare because the act of summarizing requirements seems to stimulate an immediate rough assessment of how the requirements are to be met. Example 8.1 is something of a rarity in this respect because it shows only the planned forward requirements on a month by month basis over a two-year period, concentrating on the timing of the requirements. As previously noted, there would be accompanying analyses on sourcing to ensure provision of manpower to schedule.

Example 8.2 also concentrates on requirements only. It is part of a working sheet summarizing the needs of three sections in an engineering department. It covers the supply plan for an applications engineering department over a period of five years. This company chose to build up its assessments of future manning requirements on two bases, which it subsequently blended. Using current ratios of work volumes to manpower produced different conclusions from line managers' conversions of the expected work volumes into manpower requirements. In this case the type of work was expected to change, and work analysis indicated that the technical requirements would generally be higher than with current work, so that future manning requirements would not follow the trend line of current ratios.

The balance required column contains the key set of figures, and shows against each of the types of jobs the additional number that will be required during the period of the forecast. The analysis might alternatively have shown impending overstaffing for a category.

These detailed departmental analyses become the work plans for implementation. As a generalization, an organization will aim to meet as much as possible of its requirement from existing people. This policy is normally less expensive and has a considerable impact on retaining the best people as it shows them that internal promotion is a reality.

The requirement plan, if it is to be of value, needs to contain more than simply the categorized manpower levels at the beginning and end of a one-year period and the calculated external requirement for

Departmental One-Year Manpower Requirement Forecast

Types of Jobs	Number of staff at 1 Jan 92	Anticipated loss		Anticipated gain transfer/ promotion	Net	Total requirement forecast at 31 Dec 92	Balance required during year
		Termina-tions	Transfer/ promotion				
Department manager	1				1	1	-
Cost accountant	1				1	1	-
Billing supervisor	1				1	1	-
Accounting operations supervisor	1		1*	1	1	1	-
Assistant accountant	1			1	2	2	-
Cashier	1				1	1	-
Book-keeper	2	2	1		1	2	+1
Accounting operations clerk	6		1	1	4	6	+2
Billing clerk	5	1			4	5	+1
Records clerk	2	1			1	2	+1
Filing clerk	1				1	1	-
Secretary	1				1	1	-
Shorthand typist	2	1			1	2	+1
Billing typist	5	2			3	5	+2

* To H.Q. Dept.

Example 8.3 Departmental one-year manpower requirement forecast – prepared using *HR/View* Spreadsheet with forecast data from the business plan

Building Group Manpower Requirements Areas

Category	End 1991 actuals					End 1992 forecast total		Estimated loss rates inc. retirement		Estimated promotions required		Estimated retirement from outside group	
	Company A	B	C	D	1991 Total	Inc	Total	%	Total over 5 years	Promotion from	Promotion to	Total over 5 years	Average annual rate
MD/Manager	1	1	2	1	5	-1	4		1				
Branch Manager		1	1		1	3	4		1		2	2	
Chief Contr Mgr/Dir	1	1			2		2						
Contract Managers	8	5	3	3	19	+3	22	10%	10	1	3	11	2
Foremen	13	12	20		45	+10	55	20%	50	3	20	43	9
Trainee/Asst Foremen	11	7	3	3	24	+41	65	20%	44	20		105	21
Chief Surveyor	1	1	2		4		4	10%	2		2	11	2
Surveyors	10	8	3	1	22	3	25	15%	18	2	12	11	2
Asst/Trainees			1		1	11	12	20%	6	12		29	6
Chief Est/Plnrs/Buyer	2	2	2		6	2	8	10%	3		2	3	1
Est/Plnrs/Buyers		4	4	2	10	4	14	15%	9	2	4	9	2
Asst/Trainee Est/Plr/Buyer	1				1	11	12	20%	6	4		21	4

Example 8.4   Summary of building group manpower requirements – prepared using *HR/View* Spreadsheet with forecast data from the business plan

Business Plan Summary of Manpower Requirements and Remuneration

Manpower category	Planned year end 1992	Change 1993	Planned year end 1993	Change 1994	Planned year end 1994
DIRECT:					
Manufacturing	2074	143	2217	191	2408
Engineering	245	35	280	20	300
Distribution	301	(12)	289	3	292
Total:	2620	166	2786	214	3000
INDIRECT:					
Manufacturing	305	4	309	10	319
Engineering	48	1	49	6	55
Distribution	35	(3)	32	(2)	30
Marketing	86	(6)	80	8	88
Admin & Finance	134	14	148		148
Total:	608	10	618	22	640
GRAND TOTAL:	3228	176	3404	236	3640
REMUNERATION:	£36.91m	£3.66m	£40.47m	£6.03m	£46.50m

Example 8.5 Business plan summary of manpower requirements and remuneration – prepared using *HR/View*
Spreadsheet with forecast data from the business plan

the period. For the immediate short-term future, say, for a minimum of six months and possibly up to two years, it is desirable to develop the plan in sufficient detail for anticipated requirements to show on a month-by-month basis (as in example 8.1), together with notes on the actions planned to meet these needs from both internal and external sources.

The detail of the breakdown is discretionary, subject to it being meaningful in the particular case. Separate identification of individual positions, as in example 8.3, can then show detail of the timing of requirements, but this could equally well be covered by footnotes. This detail is particularly vital as it is the basis for comparison with the internal manpower supply, and leads on to the assessments of anticipated external manpower requirements.

Example 8.4 shows a group summary which is more generalized in nature, but which has been built up from a series of more detailed departmental and company documents. At the beginning of the summary, the current positions in a series of subsidiaries are shown, together with totals, followed by data on the total extent of change expected over a five-year period. This presentation is invaluable for giving an overall view of the scale of corporate problems for discussion at board level, but it can be rather misleading about timing.

Summaries of manpower requirements, and appropriate costings, are essential inputs to business planning. The costing is usually more significant at this stage than expected head count, although questions of accommodating and equipping numbers of people need to be identified and fully covered in the plan.

Example 8.5 is taken from the business plan of a large company and covers the next two years, illustrating the changes expected by major functions and divided into direct and indirect categories. Cost figures are added below. It is, of course, possible to explode these data into something far more complex if you wish, given that the background detail should exist. Further, the manpower numbers used are year-end figures; some other organizations prefer to use average numbers, which tie in better with total remuneration.

The Manpower Requirement Plan

The examples above were taken from a variety of companies' requirement plans. In this section, I have used a series of cases to illustrate aspects of building up the components.

I have chosen to use as a case study the development of a requirement plan for the management levels of a division, which shows the process in operation, illustrating many detailed points which needed to be resolved. It is followed by shorter sections commenting on requirements in functional areas.

It is not practical to include the total plan as the detail is drawn from the manpower elements of a detailed business plan, the extracts being taken from various parts of business objectives and strategies, anticipated scenarios and assumptions. The core material for the manpower plan is the detailed business objectives through the period to be covered. If greater detail is concentrated on selected years, say one, two, five, ten and 20, then the same years (or a selection of them) should be used for organization and manning projections.

In building the manpower requirement plan, note should be taken of statements of alternative scenarios, related to various aspects of environment, and alternative major strategies should be designed to enable the plan variations to be achieved. These are critically important in that they add information on the work which may need to be done and which may require significantly different organization and manning standards to be covered by contingency plans.

The basic organization plans are developed against this total picture, and some assumptions will be included in the business plans about the scale and costs of the management structure. The task is then to use this information about each part of the structure to develop a detailed forecast of management requirements.

The pace of change in environment and in organization, plus company mergers and rationalizations, make these forecasts particularly difficult to achieve for the longer term. It may be necessary to record reservation about even the shorter term forecasts. The best available estimates are essential for meaningful development actions. As business managers, we are obliged to predict the future. By recording the assumptions we make, forecasts can be reappraised rapidly following any change of scenario.

Other chapters cover the development of organization plans, which set out the ideal groupings of activities and the top structure of management jobs expected to exist in the future, plus a statement of the general concept of organization expected to apply, and any changed cultural factors. Additionally, there should be competency profiles of these future managers, based on planned responses to environmental and other influences and the expected way of managing, and covering the types of people expected to be most effective. Finally, there will be job specific data covering the functional and general skills necessary for each post.

It is unlikely that all of this data will be assembled for every job at each of a series of points in time, but the format should be sufficient for the range of requirements to be reasonably specific. For lower levels of management, the same data are relevant and can be used for projection on a similar basis, but they will tend to be progressively more general within functions and categories as the numbers of positions increase, and less specific about individual posts.

In rough form, sketches of anticipated ideal organizations may be developed, covering the whole management strata, for a series of times, say two, five and ten years ahead, to add a degree of clarity to the evolution. In practice, it is useful to pencil in actual names on the shorter term charts to add a further critical dimension and realism to the plan and establish the individual development required. This may identify some of the hard things to be addressed (such as problems of excess or obsolete managers) in the review process of linking the identified needs with the deployment and development of individual managers.

Top down or bottom up

In the assembly of any manpower forecast, there is invariably some difference between the data assembled from top management assumptions and data built up from the judgements of supervisors and managers who will have responsibility for carrying out work. The simple view of any conflict is likely to be that top management is squeezing standards while line people are trying to provide themselves with extra cover.

Negotiation and compromise are necessary. If the top down view is tough, and prevails, it will not be long before many areas are undermanned and corners are being cut at work. There will be inadequate thinking or preparation time, overall efficiency begins to slip and there is no time for training.

Against that, there is a need for senior people to get to know how skilled their subordinates are in padding the numbers so that, in the end, the requirement and budgets which are agreed are adequate but challenging. This is no easy task, for in most organisations there are big differences in the amount of fat individual managers built into budgets. It is dangerous to carve 5 per cent off those who play things straight, while 10 per cent may not be sufficient to trim from those who enjoy haggling.

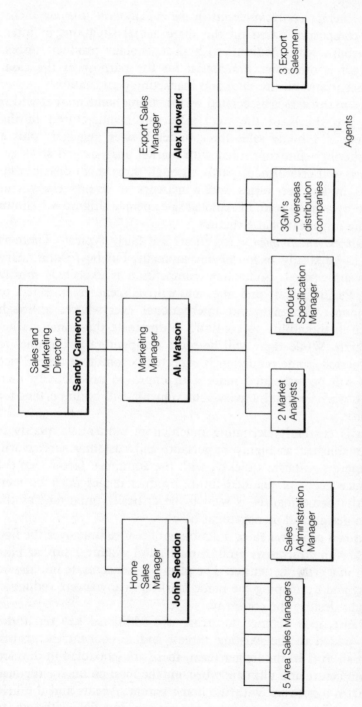

Figure 8.1 Current organization – note, clerical and secretarial grades are excluded
Source: McBeath (1990)

Case study: manpower requirements in the management structure This case is a composite, based on the three actual situations in international groups with medium- to high-technology product ranges. The product is otherwise immaterial for the purpose of the case, which concentrates on the sales and marketing organization.

The *present structure* is associated with a strong home market which produces two thirds of the total sales (all manufactured in the UK). There is a home sales force under a sales manager, plus a small marketing team concerned with market analysis and strategy. Exports are well established, partly through three small distribution companies in key territories and a network of agents elsewhere, backed up by a small team of regional sales people. Figure 8.1 shows the existing organizational structure.

The *business environment* projections are fairly typical. There is expected to be steady technical development, but no revolutionary change is anticipated. Some new competition is expected, mostly from the Pacific basin, and the competitive scene is expected to become more aggressive and international everywhere, although confidence in the ability to continue to dominate the home market remains high. While there will be more competitors in the one- to five-year period, some reduction is expected beyond that time. Price pressures will be associated more with improved productivity than with price wars, so productivity achievements will be important for profitability.

Design is currently becoming much more influential; quality is already established as highly important; and customer service will become more significant quickly, with the additional factor that the maintenance needs of planned future product ranges must be met. Finally, the home market is seen to be critically important as the long-term design and management base.

The business objectives show a doubling of real volume over the first five years, with equivalent profit growth, and assume a similar pace thereafter in a growing market. The plan is to concentrate initially on protecting and developing the home market, as any severe reduction there might destroy the company.

In parallel, it is planned to create two additional key territories overseas (added to the existing three), and to concentrate growth efforts in all five. In the longer term, these are scheduled to develop local manufacture and ultimately become the focal points for regional marketing in a network with the home parent. Agents and the field sales team will continue to press for growth, but will withdraw to niche markets (to be identified) where their markets are attacked and cannot be defended. Total withdrawal from any market will be avoided if possible. No acquisition or divestment is planned, but small acquisitions to widen the product range are thought possible.

Strategies designed to achieve these objectives include development of a full marketing activity, both at the home location and, progressively, in the five key overseas territories, to ensure the systematic gathering and analysis of data, and response to the market-place. One strategy defined will require all sales staff to prepare field intelligence reports and will link a proportion of bonus payments to implementation.

A further strategy is designed to link marketing staff more closely to product development, but does not anticipate the development of multidiscipline project teams within the duration of the plan. Development of better customer relations and concern for quality are part of culture development strategies, but are not expected to affect the organization structure directly although they will influence how some jobs are done.

The embrionic overseas companies are expected to develop dramatically; to become far more significant; to begin local manufacture of home designs, and later some local product variations; and to become bases for regional management of world sales during the second half of the plan.

The actual companies on which the case study is based found it difficult to evaluate the impact of changing organization philosophies, other than to adopt a policy of keeping organization levels to a minimum, and could identify no cultural implications other than recognizing the need for a quality manager.

The evolving management requirements are presented in the form of a series of organization charts with supplementary notes, (see figures 8.2–8.4) showing the planned requirements after two, five and ten years. Additionally, as often happens in practice, the two-year projection suggests certain people moves, while the further forecasts were less specific. Notes under each phase indicate key assumptions. (An identical process can be followed at any level or for any size of organization.)

Analysis of the top export job showed that the person specification would move from a sales orientated requirement towards a more generalist role, one able to direct the growth of a major international development. The provisional view was that a very high potential young generalist should be appointed within two years, on a three-

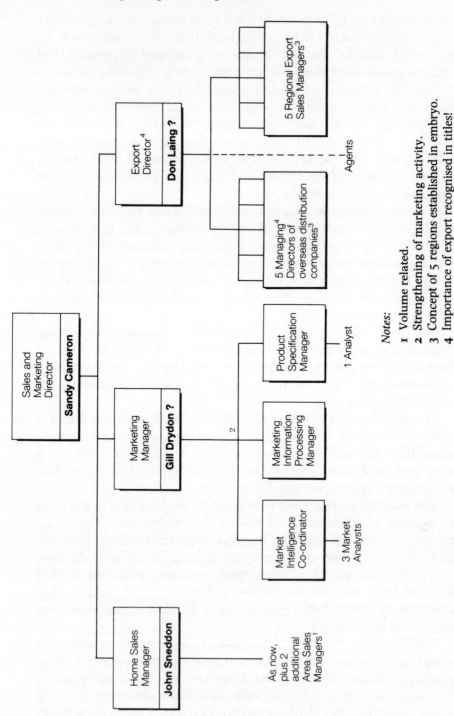

Figure 8.2 Organization in two years' time

Notes:

1 Volume related.
2 Strengthening of marketing activity.
3 Concept of 5 regions established in embryo.
4 Importance of export recognised in titles!

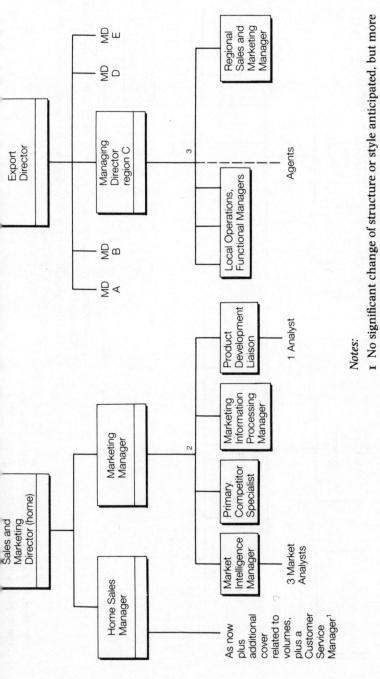

Figure 8.3 Organization in five years' time
Source: McBeath (1990)

Notes:

1 No significant change of structure or style anticipated, but more competitive selling will require increase in sales force.
2 Marketing will increase awareness of main competitors.
3 Regional structure planned for year 5, but could be earlier.

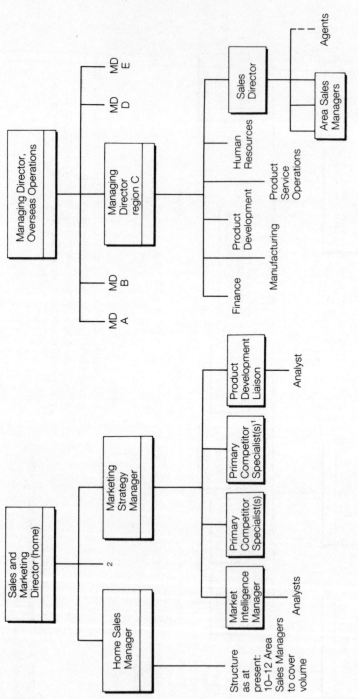

Notes:

1 Marketing information should be fully integrated into management database.

2 Possible appointment of a Product Service Manager (related to future generation of products).

Figure 8.4 Organization in ten-year projection
Source: McBeath (1990)

year assignment; followed by an older, top-ranking and proven director to lead the further rapid growth overseas. In terms of job grading, the changes in that job might justify an upward move every two to three years. In contrast, the home sales job might justify only one additional notch at some time later in the plan period.

The plan made no allowance for any major acquisitions, although the companies on which the example was based planned to look for small ones which would supplement their product ranges. Nor did they develop any contingency plans. They assumed that any acquisition would run in parallel for a minimum of one year, during which time the relative strengths and cultures could be examined and logical plans developed to achieve integration, which they did not expect would divert them from their grand design.

Analysis of the numbers and categories of managers and support staff required to fill the organization in the future involves exploding the planned organization to develop a forecast of the detail. This is possible, drawing on the full detail encapsulated within the business objectives and associated strategies and scenarios. Although the result is unlikely to be absolutely accurate in the longer term in companies undergoing substantial change, it should provide guidance on the people development programme necessary and on the level and type of graduate intake and other recruitment required.

Example 8.6 shows the top end of such an analysis of future manpower requirements from a group of building companies. This has limitations in that it does not cover the evolution in the content, objectives and specifications of positions which retain established titles, but it does provide a clear summary of the scale of the recruitment and indicates the general shape of development tasks.

Manpower requirements in manufacturing

The manpower plan for manufacturing is likely to consist of a number of departmental sections covering the production operations and supporting activities such as procurement, industrial engineering, quality and, possibly, others, depending on the product and the choice of organization structure.

The starting point is the group of people directly involved in production output, so the base information will include a comprehensive picture of planned manufacturing activities, with an explosion of planned output data expressed in units which can be translated into work-load and, through standards, manning require-

Forecast of Management and Specialist Staff Requirements in a Construction Group

Category	Totals				Losses		Total require- ments over 5 years	Supply		
								Internal promotions	External Recruitment	
	Now	5-year fore-cast	Increase	% PA	Over 5 years	Promo-tions out			Total	Annual rate
CEO of subsidiary	5	8	3		2		5	3	2	2
Branch VP	1	7	6		3	3	12	3	9	
Contracts VP	4	8	4		2	1	7	5	2	8
Contracts Director	13	22	9	10%	8	5	22	20	2	
Contracts Manager	18	32	14	10%	13	20	47	5	42	
General Foremen	38	76	38	20%	57	5	100	50	50	10
Foremen	26	60	34	20%	43	50	127		127	25
Surveyor-Director	5	8	3	10%	3	1	7	6	1	1
Surveyor-Manager	12	22	10	15%	12	6	28	24	4	12
Surveyor	16	30	14	20%	23	24	61		61	
Director-Estimator/Plnr/Buyer	12	24	12	10%	4	1	17	12	5	1
Manager-Estimator/Plnr/Buyer	18	32	14	10%	12	12	38	30	8	2
Estimator/Planner/Buyer	28	50	22	15%	30	30	82		82	16

Example 8.6 Summary of forecasted management and specialist staff requirements in a construction group – prepared using *HR/View* Spreadsheet with forecast data from the business plan

ments. From this, a picture can be built up of all the work which is directly related to production, and the people required in the various skill categories. The manpower requirements for much of the direct work will fall out from simple arithmetic calculations.

With progress towards work cells – groups of people with a range of skills which carry out complete blocks of work – the measure of manning required may be more difficult. If a team of 20 normally assembles complete cars, it is very unlikely that the throughput can be raised by adding two people to each team. The existing operation simply will not work that way. Increased volume will have to be achieved from within the groups by generating higher productivity, or by longer hours, or by adding a fresh team with their own facilities. However, the options can be determined, and decisions made.

The second general category of manpower in manufacturing covers all other manpower directly associated with production, but whose work is not measured on as precise a basis. This will cover all those working on direct purchasing or in stores, etc., covering materials handling to production, despatch, inspection and test, production cost control, and so on, and the supervisory structure. The same basic data on products to be manufactured (volumes of activities) can be used with existing manning standards for each of these work groups. Difficulties should arise only where a significant organization change is to be implemented, or where product or technical/system changes may invalidate the existing standards.

As production volumes will vary, the factors related to work volume can be identified and used to flex manning requirements in line with volume variation, but this is not very effective where small numbers of various skill categories are involved, or the work mix changes. For example, a small production volume may involve a wider range of products and require a larger number of small volume purchase orders. This may result in an increase in the requirement for purchasing staff, but reduce the demand for product inspection. However, the ability to specify changes in that way enables a judgement of manning requirements to be made.

When using a manning standard based on past practice for a particular volume, it is worth noting that a volume variation which exceeds 20 per cent should trigger a re-examination of the standard, particularly where the volume is increased and more efficient operation should be sought.

The third area in manufacture covers the indirect categories, manpower whose work is not directly related to current production. Much of their work may be adequately measurable or can be covered by an abbreviated form of manpower standard setting but measures of the volume of work required which are sufficient to determine manning requirements for the defined activity levels may be more difficult to establish.

The final category of manufacturing manpower covers any non-essential or discretionary activities (as discrete positions or as elements in other jobs) where an assumption will need to be made on likely future requirements. It may be reasonable to assume a continuation of the current volume of discretionary activity as a guideline, unless there are any special current or anticipated circumstances. In due course, all discretionary work should be fully vetted and approved to ensure proper control over this expense.

From the various analyses above, a comprehensive summary of future manpower requirements for manufacturing can be assembled, showing the total requirements at a series of points in time, and showing any changes in the skills profile over time.

Manpower requirements in research and development

This is one of the more difficult areas to plan with accuracy, due to uncertainties about how much work will be involved in particular projects, and variations in judgements of standards between research and development managers. In a large establishment, it is possible to build up extensive case law, but even this is not a reliable guide.

Some difficulty stems from the tendency for many research and development activities to carry people who have become ineffective and use people inefficiently due to poor leadership and man management. The extend of this is best revealed when another project team in the same environment breaks all the rules and achieves results in a fraction of the normal time using totally inadequate resources. One of my favourite examples arose when an 80-strong research and development team was faced with an excellent new product from a competitor. Wringing their hands, the team explained that it would take the usual three years to develop an equivalent, after which the wretched manufacturing and marketing people would delay its introduction (as usual) for a further couple of years, by which time they would be out of business. One of the more innovative development managers grabbed the initiative and, with a tiny proportion of the research and development team, supplemented with individuals seconded from industrial engineering and marketing, had a new and better product on sale in eight months. The fact that this was achieved overturned all previous manning standards, at least in theory, for there were many people in the development department who could not adjust to the change.

That example is obviously a few years old and we have moved on progressively to shorter product life cycles and faster product development times. In looking at skills in this function, the ability to work with pace and flexibility has increased in significance, and manpower planning needs to ensure an outward flow of the less effective people to other functions, or out of the company.

The principles to be followed are straightforward enough. There will be a programme of projects to be carried out (which will get amended over time), and the technical management will have to make a judgement of the volume and form of work required in each one, the skills required and the time necessary.

Some large research and development establishments have resource managers who are responsible for deploying people to projects. They have realistic views of activity volumes and how best to get work done. Given fluctuating work patterns, these individuals need to vary the pressures on their resources to extract maximum outputs at times of peak loading, and to accept lower outputs at other times, and they have to be relied on as the source of manning standards for planning purposes.

The simple fact is, if you want to develop something new, it has not been done before and, therefore, there are no established measures. An experienced resource manager will make an assessment of what appears to be required, and make some allowance for contingencies based on experience of similar projects. One limitation is that judgements are historically based but, then, so are all manning standards. A shift in technology, or organization, or a single innovative leader, may upset the predictions. In most cases these upsets will shorten forecast times and reduce manning requirements.

The major concern in research and development will always be unforeseen technological advance which may, quite suddenly, outdate corporate competences and associated products and developments, and leave a research and development team lacking knowledge of newly critical technology. Given the pace of technological change, it seems essential that the continual updating of knowledge required by all technical staff should be broad enough to take into account any development which could shake one's own field. From the manpower planner's viewpoint, recognition of danger areas, and contingency planning to cover potential hazards by acquiring knowledge of new technologies, appears necessary.

A summary of overall needs for the function should be developed, along the same lines as indicated for manufacturing.

Manpower requirements in marketing and sales

In marketing and sales, the conversion of objectives and targets into work to be done is reasonably straightforward for activities directly associated with selling, but there is an increasing amount of analytical work in market and competitor analysis which may trigger a range of special studies or discretionary projects, where manning requirements are more difficult to assess.

The requirements for selling activities are easy to forecast in the short term, based on existing standards. However, it is essential to take into account judgements of how a market is changing. In general, most markets are becoming more competitive, making sales objectives more complex and tougher to meat, which gradually alters the person specifications at every level. It follows that manning projections should not be excessively tight, and may need to be generous.

Marketing areas face the same pressures, and there may be an advantage in putting extra resources in the hands of competent marketing managers. Much opportunity for competitive advantage can stem from detailed knowledge of major competitors and their strategies, while under-resourcing of the marketing function can have an adverse impact on market share and profitability.

There are many facets to marketing, and manpower projections need to take into account the objectives set for each activity to define adequately the balance of skills needed within the future requirement plan.

Manpower requirements in HR/personnel

This may be a smaller function in terms of numbers, but it is critically important to business success. It is one of the prime functions which is increasing its use of external specialists as consultants on a part-time basis, or on a retainer basis, recognizing that many smaller companies cannot occupy or cannot afford the 'heavyweight' specialists they need on a full-time basis. The manpower plan should indicate the means of meeting these requirements in the most effective way.

The routine and administrative elements of the personnel function can be covered adequately by establishing manning standards. Some other aspects have variable work-loads, such as recruitment, where there is plenty of scope for maintaining a basic core of staff, and meeting fluctuations through a variety of forms of subcontracting. However, some critical aspects of HR work involve influencing or making things happen without having line responsibility or hands-on control, and much of this work requires relatively scarce skills. These activities need to be treated as discretionary work, with forward requirements judged on line management's expectations from the function, which will also determine the particular personal skills required.

Manpower requirements in finance

This is a reasonably simple area to cover once the necessary work has been defined. Most of the small proportion of jobs without established and challengeable manning standards will be in non-routine management positions, but the objectives of their discretionary activities are likely to be clear-cut.

As companies progress towards more general use of a corporate database and managers gain a better understanding of the overall workings of the business as well as the associated information technology, numerate people in other functions will tend to be less dependent on the finance function to interpret financial data. This should reduce manning requirements and influence.

Manpower requirements for management information

The greatest degree of change in the 1990s is likely to be felt in the management of information as computer and telecomms technologies continue to advance rapidly. It is my experience that line managers (including those managing information technology) continually understate the extent of impending change beyond the immediate 12- to 18-month horizon, so manpower projections are likely to underestimate the potential for change and the impact on manning requirements across the company.

In theory, it should be possible to use current IT projects as a basis for estimating future work-loads and skill requirements, but these are rarely precise beyond 18 months and caution should be exercised about the pace of further developments.

My view is that the manpower requirement plan for this function needs to be updated quarterly to give the best advance warning of future developments. Skilled people are likely to remain in relatively short supply, but the form of the skills required will evolve quickly in line with software technology. Lengthy warning of changing requirements is therefore necessary to enable existing staff to be retrained.

Requirements for other functions and activities

The functional guidelines set out above are adaptable to most other situations. As the range of specialist groupings seems likely to increase in future organizations, the tendency to use retained, part-time specialists will also increase. In manpower terms, these resources will need to be planned for and managed as though they were full-time ordinary employees.

Flexing Requirements for Volume Change

Manning standards relate manpower requirements to work volumes, but if the volume of work doubles or halves, it is unlikely that the relevant manpower ratios will follow exactly.

Those elements of the work which are completely volume related will remain directly proportional, unless new equipment or systems affect productivity. For less directly affected work, the volume change will have a lesser impact. For example, if work volume doubles, supporting services and supervision may need to increase by no more than 30 to 50 per cent. The assumption of such a figure is realistic, but subject to analysis and challenge.

We might expect to make similar adjustments if the volume falls drastically, but the financial receipts of the business will fall in direct proportion and this will necessitate commensurate reductions in all expenditure, including manpower. While volume change is rarely as tidy as these figures assume – for there may be many complications such as a changing mix of work as well – the principle is sound. If volume is declining, the business must reduce manpower in direct proportion whereas, if volume is increasing, there has to be scope for real productivity improvement.

Forecasting the timing of some changes in manning requirements is so difficult that there may be occasions when we have to respond to options of equal probability, but rather different end results. Then, the manpower projections need to indicate ranges of requirements, such as maximum and minimum figures, or an envelope defining the limits within which the ultimate manning requirements are expected to fall.

Contingency planning

In the preparation for a business plan, a number of possible occurrences will be identified which are not built into the most likely scenario, but which cannot be ignored. In such cases, a contingency plan should be developed, setting out the course of action to be taken in response. The most common events covered by contingency plans include allowances for greater or lesser volumes of orders and, therefore, manufacture; early or delayed timing of technical change and product change; various actions by competitors; and timing or impact of significant legislation.

We are concerned here with the impact both on manpower requirement and supply plans and the mechanisms which we can use in the event of all short-term changes of plan to ensure provision of manning needs. The actions will depend on the nature of the possible change, whether it involves changed phasing of planned events, increased or decreased activity, and whether the change is expected to be of short duration, or become more or less permanent.

The options available can be built into manpower plans with greater ease than used to be possible. For example, possible downward fluctuations in business volume can be covered by setting the level of core staff as the essential minimum, with a contingency manning provided by temporary manpower for peaks of higher volumes. This enables the expenses of non-core staff to be trimmed off when not required, subject to the availability of necessary skills and experience. Small increases in work volumes above a base level may be covered by some extra effort and overtime. For short periods it may be possible to cover an excess of up to 20 per cent in this way, but it will vary with activity and also with corporate pace and culture. By that level, recruitment of temporary help is essential to enable higher volumes to be achieved. The practicability of this will be dependent on the availability of spare capacity on equipment and other resources, of course. However, it may be straightforward if an additional shift can be accommodated.

An alternative option would be to subcontract a proportion of work, keeping the in-house volume close to the core base level. If it is possible to do this with reliable suppliers who accept that they are covering a peak which will come to an end, this may be the preferred option. The choice of work subcontracted can be adapted to match the combination of internal competences and those of the subcontractors.

The value of contingency planning is only truly evident when a contingency occurs and the plan, rapidly pulled out of the bottom drawer, is seen to provide clear and thorough action plans to deal with the situation. Hopefully, the need will not occur too frequently, but with an increasingly volatile business environment, contingency plans are likely to be more relevant in the future.

The plan itself will be unremarkable. It is likely to be identical in content and form to the rest of the business and manpower plans. The only difference is that it is an appendix – a supplementary plan which just may be needed. Planning for short-term flexibility in the use of manpower is an important subsidiary objective for manpower planning, and an area where substantial success is possible at the supply stage.

Special situations

Not all planning takes place within tidy, established business scenarios, and this section looks at some of the unusual situations for which special treatment is necessary.

Fast growth companies: In fast growing organizations, the number of top-level or director-level jobs may not change significantly over several years, but the scope of the responsibilities and the complexity involved may alter enormously. This will show in tougher person specifications and rising valuations of the jobs; for example, job values may double rapidly.

At the base of the jobs pyramid, the numbers of employees in clerical and manual categories, and the attendant supervisors, may increase substantially, but growth means only more jobs at the same levels. Between the base job levels in the expanding lower strata of the pyramid, and the rising peak of the growing structure, additional levels will emerge, with some individual jobs growing and rising in value, and others remaining static and being capped by new higher posts. It is important that these changes are recognized in the organization, manpower and career planning.

Where a grading structure exists, forecasts of requirements by grade levels should be developed to help clarify the degree of change in job requirements. While this does not tell the whole story, such an analysis can be extremely informative. Example 9.7 later in the book shows a forecast of such a situation which adds significantly to an appreciation of the problems.

The young division: Most companies set up a new division, a new department, or some form of new organization from time to time. Up to a point, the manning of these new organizations can be planned for, and staff developed in advance to fill the key posts. However, there are many other cases where a decision needs to be taken before planning is complete, such as key appointments required urgently to launch the project, leaving no time for preparatory development or training. This can present considerable difficulty as management development traditionally concentrates on future succession requirements, rather than developing an inventory, but it is an inventory which is needed to help identify suitable candidates to man possible new divisions if and when the company engages in new activites.

One of the major companies in the paper industry adopted the deliberate policy of overstaffing with high-potential people to meet its unplannable requirements for new departments or product divisions. The result was a useful stock of experienced people, but a higher than usual turnover of those good people. The company accepted this situation because it was able, from time to time, to meet a sudden demand for additional managers following some commercial development. However, the approach was costly and caused as many problems as it solved. Other companies have found it necessary to recruit whole teams externally to meet the management requirements of an unplanned new organization, and accept the time delay involved.

A system which incorporates a detailed inventory of existing skills, experience and potential provides the most useful database when a new unit is proposed at short notice, particularly if the database includes comprehensive cover of individual competences. Existing manpower strengths can then be displayed to optimum advantage, and the deployment of all resources reviewed in order to develop an optimum solution for the immediate situation.

Ideally, we should think immediately of the manning requirements and any potential staffing problems whenever a new organization of any sort is being considered. Then, as it jells, the staffing plan will consolidate and the supply mechanisms which build up the required teams can be running quietly, even before the final decisions to go ahead are taken.

Rapid Change: A significant advance in technology may have a rapid and potentially catastrophic impact on a business, leaving little time for planning change. Many companies tell me that any new product they launch which gives them competitive advantage will face new competing products in no more than three months. This spells out the pace of response required in the market-place. In turn, this will require very fast manpower deployment actions and emphasizes the need for contingency plans where competitor exposure can be identified.

The entrepreneur: In a large private company, the top man announced a new venture which was to be put into operation immediately. As the new venture was to have a seven-figure turnover within a year, a great deal of furious pirating was considered essential to obtain the necessary staff. In spite of the skills which were pressed into operation, there must have been a substantial element of luck in the successful, but scrambled, launch of this new enterprise.

It has been put to me that entrepreneurial attitudes and planning do not mix. This is true enough, but they do need to coexist peacefully so that the ground is prepared in advance for major developments in the way outlined for the young division above.

Not all ideas come to fruition, so why plan? The answer, I think, is that the success of many business options is critically dependent on the availability of key human resources. This availability has to be a prime factor in the planning study, to confirm or refute the soundness of the proposal and to determine either its speedy and successful launch or its logical cancellation.

9

Planning Manpower Supply

The supply side of the manpower planning equation logically follows on from determination of requirements, but the very long lead times sometimes involved in supply mean that many aspects of supply need to be established in long-term patterns. The clearest example of the long-term nature of manpower supply is to be found in the systematic annual recruitment of graduates to provide a strong internally generated flow of managers five, ten or 15 years into the future. Interfering with this intake is hazardous if the longer term objectives are to be safeguarded, as graduates and graduate sources have long memories where career prospects are concerned.

There is also a significant shorter term factor in that business fluctuations have an immediate impact on manpower needs, which the company may not be able to cope with quickly. If there is a sudden downturn, it is difficult and expensive to reduce the numbers of permanent employees, even if it appears to be in the best interests of the business. On the other hand, an upturn in business opportunity may present even greater problems in resourcing the manpower needs quickly.

To begin planning how to satisfy manpower requirements, we need to establish an opening position. This includes:

- A clear picture of forward manpower requirements, in exploded form, to detail the function, category and level of each position at a series of points in time.
- A clear picture of our current manpower inventory, also in exploded form, using the same breakdown into function, category and level.
- Data on flows through the structure, loss rates, and various analyses which provide information on how the present inventory is changing.
- Data on the availability of various skills and experience we may need to recruit externally, and cost levels, so that we can assess the economics of possible business intentions.

The supply plan involves matching the evolution of the inventory with the future requirements. To do this effectively, it is essential to know a great deal about the make-up of the current inventory, and about the personnel flows into, through, and out of the structure. This should enable the intakes needed to maintain the balance between inventory and requirements to be calculated, and recruitment actions to be scheduled. Similarly, it will clarify the development and training required to prepare individuals for moves to higher levels when the needs arise.

Planning supply requires close monitoring and fine tuning because people management issues are not precise. Apart from the likelihood of a continuous flow of modifications and changes to the detail of future manpower requirements, it is difficult to match recruiting specifications precisely and ensure that recruits start on planned dates. Also, individual development rates are variable which means that planned readiness is frequently uncertain; individual preferences and ambitions change, so that planned candidates do not accept planned appointments; assessments of job content and required competences are misjudged and candidates do not match needs; and flows or loss rates vary unpredictably.

Planning should ensure that the anticipated manning requirements are being met reasonably closely, but there will always be some mismatch which has to be covered by emergency action to meet essential business needs. I am reminded of the CEO who, at the end of a detailed review of his management succession plans, observed ruefully that, for the past several years, each of his carefully prepared plans had failed to recognize the need for at least one significant appointment which had had to be made within the following twelve months due to some development in the overall business environment. While some of these might have been anticipated, it seems inevitable that plans will never cover all eventualities.

Our task starts with overlaying requirements with available supplies and analysing the differences, taking parts of the organization and functions piecemeal in view of the complexity and the opportunities within the total frame. The resulting pictures are likely to show a great range of mismatch situations, with an excess in some categories, skills and levels, short supply of others, and opportunities for some transfers between areas. The remainder of our task will be to determine the extent to which we can bring the two parts together by modifying both our requirements and our stock through retraining and redeployment to shift any excess of manpower into short-supply areas.

Flows

Our analyses of flows should tell us a great deal about how the inventory has been evolving over the past several years, and how it may be continuing to evolve. This is of fundamental importance, as it will determine the achievable levels and points of intake of fresh manpower, and indicate the availability of people who meet broad specifications throughout the functional areas.

Flows are examined in detail in the next chapter, showing the potential impact of changes in flows which can drastically alter supplies.

Recruitment

The most significant and immediate supply action is recruitment. However, it is necessary to ensure that the numbers and specifications of recruits match the immediate and longer term requirements of the company. Relatively few recruitments are made solely to cover an immediate need. It should be recognized that a 25-year-old may stay with an organization for some 30 years, accumulating knowledge and skills over that period, and being employed in a sequence of positions. Given that situation, the recruit features immediately in the flow patterns as well as in the initial post.

A company recruits graduates to fill a series of opening level positions, and expects that they will move up after about a year to make way for the next wave, and that successive waves will progress up the structure. The form of that progress is detailed in the flow patterns. It is expected that a certain proportion will move into supervisory and then managerial roles – again identified numerically in the flows – and the organization is dependent on the recruits meeting the standards required to achieve relevant promotion in the expected times.

The specifications for recruitment need to be carefully drafted to help meet future, as well as the immediate needs. For example, the increasing importance of future managers having good leadership skills means that we need to look for those qualities, or that potential, in a proportion of our graduate recruits.

Of course, not all recruitment is at the major intake points (school and university leavers) but the same general principles should apply when recruiting mature entrants. As well as meeting the immediate need, they should fit into the pattern of future needs, perhaps being potential candidates for some category likely to be underresourced according to the plan.

Development

There is no harm in repeating that it is not enough to recruit people to meet immediate requirements. We should expect them to grow (and flow upwards), so there is a need for a corporate culture which encourages that growth, and for active management support and participation in the process.

Development requires activities such as appraisal to identify how people can improve their performance in their present jobs, and forms of assessment which will help to identify the shape and content of future potential. Development can then be planned individually, by arranging a sequence of planned experiences or assignments which expand capability and prepare individuals for more senior or varied assignments which match both personal and corporate needs.

Training

Training contributes to development. Before an individual moves into a fresh position, it may be necessary for him to have a sound theoretical grounding beyond that which he could have acquired at a lower level. Training sets out to ensure that necessary theoretical knowledge is absorbed at appropriate levels, to provide a clear base for practical learning by experience.

As one example, many graduates go into marketing careers with no theoretical framework of understanding of the function. A few may subsequently do an MBA with a marketing emphasis, but many will do little more than accumulate knowledge from assignments in different aspects of marketing and, subsequently, in general management. When a non-standard question arises, the difference in the quality of response possible from employees with MBA training compared with that from those whose experience is solely on-the-job learning will be massive. This gap can be reduced by providing as much theory and action learning as possible to supplement the lack of in-depth learning, and some companies are excellent in this respect.

Excess manpower

If there is a high probability of an excess in manpower, planning is vital to minimize its extent and to minimize damage. It is possible to take a variety of courses of action to achieve these ends, and many of these are touched on in chapter 14.

Loss rates

Beautiful manpower plans which identify needs and produce matching people are of limited value if an excessive proportion of those people do not stay around to fill the vacancies. It simply is not possible to retain everyone you want, but a high proportion will stay around while they are convinced that their careers can develop satisfactorily with their present employers. Communications about future opportunities, and real involvement in personal career development have remarkably positive effects.

Strategies from a plan summary

Projections from the current inventory and flows analysis will show that the current stock of managers is declining due to retirements and terminations and that the supply of potential managers has an anticipated output over the period of the plan, with that supply also subject to some losses. If these data are plotted against the

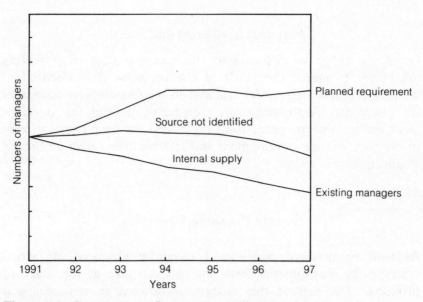

Figure 9.1   Requirements for managers with indication of sources

management numbers determined in the requirement plan, any excess or shortfall is clearly visible, as in figure 9.1.

Any shortfall may be overcome by a number of supply strategies. If people can see that their career ambitions are likely to be met within the organization, they are far more likely to stay. Improved involvement in career planning and communication of opportunities may reduce loss rates. A second action may be to speed up the development of potential future managers, to bring more of them through quickly to match requirements. Finally, if internal sourcing is not possible, then an external recruitment plan needs to be created to bring in people of the calibre required over the duration of the plan.

Management continuity

At the top end of manpower planning, management continuity or succession planning has a specialist role within manpower planning. There is a point where the numbers which make up the bulk of corporate manpower come down to being one of everything, and the specifications of those individual slots are both personal and evolutionary. Then the planning comes down to individuals as well, but the same processes and activities are relevant across the board.

Continuous monitoring and review

Given the range of elements in the whole process of providing manpower to match the needs of the business, it is essential to monitor progress frequently, and also to monitor the end objectives for movement. This is not solely a matter of ensuring that development and training are proceeding as planned, for people tend to vary in the pace of their development and rethink their career ambitions in unpredictable ways.

Supply Planning Examples

As with requirement planning, I recognize the need for actual examples to illustrate the form analyses can take at this stage of planning. The rest of this chapter is devoted to examples and associated commentary, ranging from simple, single-department,

Job title	Action
Accounting operations supervisor	Jenkins marked for promotion to HQ in April. Accounting operations clerk Patteson to replace him
Assistant accountant	Promotion of Salmon to new post – September or October
Book-keeper	Replacement for Salmon – recruit July onwards
Accounting operations clerk	Three replacements anticipated. Plan intake of one from training course September. Recruit as required
Other categories	Recruit as required

Figure 9.2   Notes on detailed phasing of forecast

short-term plans, through to extracts covering critical areas in company five-year plans.

Example: Action to meet requirements   In the previous chapter, example 8.3 covered the manning requirements of an accounts department for one year. Actions initiated or planned to fulfil those requirements were set out in an appendix (figure 9.2) to the department manager's planning memorandum. It makes some allowance of hand-over of responsibilities, induction, etc.

Supply planning involves selection of sources for each category of staff (where these people are to come from); planning how they will be obtained; what training and development or induction they will need before they will become effective; and so on. From this exercise, an overall recruitment and development operating plan can be evolved, incorporating the required flow data.

In the short term, this involves scheduling recruitment, taking into account the time necessary to define the post, prepare and publish any advertisement, sort and interview candidates, select the most able and perhaps negotiate terms, and then wait while notice is worked before he joins. The times will vary for a number of reasons, such as the ease or difficulty of attracting suitable candidates and the differing lengths of notice required. The result is that a recruitment campaign may need to begin anything from three weeks to a year before an individual is required to become effective.

Example: Identifying manpower problems to be addressed　A second example from the previous chapter which I would like to follow through is example 8.4, taken from a subsidiary within a building group. This example sets out the current position and the five-year forecast without showing year-to-year detail, which was added later. The purpose was to get a view of the implications of its growth plans while ignoring short-term fluctuations expected along the way. As the subsidiary is structured with four divisions, some of which are subdivided into branches, the opening actuals show a more detailed breakdown than is available at the year five stage. A business volume growth of the order of 30 per cent was anticipated.

The loss rates being experienced by the company were very high and, even with some reduction in those levels, the impact of losses on availability was severe in several categories. For example, losses of foremen were revealed as not being offset by the planned training programme by a wide margin although the intake of trainee/assistant foremen was almost trebled. There was a clear need to review the calibre of the intake and the content of training in order to speed up the throughput and achieve better retention of new foremen. The next update of the plan will need to reflect an improved picture if the business ambitions are to be achieveable.

The creation of intake categories of surveyors, estimators and buyers is in response to shortages within these groups but, again, the expected loss rates and the duration of trainee/assistant periods make this tactic look of doubtful value. A revised programme to bring in individuals capable of responding to speeded-up training and development may produce a more satisfactory end result; lower head count, lower costs, lower loss of skills, less frustration of the established skilled people, and an earlier supply of competent support staff.

Example: An application of flow analysis　Example 9.1 represents a five-year forecast by a civil engineering company, to determine the scale of needs it was unlikely to be able to meet from internal sources. The opportunities for promotions within the site management structure were seen to provide very attractive career opportunities and, as a result of the plan, much greater attention was given both to the identification and recruitment of people who might be promoted and to their subsequent training and development.

Curiously, little attention was focused on the engineers in this company – possibly this was because the bulk of the business was

Civil Engineering Group - Manpower Survey - Five Years 1991-96

Category	Present strength	Immediate require- ments	Current proposed strength	Resignations and retirements anticipated	Promotions from staff	Additional requirements					Strength 1996 (Year End)
						1992	1993	1994	1995	1996	
Managing Director	1		2			1					1
Contracts Director	1	1	4		(1)^1		1				2
Contracts Managers	4	2	10			2			1		5
Site Agents	8		4	2	(1)^1				1	1	12
Senior General Foremen	4		4	1	2	1					4
General Foremen	8		4	2	(2)^4	1		1		1	6
Foremen	8		8		(4)^4			1	1	1	12
Section Foremen	9		9		(4)^4			1	1	1	12
Chargehands	N/A		N/A		(4)^						N/A
Quantity Surveyors	4	2	6	4		2	1	1			7
Engineers	9		9			2		2	1		12
Senior Estimators	1		1			1					1
Estimator	1		1								1
Prod'n Planning Engr			1								1
Group Secretary	1		1								1
Accountant	1		1								1

Chargehands, skilled men and labour omitted. Note: ^ - indicates promotions within the company.

Example 9.1   Five-year manpower inventory projections of a civil engineering group – prepared using *HR/View* Spreadsheet with data from the business plan

Extract covering Part of a Manufacturing Unit affected by Product and Technology Change

Category	Actual Jan 1992	Movement 1992 Out Was	Out Red	Out Trs	In Trs	In Fop	In Rec	Plan Jan 1993	Movement 1993 Out Was	Out Red	Out Trs	In Trs	In Fop	In Rec	Plan Jan 1994	Moveme Out Was	Out Red	Out Trs
AMP Dept																		
Semi-skilled 2	6	4	2					4	2	2	4				0	100		
Semi-skilled 1	48	4	18					26	2	8	22				0	50		
Skilled 2	36		14		2			20		6	10				0	5		
Skilled 1	10		4					6		2					0	3		
Highly skilled	4		2					2							0			
TOTAL	104	8	40	6	2			58	4	18	36				Nil	158		
BRLE Dept																		
Unskilled	9			3				6			6				0			
Semi-skilled 2	9	3		3				6			6				0			
Highly skilled	87		27					57		51	6				0			
TOTAL	105	3	27	6				69		51	18				Nil			
JPB Dept																		
Semi-skilled 2		20			60	10	60	110	80			150	10	95	275	100		
Semi-skilled 1		10			30	10	30	60	80			70	15	90	150	50		
Skilled 2		1			11	7	2	19	12			25	5	1	48	5		
Skilled 1					2			2	3			5		3	12	3		
TOTAL	Nil	31			103	27	92	191	135			250	30	179	515	158		

KEY: Was - wastage; Red - redundant; Tra - transfer; Fop - from other plants; Rec - recruit

Example 9.2 Extract covering part of a manufacturing unit affected by product and technology change – prepared using *HR/View* Spreadsheet with forecast data from the business plan

in subcontracting on major contracts where the engineering work has been done already, and possibly because the company's top management was a mix of accountants and construction men. As a consultant in this situation, two of my key recommendations involved a review of the engineering input to company objectives and the strengthening of the association between the engineering resources and operations to encourage career flows.

The company resolved to develop career flow pictures to give themselves a greater vision of potential sources of candidates for advancement, which resulted in clarifying opportunities for some of their graduate engineers. They also modified their engineering intake profile to improve the match with their development needs, and began to create development plans for individuals, to ensure people were properly prepared to progress as anticipated.

Example: Planning for technology change   Example 9.2 covers part of the manpower plan for a manufacturing unit affected by substantial product and technology changes. It includes some product areas in rapid decline and other areas about to be launched. Significantly, the plan identified the fact that many skilled men on declining products were unlikely to accept the job opportunities on the new lines, which were largely semi-skilled or automated assembly, so an active recruitment and training programme would have to be implemented during a parallel programme of redundancy.

For brevity, only two of the departments scheduled for closure are shown, plus a summary of the group of departments in the new area. These are sufficient to show the form of analysis, and the types of movement expected to take place. Further, all supervision and all service departments are excluded from this extract.

In summary, the bulk of the lower skilled employees no longer required in the old areas can be offered equivalent graded jobs in the new organization, although a proportion may prefer to take redundancy or early retirement. In the early stages, the run-down will be out of phase with the timing of new requirements and some redundancies will arise for that reason. (In reviewing the plan, some rescheduling of work was arranged to bridge the gap, reduce redundancy needs and increase opportunity for transfers.) Very little scope for absorbing the highly skilled group is revealed in this summary, but the new equipment did require their skills and redundancy was largely avoided.

In addition to generous severance terms, employees were given every assistance in obtaining alternative employment. A few in narrowly specialized categories faced some difficulty in this respect. Some other people ultimately expressed a preference for taking the redundancy package rather than the alternative jobs, which were at the same grade and pay levels but involved different work.

This case is a classic example of the need for a change in skills-mix, where assumptions about necessary redundancy and scope for retraining and redeployment may be affected by the generosity of redundancy packages. Continual review of actual events against plan is essential and it is likely that a manning situation such as in example 9.2 will require updating on a quarterly basis – in fact, the company used an expanded version of this plan giving quarter-by-quarter figures which was updated at the end of each quarter.

Concealed within these figures can be skill mismatches where the

---

To the Board
SENIOR MANAGEMENT REQUIREMENTS AT DECEMBER 1988

The top slice of a manpower plan becomes personalised. The number of jobs tends not to change, but there is some change in job contents and incumbents.

South East
1 The appointment of an MD to replace LMT on his promotion is required now. Short list attached.
2 Chief Buyer E.C. Able reaches retirement age of 62 on 7 December 1991.
3 Chief Contracts Manager, J.C. Beeson, is 62 on 1 December 1993.
4 Senior Contracts Manager, T.D. Connock, is 49 but suffers ill health and will need to be transferred and replaced.
5 Finance Manager, A.H. Dennis, is 31 and is unlikely to be in the same job beyond 1991.

Central
1 Chief Buyer, G.R. Easy, is over retirement age, and is 65 this year.
2 Chief Contracts Manager, G.G. Fredericks (38), is likely to have justified promotion by 1991.
3 A Branch Manager for the western areas may be required by 1990.

South West
1 Joint Managing Director, H.B. Griffiths, is 60 in July 1989 and wishes to retire at that date. The other Joint MD, B.S. Herbert (46), will become sole MD.
2 Chief Contracts Manager, S.P. Tilley (37), may be promoted before 1990.
3 Finance Manager, S.B. Jacobs (29), is unlikely to be in the same job in 1991.

Midlands
1 An MD for the region has been selected and will be appointed shortly.
2 The present MD, H.P. Kennedy, is 62 in January 1988.
3 Finance Manager, A. Litton, could be a regional MD within two years.
4 Chief Contracts Manager, L.W. Mitchell, is 59. He will be succeeded by F.N. Oswald.
5 Etc.

Figure 9.3 Extract from a senior management requirement plan prepared as at 1 December 1988

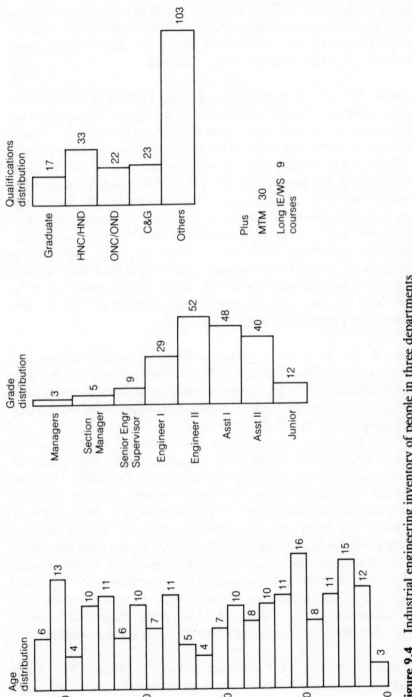

Figure 9.4 Industrial engineering inventory of people in three departments

grading of different skills is identical but there is no possibility of interchange between the employees concerned. For that reason, the use of skill grading as used in this case is not ideal, and relevant competency or skill categories should be used.

Example: The need for management planning Figure 9.3 shows (in a suitably disguised form) a summary of management requirements across a group of building companies (although it could be any industry). It reveals a picture of needs but gives very little evidence of people ready to take over. It was, in fact, a first statement of management needs prepared in this group. Subsequently, plans were developed along the lines of those set out in chapter 16, but at least once each year the board continued to review a current analysis in this simple form to reassure themselves that planned action was sufficiently specific to cover all managers likely to move within roughly three years. In subsequent years they added lists of managers whose performance was falling short of requirements in order to spotlight the need for corrective actions, plus lists of those thought to have high potential for early advancement.

Example: Restructuring to upgrade manpower quality Figure 9.4 shows a rather different picture. This analysis followed a conclusion that the company had an increased need for industrial engineering effort, but that the existing total head count in industrial engineering departments was too high. The example illustrates part of the problem: an ageing population of low grade and poorly qualified people. The task of building an efficient, technically up-to-date department from this starting point could only be achieved over an extended time period, or by deliberate surgery. A target structure was developed in full, with every job detailed, and short lists were developed for every post in the new structure. Where the new specifications could be met internally, existing people were appointed, and some compromise appointments were made on a probationary basis to minimize the upheaval. Some 80 per cent of posts were filled internally, while external recruitment was necessary for the rest. The remainder of the existing workforce was deployed as far as practicable, but there were many transfers and some casualties.

Example: Retraining in response to technology change Any major change in technology is likely to have an impact thoughout the entire organization. In the company from which this example is taken, a shift from electromechanical to electronics technology has a serious effect on skills and manning levels across product development, across all of manufacturing, and across the large product service operations, and a lesser impact in most other departments. The effects would be spread over some five years as the new generation of products built up and the old was phased out.

One of the clearest areas of change was in the service department where the major activity was installation and commissioning of new equipment, with a small proportion of people engaged on maintenance support of the customers' own maintenance teams. As a result of the technology-cum-product change, the existing service team was faced with a rapid decline in demand for their traditional skills, while a fresh team was required with new skills.

An analysis of existing and required skills showed much in common, the critical difference being knowledge of, and experience with, the new product technology. A small pilot group of engineers was taken into the technical training centre for three months and given an intensive course on the new technology, and then put into the field alongside newly recruited electronics people. The customer and company knowledge of the established engineers was seen to be of immense value, while the quality of their newly acquired knowledge varied.

A programme was developed which invited applications from established service engineers for retraining places, as an alternative to probable redundancy. The opportunity to acquire new skills proved very popular, with substantial take-up. However, some psychometric tests were developed progressively to identify those applicants who would be more or less likely to cope with the learning. The time in training became flexible (up to 12 months), with graduation from the course based on reaching measurable levels of knowledge and skill.

The effect was that the initial external recruitment programme was phased out quickly as the internal flow developed. Although the total number of service staff declined by almost 20 per cent over the period, all of the existing staff who wanted to change, and were thought to have the ability to learn and adjust, were given the chance and failure rates were very low.

Example 9.3 shows the initial manpower requirement forecast for service engineers, and 9.4 shows progress around half-way through the change. Any programme which takes reasonably expensive people off productive work for three to 12 months is bound to be expensive, but the costs were offset by avoidance of substantial

Manpower Plan covering Shift of Skills over 5 Year Period in a Service Department

Category	YEARS					
	0	1	2	3	4	5
Electromechanical						
Operational	301	260	220	160	100	40
In Training School	20	50	60	60	50	20
Subtotal	321	310	280	220	150	60
Electronics	20	55	90	135	175	200
Total Headcount	341	365	370	355	325	260
Total Operational	321	315	310	295	275	240

Example 9.3   Manpower plan covering skills shift – prepared using *HR/View* Spreadsheet with forecast data from the business plan

Category	YEARS					
	0	1	2	3 Plan	4 Plan	5 Plan
Electromechanical						
Operational at year end	301	248	206	150	100	40
To retraining during year	20	50	55	60	50	50
Completed - to Electronics		33	44	52	50	40
Left Company		18	12	6	5	5
Continue in training	20	19	18	20	15	20
Electronics						
Recruits in year	25	12	10	10	10	
From retraining		33	44	52	50	40
Losses	5	14	22	15	15	15
Operational at year end	20	51	83	130	175	200
TOTAL OPERATIONAL	321	318	307	300	290	260

Example 9.4 Mid-term revision of manpower plan in example 9.3 – prepared using *HR/View* Spreadsheet with forecast data from the business plan

redundancy payments, recruitment costs, and efficiency losses likely with large numbers of new people. Morale and efficiency remained high through the exercise.

Example: Gradually evolving position specifications　Not all situations are as clear cut as that in the previous case. The product change in a hydraulics engineering company, employing about 500 people in total, was slower but was gradually having a cumulative effect on the sales side of the business. The sales director observed that his customer base was changing and that selling was getting tougher. For the first time in this company, he found that he needed to use the marketing skills which he had learned elsewhere, much earlier in his career, and that he needed support on competitor analysis and marketing strategy. Separately, he realized that his sales people were needing a lot more understanding of the applications of their products, and that the less technically qualified people were not coping.

He created a new specification of sales engineers, emphasizing knowledge of product applications, and rewrote his manpower plan to reflect the changes he required. Initially, only a couple of his existing staff were up to the new specification but all his sales recruiting was in that grade. He set out to bring the rest of his staff up to the new standard over a couple of years. Those who didn't make it would become obsolete in that time.

His numbers were eleven sales people. His new plan (example 9.5) was quite simple but, because his numbers were conveniently small, he created short development plans for each of them to identify specific actions designed to bring them up to scratch.

In parallel, the sales director found his own role continuing to change fast (alongside some other members of the management team), and his biggest task was self-development to bring his own knowledge and skills up to the new requirements.

Example: The problems of rapid growth　The sheer growth in volume of work can create substantial problems of management in a rapid growth situation. At the smallest size, an activity may require 12 people, one of whom might have supervisory responsibility, but when the numbers exceed 20, a second manager will be needed. Somewhere above 50, the managers would need to be co-ordinated.

Few companies go through those phases quickly, but rapid growth will frequently raise the pressure for an additional level or an

Planned Shift to higher Specifications in a Sales Team

Category	Current	+ 6 months	+12 months	+ 18 months	+ 24 months	+ 30 months
SALES PERSONS						
No. of Sales Persons	11	8	6	4	2	
Upgraded to Sales Engineers		2	1			
Left Company		2	1	1	1	1
Recruited		1	1	1	1	1
SALES ENGINEERS	New category					
No. of Sales Engineers		4	5	8	10	12
Left Company			1			
Recruited						
TOTAL	11	12	12	12	12	12

Example 9.5 Planned shift to higher specifications in a sales team – prepared using *HR/View* Spreadsheet with forecast data from the business plan

alteration in management practice so that restating 'how we do things' is necessary for manpower planning.

In the case selected, the company was expanding its field sales force very rapidly. It planned over the coming year to double the number of representatives and its numbers of sales managers. It had to consider what this would mean to its field sales administrative staff, as it was far from keen to double those numbers as well.

Two other factors influenced this situation. The first was that, with larger numbers of administrative staff make some increasing specialization possible, with higher output per individual as a result. The second factor was that a clerical methods study was undertaken as part of the expansion programme and concentrated initially on the field operations. Streamlined administrative procedures were subsequently introduced and helped to cut growth of the administrative side to only one third more people over the previous year.

Figure 6.1, earlier in the book, showed pictorially the build up of the sales force and the point at which the decision was made to introduce an additional managerial level due to declining sales-force effectiveness. At a later stage, where growth was again slowing due to some slippage in efficiency, the company introduced a new specialist job rather than management level. Business analysts worked with the field force to identify areas where efficiency might be improved by either systems changes or by very specific training; these analysts had enough clout to follow through and implement their proposals rather than just make recommendations. This approach proved successful, and enabled the company to expand with much wider control spans instead of additional levels.

Similar stories can be found in numerous companies in financial services which have built up substantial sales teams. Part of the key to success lies in growing quality of sales management. Initially, some of the better salesmen were persuaded to switch to managing by offers of override commissions on the earnings of their subordinate salesmen but, progressively, more professionalism was wanted and, as the relevant skills were identified, a parallel stream developed of managers who could understand and motivate sales people, but spend only a limited proportion of their time selling. In time, a cadre of sales-orientated managers had taken over the task of managing the sales force.

As sales functions tend to have a relatively high staff turnover, and the primary motivation is movement up the earnings scale, individuals' career ambitions should be related to the potential of the

Category/Year	Year Start	Recruits +	Promotions out	Losses	Year End
SALESMEN					
Year 0					50
1	50	50	10	22	68
2	68	90	15	37	106
3	106	160	25	53	188
4	188	210	30	71	297
5	297	250	40	80	427
		Promotions from Salesmen			
SALES MANAGEMENT					
Year 0					3
1	3	10		6	7
2	7	15		10	12
3	12	25		16	21
4	21	30		21	30
5	30	40		28	42

Example 9.6 Growth of the sales force in a rapidly expanding company

commission plan, without the distraction of invitations to put aside their real skills and attempt to manage. The separate manager stream may include some people recruited initially as sales people, but they should understand from day one that they will progress into managing.

Not every sales team finds that course of action appropriate and example 9.6 is taken from a company which expected to grow very quickly and set out to include in its intake of salesmen a proportion who would be channelled from an early stage towards management. The objective was to show that the sales managers has first-hand selling experience, thereby ensuring respect from the salesmen.

The casualty rates were anticipated to be relatively high, but that can happen during rapid growth while specifications are still evolving and selection is somewhat imprecise. Within the management category, a more senior level was expected to emerge around year three or four, but was not specified separately at the early stage.

Example: Planning the provision of management in a growth company
At a more senior level in a growth company, the same issues apply. It is the changing scale of jobs which is one of the key measures of corporate growth, and grading can provide some indication of the adjustments required.

Example 9.7 illustrates this for a management team progressing through a period of rapid change, but for management planning (or management succession) we need to know the form of change as well as the measure.

The organization from which this example was drawn was able to outline most of the jobs in the evolving structure and evaluate the changes required in associated competences. In effect, it had to think of all of its senior managers as having high potential and being capable of advancing two or three distinct grade levels within a comparatively short period of time. In reality, although the team was very strong, not all of the members did have that sort of potential.

From this data, the company team was able to feed realistic future requirements into their planning, to make rational judgements on individual placements and accept the need to recruit higher capability into some future positions.

Example: Planning for a small function in a large company In large organizations which are divided into a collection of businesses, the numbers of people in any one company in the smaller functions may

Forecasts of Manpower Requirements by Grade from a Rapidly Growing Company

Grade levels	Present establishment	1-year forecast	2-year forecast	5-year forecast
18				1
17				
16				2
15		1	1	2
14	1	3	3	3
13	3	2	2	7
12	2	6	8	14
11	7	11	13	18
10	11	12	18	29
9	14	21	32	35
8	25	23	36	41

Example 9.7 Forecasts of manpower requirements by grade in a rapidly growing company – prepared using *HR/View*
Spreadsheet with forecast data from the business plan

Grade Distribution on legal Departments of HQ and Divisions of a Group

Grade levels	HQ	DIV A	DIV B	DIV C	DIV D	TOTALS
Board	1					1
Grade 12		1*		1	1*	3
11			1*			1
10				1*		1
9	3*	1			2*	6
8		2**	2	2*	1	7
7	2		1		2*	5
6		1*	1	2*		4
Graduate entry	1*	1*	1*	1*	2**	5

Example 9.8   Analysis of grade distributions within the HQ and divisional legal departments of a group for career planning – prepared using *HR/View* with data held in *Executive TRACK* management development planning system

be insufficient to allow full career progression planning. Yet if these small units could be seen in total, there could be a great deal of scope. Some organizations manage to handle these categories as single entities for career purposes.

The legal director of one group found that, in grading terms, (plus experience and career potential), there was a vast gap between himself and his direct subordinates, and that he had no obvious successor. However, within the subsidiary companies, the top legal people were at grade and competence levels which were well within the range in needed for succession to the group position. The logical career flow of his supporting staff in the headquarters was to top posts in the divisions, in preparation for becoming candidates for the top group job.

The analysis shown in example 9.8 shows the distribution of professional legal staff by grade level, with an asterisk for each member likely to be ready for a promotion to a higher grade within five years. It is likely that some of these staff will seek external appointments within that period in the absence of sufficient internal opportunities. Career flow patterns for small professional groups have to be partially between companies, simply because only the biggest can absorb all of those candidates ready for advancement, and even that requires skilled career development planning.

Manpower quality and supply planning

Quality is an essential facet of manning but, if you need to upgrade quality, it will require careful and deliberate planning over several years. If a company seeking major change is willing to allocate, say, three years to implement the change, it might start by redefining the departmental missions, updating jobs, and reviewing the competences of people. The second year might be seen as a consolidation year, with slower pace redeployment of unsuitable staff and a steady loss of individuals who realized the form of the change taking place and the fact that they did not fit. Intake of higher calibre people into the bottom levels would also have been a significant second-year development. The programme would be completed in the third year with a final comb out of old guard, unsuitable people, and the new style structure should have become fully effective.

Summary

These examples illustrate a diversity of problems and approaches. Common to most of these are the factors I started with, namely, a clear picture of the level, function and category of forward manpower requirements, a clear picture of our current manpower inventory, data on 'flows' to show how the present inventory is changing, and data on the market availability and costs of various skills and experience we may need to recruit.

The review process integrates manpower plans and actions with the evolving needs of the business. The process operates on an ongoing basis at every level, with periodic total reviews from the bottom up to the top levels of the business.

The supply plan sets out to meet the business requirements through manipulating the content and evolution of the inventory. It covers decisions ranging from specifications, numbers and levels of recruits, changes in the pace of individual development and career flows through the organization, development of skills relevant to the business, and so on.

The process is fluid in that evaluations of the business are progressive, the environment and the pace of individual development are changing continually, so that the review takes place against a current position which is ephemeral rather than fixed. Options and contingencies require the process to be continuous, allowing current decisions about organization and people to be well thought through, but always providing a basis for re-examination before implemenation.

The supply plan represents a summary of the planned actions, reviews and conclusions, showing the current view of how the full manpower requirements will be provided through the period of the plan. It includes assessments of developing and future flow patterns and loss rates, so that the full pattern of internal and external actions, and their timing, can be incorporated into the scenario. Against this, all unanticipated change can be assessed so that the plan can be updated.

10
Supply Planning: Manpower Flows Within the Organization

One of the most important elements in constructing manpower requirement and supply plans is the analysis of the ways in which people flow through the organization. These analyses cover all movements from the points of inflow to the career structures of the categories involved, the rates of progress through various grades or levels in these structures, and the rates of outflow by retirement and leaving. By matching these analyses to the evolving needs of the future business, the major supply issues can be identified.

The basic structure of flows can be seen clearly from figure 10.1. It is necessary to manage both the flows into and out of an organization as well as the flows up through the structure.

It is reasonable to assume that the regular annual intake of graduates into, say, a technical department will progress through the structure of the organization in a regular pattern, if there are no significant influences for change. Establishing the existing pattern is fairly easy if data from the past several years are available, and predicting the future pattern is equally straightforward.

Such a flow analysis would show how the regular graduate intake moves on at the end of its first year to make way for its successor, and the ways in which people at each level progress within the function, or move to other departments or outside the organization. If the number of people required at each level is assumed to stay roughly proportional to and reflect overall work volumes, the flow into any level must be related to the outflow, or the balance may be upset.

Part of the purpose of analysing flows is the need monitor changes in patterns which can be harmful to the manpower supply. A disturbance or blockage of the flow which leads to any sort of build up at any level will quickly alter the career advancement prospects

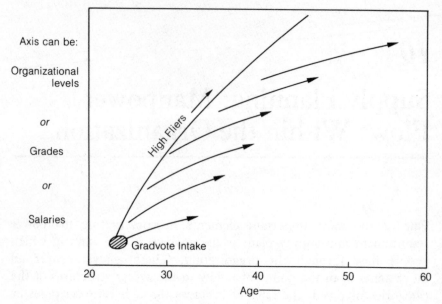

Figure 10.1   General view of flows up through an organization

for individuals below the blockage in a highly visible way and trigger resignations of the most mobile people.

The flow of people through the career structures of a company must take into account the availability of posts and the varying capabilities of people. Given the general pyramidal shape of many organizations and the associated distribution of people by grades, it is evident that any cohort of recruits will find personal career ceilings at a variety of levels. For example, a graduate entry of 100 may include only one person who ultimately reaches the main board, while a further one or two may never rise above the entry level. The remainder will progress at varying rates according to their abilities and inclinations, spreading throughout the whole range of levels as indicated in figures 5.5 and 5.6 in the earlier chapter.

Looking within flow patterns, those individuals with little potential for growth are likely to have moved into their ultimate levels at young ages. There will be very little flow of graduates out of their intake level to the next level after about the age of 30. (However, this pattern may be changed by an increased number of women returners, and late qualifiers, and will need to be monitored.)

As we move up the structure, the fastest developing stream set the minimum ages at which particular levels may be reached, and the prospect of advancement is distinctly less good for people more than ten years behind those markers.

The structure of flows needs to be looked at in three-dimensional terms because, while we can look easily at a sheet summarizing flows through, say, one function, there are sets of similar sheets with the same axes covering all the parallel flows for other functions, specialist areas and generalists. There is some movement between these flow pattern sheets, and there are some situations which require a total company picture. For example, stagnation in one flow may be eased by identifying a fresh flow into a different career stream, such as those flows needed regularly to take people whose creativity has declined out of research areas and move them to other areas where their expertise is valuable.

The driving force for flows comes primarily from the intake waves at the bottom, and from losses and retirements further up. It is necessary to have regular clearances of intake posts to make way for the next wave, and equally necessary to have upward pressure to fill higher posts which are vacated.

Push and pull flows

A distinction is made by some writers between push and pull flows. The great bulk of movements are described as pull; a vacancy occurs and someone is pulled into the position by recruitment, promotion or transfer.

In contrast, a push movement does not necessarily require an approved vacancy. Here, the initiative is more to push someone out of an existing slot. The clearest example occurs where last year's graduate entry must make way for the new intake, and are pushed forward into positions needing some experience.

While I recognize that there are various pressures for movements, I have not found the push and pull labels of value in my analyses. However, I acknowledge that others evidently find some purpose in the separation.

Most of the analyses of flow patterns consider individual functional or other discrete segments as being more meaningful and relevant to manpower supply than company-wide data. There is, after all, relatively limited movement between engineering and accountancy, and the career structure and flows in one category will be largely unaffected by whatever exists in the others.

Flow Patterns

There is likely to be a complex network of flows within any organization. Most will be reasonably stand-alone paths, while some involve interrelationships between several parts of the business. Some of the separation is related to functional (or job family) divisions where differences in skill requirements limit movement, and some is due to geography as people are not mobile in ways which facilitate interchange. In contrast, some flows from research and development into production or sales appear surprising until you analyse the skill transfers which make the flows desirable.

One of the simplest flows can be seen in the progression through an intake and training programme; figure 10.2 shows a flow through an apprentice ship training scheme. This five-year scheme is now rather dated, but shows the intake of recruits and flow through the years with minimal wastage *en route*. After the fourth year there is some choice of career and mixing with other flows.

Basic flow patterns can be drawn for a range of activities. Progression through a research and development function is shown in figure 10.3, and other functional streams would be similarly

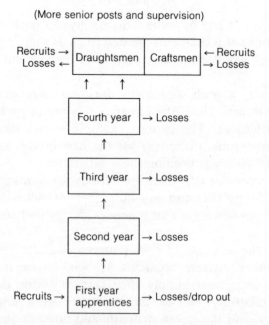

Figure 10.2 Flow structure through an apprenticeship scheme

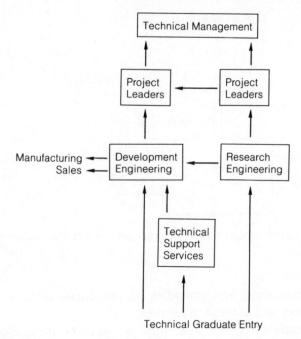

Figure 10.3 Career flow structure in research and development

structured. Movement between functional streams is limited due to skill differences, but does occur for planned individual development. As this is rare rather than normal, it would not appear on a chart of normal flows.

Other organizations may have more complex patterns. For example, an insurance company is likely to have intakes at several levels from schools and universities. Starters with GCSEs and A levels will start at different points in their progression towards professional insurance qualifications compared with the graduate intakes. In due course, gates in the flow pattern will make those professional qualifications prerequisites to further progress along some streams. In such a situation, a flow diagram might usefully include indications of relative volumes, as in the next example.

Some flow charts incorporate data to show the relative size of the different populations, and the size of the flows over the past year. Rather than simply adding numbers, figure 10.4 uses the relative size of each box to represent the different sizes of each population, and variable-size arrows to indicate the scale of flow. This is a most

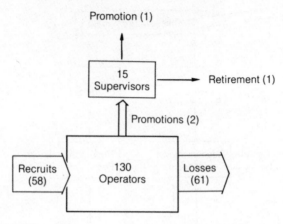

Figure 10.4 Flow structure to scale – areas are proportional to numbers

effective visual representation, providing an immediate understanding of the direction and scale of movement.

Career advancement is rarely as tidy as some of these charts suggest. Even within a single function, there is movement between the more general coverage of the function and the more specialized aspects. Flow charts may need to cover several years to capture a full picture, for there may be phases when movement is restricted to narrow chimneys. Further, there may be some value in defining grade levels in such a situation, to show sideways moves which may be part of development strategy.

Figure 10.5 is taken from a large company with closely associated technical and production sides, and planned interfunctional development. Such a complex model needs close monitoring to ensure that the flow stays balanced. For example, it would be easy to allow too many people to flow into favoured aspects, or to stay too long in posts, so clogging the path for others.

Analyses of the groups of individuals at different points in the flows are vital in showing the distributions of age, qualifications, competence, etc. A build up of one age group, for example, can become a problem. Figure 10.6 shows an extract from the previous example which looks at the flow at one middle level by age plus time at the level. It appears that a number of older people have become rather stuck at that particular career stage, but there is still enough room for younger people to flow past them. In contrast, figure 10.7 is taken from a more senior level, and shows virtually no movement

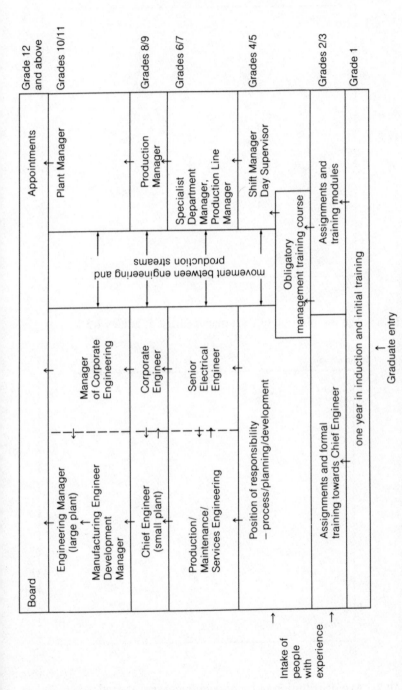

Figure 10.5 Internal career flow structure through technical and production

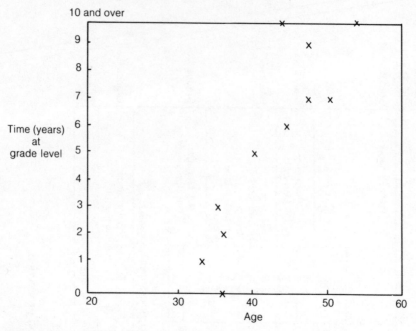

Figure 10.6   Age distribution of shift management at grades 4/5

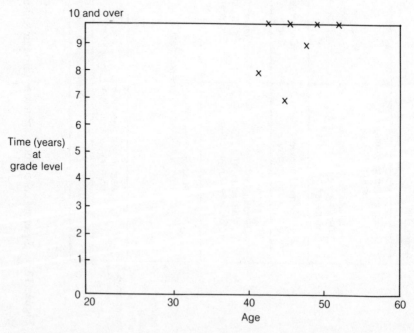

Figure 10.7   Age distribution of production managers at grades 8/9

Table 10.1 Analysis of manpower movement in an engineering department

Category	Strength 1 January	Promotion from (1 grades)	Promotion from (2 grades)	Transfer to other Divisions	Leavers	Total movement	% of total	Promotion to (1 grade)	Promotion to (2 grades)	Transfer from other Divisions	Recruits	Strength 31 December
Managers	6	1	–	–	1	2	33	1	1	–	–	6
Senior Engineer I (Supervisors)	8	1	–	1	1	3	37	1	1	–	–	7
Senior Engineer II	10	1	1	1	1	4	40	2	1	–	1	10
Engineer I	21	2	1	–	3	6	29	8	–	1	2	26
Engineer II	37	8	1	1	6	16	43	8	–	–	10	39
Assistant Engineer	14	8	–	–	1	9	64	–	–	–	8	13

Plus further analyses by age groups, qualification levels, years of service in grade, etc.

as most incumbents have reached their ceiling and all progress is blocked. Further analysis of people at this level revealed average service of between seven and eight years: clearly a stoppage in the flows.

Analyses of flows generally start with the assembly of raw data, as set out in table 10.1, covering the functions selected, and various levels or management categories. Different divisions or units should be analysed separately as this may reveal differing flow patterns, and a whole series of subsidiary analyses may be generated to examine the relevance of age patterns, qualifications, length of time at a level, differences in competences, and so on.

From these data, we can build up statistical norms, such as those shown in example 10.1, which summarizes the probability of promotion for a category of engineer in one company, given a particular set of circumstances. This is one of a series of analyses covering the various engineering categories. The value of this analysis is dependent on the assumption that flows will continue at

Engineer I: Probability of Promotion within One Year

Service in Grade	Age Range				
	21-23	24-26	27-30	31-40	41 +
Up to 1 year	12%	15%	9%		
1 year and up to 2 years	21%	30%	28%	15%	
2 years and up to 3 years		38%	30%	10%	
3 years and up to 5 years		12%	18%	16%	8%
5 years and up to 10 years			7%	12%	8%
10 years and over				10%	

Example 10.1 Promotion probability analysis for engineer I level – prepared using *HR/View* with data held in *Executive TRACK* management development planning system

the previous rate. If there is any significant change of circumstance and throughput, such as a blockage, or a need for an increased supply, then the assumptions on promotion opportunities will be changed.

If the established percentages of engineers ready to move into higher positions cannot be accommodated, the result is not a simple slowing up of promotion opportunities. The engineers ready for promotion are likely to react by seeking other opportunities and the reduction in internal promotions is likely to be offset by an equivalent increase in the rate of losses to outside organizations.

Data on promotion patterns are invaluable as an input to manpower supply planning in that they quantify the probabilities of your being able to provide the required numbers from internal promotion, category by category. Equally, this analysis will quickly highlight where promotion potential cannot be absorbed and higher turnover may be expected.

If future promotion requirements are greater or less than previously experienced, some contingency actions are possible, provided that the situation is recognized early enough. For example, if the requirement increases, the stock from which promotions will come can be upgraded to increase the numbers of people in the high promotion rate categories. Referring to example 10.1, this would force us to ask whether we can increase the numbers aged between 24 and 26 with one to three years' service by more selective recruiting. In contrast, if the promotion opportunities are likely to decline, it is probably worth adjusting our recruitment to include more 30- to 40-year-olds, who will ensure stability and retention of knowledge without high promotion expectations.

Normal career projection lines may become much clearer from these analyses, with obstacles and bottle-necks identified so that arrangements can be made for their removal. Loss analyses may reveal part of the story, by showing heavy losses of people at one grade level in question, pin-pointing the problem more precisely.

It is interesting to monitor and compare the progress of the cohorts of annual entrants; what has happened to the intake of '83? Gradual shifts in recruitment sprecifications can be noted, together with gradual changes in the rate and direction of career progression, all of which provide valuable data and pointers for planning future intake levels and progression rates.

One manpower group for which promotion flow analysis is particularly important is that of the graduate intake. All too frequently, the loss rates of graduates after two or three years with the organization tend to make a nonsense of the expense and effort to recruit them from universities to fill future supervisory, managerial and specialist positions. The reasons for losses may become much more apparent when the flow analysis shows a lack of movement or promotion opportunities into suitable positions. But remember that these analyses only identify the problem. They do not alter attitudes or increase promotion opportunities. An action plan must be designed separately and implemented.

The best means of presenting the value and applications of flow analysis is by using a number of real examples, using data on intakes, flows and losses of people in a category, and analysed by level, time at that level, qualifications, age, and so on.

Example: Steady flow through research and development   The research and development department illustrated in example 10.1 consists of just over one hundred professional staff headed by a technical director with six supporting managers. The company has an established pattern of recruiting about 30 graduate engineers each year, and a policy of transferring a proportion of their staff at several levels to sales and marketing and to production engineering each year. The flow pattern has enabled the organization to keep the young innovative engineers in research and development, with fast promotion prospects, while ensuring acceptable alternative career progression for those deemed to be less creative. Separately, sales and marketing welcomed the flow of engineers, who were knowledgable about product design, to progressively upgrade the sales force; the production departments, too, appreciated the influx of technical product knowledge.

Example: The research and development flow pattern changes   The flow pattern of example 10.2 lasted for six to seven years before the process of upgrading the sales staff was completed, sharply reducing the sales opportunities, and the ability of production to absorb more engineers was reduced. As this cut off was not appreciated by the research and development staff, the position illustrated in example 10.3 developed by the end of two further years.

During the first year after the change, the total staff rose sharply, but in the second year, after the second graduate intake, the loss rate doubled as the better, upwardly mobile people began to feel the

Salary Grade	No at 1st Jan	Recruits	Promotions		Transferred out to other Departments	Left Company	No at 31st Dec
			To	From			
YEAR 1							
Graduate Intake (sab)	30	30		28		2	30
Grade 7	40	2	28	20	11	3	36
8	25	2	20	8	8	4	27
9	14	1	8	1	5	2	14
10	6		1		3	1	4
Tech Directors	1						1
TOTALS	116	35			27	12	112
YEAR 2							
Grade 6	30	30		28	1	2	29
7	36	5	28	22	7	3	37
8	27		22	8	8	4	29
9	14		8	3	4	2	13
10	4		3		1		6
Tech Directors	1				1		1
TOTALS	112	35			21		115

Example 10.2   Analysis of flows through a research and development department over two years

Flows through an R&D Department after the in-company Outflows had become blocked

Salary Grade	No at 1st Jan	Recruits	Promotions		Transferred out to other Departments	Left Company	No at 31st Dec
			To	From			
Grade 6	42	30		21	1	3	47
7	46		21	14	1	8	44
8	26		14	7		5	28
9	15		7	1	1	3	17
10	6		1			1	6
Tech Directors	1						1
TOTALS	136	30			3	20	143

Example 10.3 Analysis of flows through a research and development department showing the impact of career blockage

resistance to advancement opportunities and began to vote with their feet. The immediate actions required are a search for alternative outlets for people who need to be moved out of research and development, and a reduction in the intake level to rebalance the input-output flow equation.

The overall staffing level rose by over twenty. Almost inevitably, there will be further losses of good people from a situation which has visibly gone wrong, and some positive action will be necessay to retain key people. Some selective redundancies may be the optimum way of dealing with the excess staffing and regaining a more stable structure and flow quickly.

The essential message from this example is that it can prove very difficult to recover from a situation which has gone wrong. The manpower plan for the sales and marketing area ought to have highlighted the ending of that particular outflow a year or more before it happened, not a year or so afterwards. A practical long-term approach to this type of situation is illustrated in the next example.

Example: Planned flows in an electronics research centre   In a different organization, the head of the research centre took the view that the most creative period for his engineers and physicists started when they arrived from university and lasted until they reached the age of 30 to 32. By then, the training and development time which he and his managers had invested in them should have been paid back. After that, most of them would become liabilities if retained in research.

His thinking was reflected in the corporate resourcing strategy, which recognized that most research people should move, with their projects, into production division development teams or industrial engineering, over a three-year span around the age of 30. Of those retained beyond age 30, smaller numbers would follow similar routes at later stages.

Positive action was required, on a year-to-year basis, from all of those retained deliberately in research. They had to have particular research strengths or be skilled team leaders/mentors. As time passes, research manager and research specialist career streams evolve and there is a continuous re-selection process to retain the very best and transfer all non-essential people into other career streams.

Ultimately, at the top level in research, this leaves a small number of outstanding research directors, plus a similar number of world-class researchers, but maintains the manning standards and quality at every other level.

Such an approach must be fully integrated with the manpower requirement plans of all the catchment departments, and there needs to be agreement on how to handle any oversupply which may occur. In this company, the procedure is quite simple. The research centre has absolute priority on decisions to transfer out and any excess must be accepted in product division development departments. From there, opportunities for redeployment may be sought in other parts of the business.

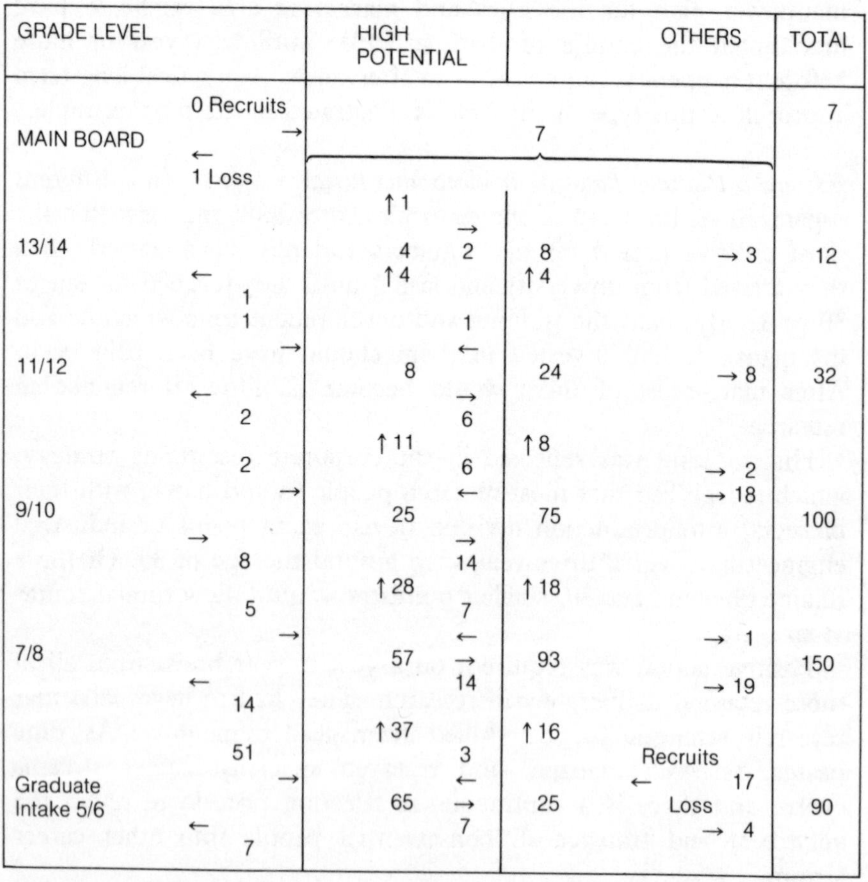

GRADE LEVEL		HIGH POTENTIAL		OTHERS		TOTAL
MAIN BOARD	0 Recruits → ← 1 Loss	7				7
		↑1				
13/14	←	4	→2	8	→3	12
		↑4		↑4		
	1					
	1		1			
11/12	→ ← 2	8	← →6	24	→8	32
	2	↑11	6	↑8	→2 →18	
9/10	→	25	← →	75		100
	→ 8		14			
	5	↑28	7	↑18	→1	
7/8	→	57	← → 14	93	→19	150
	← 14					
	51	↑37	3	↑16	Recruits ← 17	
Graduate Intake 5/6	→ ← 7	65	← → 7	25	Loss →4	90

Figure 10.8 Flow through levels, from graduate intake to senior management – the high potential stream

Example: Monitoring flows in a high potential stream Of all the manpower resources, the individuals classified as high potential must be among the most important, and we would expect them to be progressing steadily. Figure 10.8 shows an analysis of the total flow up through a company, with a separation of the high potential stream for comparison. The analysis shows a heavy intake at the graduate intake level, but not all of them are graduates as some have progressed to this level internally (not indicated separately on the analysis).

This analysis shows movements over one year, including the continual reassessment of people into and out of the high potential stream. Interestingly, not all the upward flow is from the high potential stream. Overall, it looks like a reasonably healthy picture. The analysis indicates stability in terms of overall numbers but, if an organization is growing, the creation of new posts will provide an additional upward suction to be met from internal or external sources.

Of course, the term high potential must be defined for the company, and appears to have been used somewhat loosely in this example. The important factor is always that the basis should be understood locally, so that the analysis can be interpreted sensibly.

Summary

The provision of manpower to the career staff areas of an organization is heavily dependent on planned manpower flows. It is frequently a corporate objective for the great majority of supervisory, managerial and specialist posts to be filled from within the company, by people who were recruited at a lower level and then developed. This is fine, so long as the intake is governed by an appropriate specification and quality; that the required development takes place; and that suitable posts are vacated or created to enable planned advancements to happen. Then the manpower requirements can be met by the flow.

However, many things can go wrong with a flow and they can have far-reaching repercussions, which makes regular and careful monitoring very necessary. This gives early warning of difficulties and allows timely corrective action to be taken. Even relatively small changes in a flow can have dramatic effects. For example, an accumulation at any level of people from one age group may build a clot in the flow and block it, or an apparently small increase in a flow can drain people away from a key activity.

Analysis of flows involves searching for changes in any key elements (age, qualifications, experience, etc.) within a flow pattern, and reviews of other elements of manpower mix. If the proportion of high potential people diminishes, does that precede some slowing of the flow? Or, is there significance in the changing proportion of women or minority groups in a population? These and many other questions need to be permanently in the mind of the manpower planner.

11
Supply Planning: Resourcing and Recruitment

Every vacancy provides an opportunity for advancement for an existing employee. Decisions to recruit from the external market when it is not essential can lead to serious demotivation of existing staff. Resourcing strategy therefore needs thoughtful evaluation. The strategy should be long term and incorporate the systematic intake of school-leavers, graduates and other appropriate people to be developed to flow up through the structure to meet the majority of planned needs. It is unlikely that all needs can be satisfied from internal sources, but the strategy should ensure that the internal option is always considered first. (At times when an organization is reducing numbers, particular effort should be made to avoid recruitment, but, where the essential skills required are simply not available internally, it is better to avoid excessive compromise and initiate recruitment.)

Recruitment strategy for career staff, specialists and management should be designed to meet present and future requirements by bringing in calculated numbers of potential future candidates, such as young graduates and professionally qualified people, who are capable of being developed to provide the flows up through the structure. External recruitment to more senior positions should be tightly controlled. It will always be necessary to bring in some people to specialist positions where numbers within the company are small and career opportunities limited. For other management positions, there is a value in bringing in new blood occasionally. It prevents the organization from becoming stagnant and injects new ideas or fresh ways of looking at a subject. This action may be part of a programme of cultural change, or it may be done to rejuvenate a function when the environmental demands are becoming more challenging.

If decisions to recruit externally are evaluated to assess whether the development process is failing to meet company needs, it provides an adequate safeguard. For example, few manpower plans seem able to identify all of the new skills required as an organization grows and evolves, and some intake can be healthy. If the proportion of placements from external sources becomes excessive, the company is either not anticipating impending environmental change or its career planning and development processes are not effective.

Forward organization design may require future person specifications which are difficult to match from stock if critical new competences cannot be developed quickly. For example, flexibility will be a necessary competency in many future specifications. Evaluation of any possible flexibility in structure and specifications, utilizing the strengths and accommodating the limitations of available people, must be done before resorting to external sourcing.

Lastly, the filling of any position involves fitting an individual into an established team situation. Unless it is decided that the team style or culture is to be changed, candidates should be matched both to the requirements of the job itself and to the team. If the previous incumbent had brought a particular quality or competence to a team, finding a fresh team balance may require more than just finding a competent performer for the vacant position.

Planning Recruitment Action

All recruitment action and, indeed, all actions which lead up to the appointment, is handled best through a series of logical steps.

1 The organization in which the job is located, and the purpose, content and objectives of the job, should be clearly defined and approved. These factors should have been reviewed to ensure that they are all current and valid. The ongoing need for the job to exist for at least a year into the future should be confirmed.
2 The job should be planned and budgeted, or similarly authorized.
3 There must be visible effort to fill the post from internal sources.
4 If no internal candidates are suitable, the external market should be assessed to determine the availability of suitable candidates and the financial package likely to be required for successful recruitment.
5 The degree of flexibility acceptable in meeting the person specification should be clarified.
6 Recruitment and selection actions should be initiated.
7 Applicants should be evaluated.

8 The selection process should lead up to a decision and formal offer of appointment.

1 Establish the vacancy

'Jones is leaving. Replace him!' 'Get another person to manage the design team.' Simple enough instructions admittedly, but why is Jones leaving? Could it be that the organization is changing imperceptibly and that the change in work has unsettled him? Throw in one doubt of this sort and it becomes worth checking carefully on the real vacancy before steps are taken to fill it. It is essential to know what the vacant postition involves, and also to examine the likely future of the person to be recruited.

The review of requirements is best done by interviewing the preceding job holder, where one is available, or the immediate manager. If a job description and objectives exist, they provide the starting point, and the review should determine if and how these have changed. However, the lack of an earlier description is not critical, as it need not take long to obtain a complete outline of the post. If the post is a new one, its requirements and duties need to be adequately defined.

More important at this stage is an evaluation of the particular tasks and problems which the new person will have to face; the objectives, and the competences required. For example, a marketing manager may have to be prepared to cope with rapidly growing and undefined new competition; a personnel manager may have to create a special retraining programme to prepare for impending office automation; and clerical recruits may need high levels of computer terminal familiarity. The person specification will be influenced by the particular skills needed, the degree of difficulty faced, and the performance standards expected. Remember that, the higher the position, the more unique the role and specification.

At many levels, further evolution in the content of jobs must be considered to minimize the possibility that the skills of the new job holder may become obsolete quickly. Impending changes should influence the specification so that new job holders show the ability to acquire anticipated skills within the available time frame.

Once the job content, objectives and person specification are confirmed, the job level can be checked and a recruiting pay level or salary range determined. Within a grading structure, the overall salary range will be immediately available but, occasionally, special factors may apply to the particular market group, so a proper check on values should be automatic. Additionally, the precise person specification required will influence the commencing level. For example, someone having only the minimum experience required to meet a specification would justify a minimum salary, or a higher rate would be appropriate to take account of the substantial experience and track record of another candidate.

As future organizations move away from hierarchical structures and become more knowledge based, and as structures become less power/authority dominated and more influenced by knowledge and the ability to contribute at all levels, then the emphasis within salary structures and policies will shift.

The most significant change is likely to arise in the approach to grading practice and we should begin to take this into account in our manpower planning now. There will be a move from job grading (based on the responsibilities and authority vested in the job) towards some form of personal grading based on the individual's ability to contribute to the business. The basis for this in fluid structures will be two or three prime elements: knowledge, application ability and, possibly, a position-related factor.

Knowledge will be judged initially on qualifications, as with the graduate intake at present, but also including professional qualifications. It will be supplemented progressively by measures of wider and deeper professional knowledge, experience-based knowledge and knowledge of other functions, including generalist knowledge.

Applications ability will be judged on the ability to use that knowledge effectively in the business, and the ability of the individual to contribute generally in his specialist area, in multidiscipline projects, or on business strategy.

The third factor covers management/leadership skills, which will be critically important, but the overall approach to establishing personal ranks will ensure that high level specialists will rank equally with leaders on the basis of their potential contribution to critical elements of the business.

2 Establish that the vacancy is budgeted

However clearly the need for a job is established and urgency stressed, it should not be possible to proceed with filling the post until it is clearly established that the position has been budgeted for, and the expense is expected. At any time, a variety of smooth-tongued managers can justify recruiting additional people but, if these additions were not taken into consideration in business plans and budgets, what will be the impact on the bottom line? If the job does result from a post-budget reappraisal, it takes little enough time to set out a brief supplementary plan to justify the action and show the expected financial impact. This is an essential discipline in manpower control.

If the position is budgeted or covered by an approved supplementary plan, take a final look at the requirement to confirm it is for essential work or necessary discretionary work.

3 Internal sourcing

Only when the vacancy is clearly established and approved should any sourcing activity begin.

Outside recruitment of any sort is expensive and takes time so, quite apart from all of the other reasons, the need to examine and make use of the existing stock makes economic sense. Sometimes the decision is not clear cut and it may be decided to include internal people on a short list, in competition with external candidates.

The search within a company can take one of two main approaches. It can leave the initiative to the individual, after advertising internally what vacancies exist, or it can make use of all available information on employees and endeavour to match the job requirements to suitable candidates, providing an opportunity to further an individual's career.

Taking the former case first, this approach may overlook the best candidates as they may not apply for a variety of reasons. These may vary from a simple lack of adequate understanding of the vacant post, or underrating their own abilities, to straightforward pressure from a selfish manager not to apply. Where the employee initiative approach is adopted, I prefer to do a back-up internal search as a cross-check to identify candidates who have not responded.

Where the company adopts the second approach and searches its database for candidates, there is no reason why internal advertising should not be used as a cross-check. Internal advertising also serves a useful purpose in drawing attention to previously unknown potential transfer and promotion prospects within the organization, and emphasizing an intention to develop employees from within rather than bring in outsiders. Further advantage comes from identifying people who are unsettled, or who become known to want to move for any reason. These potential leavers may be retained by taking action to deal with their concerns.

Where a company assumes the whole responsibility for internal selection, it must ensure that it has adequate database and selection facilities to identify all employees potentially able to fill a vacancy, and select the best candidate with a minimum of employee participation. If it adopts this course, it should seek appropriate publicity for its procedure, which must be visibly effective, and be prepared to answer staff who ask whether they were considered and rejected when an appointment is made.

Many vacancies are known well in advance, so the situation can be examined at leisure and each appointment planned as a potential career step with sufficient time available for training or otherwise preparing the selected employee in advance. Not least in importance is the feasibility of new appointees sitting alongside the previous job holders for a period, allowing them to pick up the reins at first hand.

At senior level, the management development process will have assembled detailed information on all managers, their potential and individual development plans, providing a valuable guide to available and suitable talent within the organization. This approach should be adopted as far down the organization as possible, and the associated database accessed whenever a vacant position has not been anticipated, possibly due to a termination, or for a newly created position.

Not all internal placements will be perfect matches to a specification. Occasionally, the only person available with sufficient experience or knowledge must be appointed, even though they lack some of the qualities specified. Occasionally, it may be advisable to modify the job content, specification and performance expectations to fit the appointee, to reduce any appearance of a poor choice, and build up to the desired standards gradually.

Such a situation might arise when replacing a technical manager, where the available deputy is a brilliant specialist but is a hopeless administrator. The organization might be restructured to support the new manager with a good administrative deputy so that the strengths of the promoted manager are used fully and his weaker areas are protected.

This leads on to a further aspect of internal selection, that of finding a job for a person, rather that the person for a job. This is an important requirement for those high potential employees who are ready for a move but whose advance is blocked. It applies also to competent people who have lost ground due to organization change but retain the abilities to manage larger tasks.

A list of readies (people ready for promotion now) probably sits on the majority of management development manager's desks, and the search for suitable places for them is constant. Opportunities may be anywhere but may need to be opened up. Chain movement may help to solve a problem by shifting a series of people and opening a position required for a key person in the process. The first stage must be to identify the special requirements, and a possible target job, in terms of man and job specifications, grade level, working relationships and so on. Then the means of achieving the opening can then be studied and planned.

4 External sourcing – the market

Manpower supply is greatly influenced by the availability of required skills and expertise in the job market. If the demand for various skills significantly exceeds the available supply, the price (the remuneration level) of those jobs will rise until a sufficient proportion of the demand has been discouraged, and supply and demand are in balance.

This is classic economic theory and, like any other part of the market-place, it is imperfect – perhaps more so than some other aspects, for it is dealing with people, and their decisions do not always appear wholly rational. However, the workings of the market are sufficiently logical for us to need to take them into account in our manpower planning.

Market structure There are two main elements in the structure of the job market. The first is job families, which restrict the ability of individuals to move between diverse occupations; the other is job level, as there is some correlation between level and mobility.

All jobs fit into families. Finance and accounting is an example of a main family within which there is some mobility between jobs because qualifications and experience are related. However, it is difficult for an accountant to become an architect because the qualifications, experience and skills required are quite different. While such a switch is not impossible, it would require the accountant to retrain and then to start a career again at the bottom of the ladder, discarding virtually all the market value associated with accountancy.

Job family structure is particularly relevant to short-supply problems, where a contributory factor may be the inability of people to enter the activity from elsewhere because of knowledge and experience constraints. People begin their careers equipped with their personal attributes plus basic education and progressively build themselves into packages consisting of knowledge, skills and experience, which combine to influence value. The evolution of these packages takes many years, and cannot be duplicated quickly if the demand exceeds the supply.

Job level adds a further dimension. At lower levels, people are rarely mobile, tending to seek work in their immediate localities. At more senior levels, there is a greater willingness to relocate and, for certain categories, this willingness extends to international movement.

At the lower levels, this lack of mobility results in the formation of local market values, which may vary substantially within a distance of 100 miles. Local job centres usually have an excellent picture of supply and demand in their area at this level. Different rules cut in at, roughly, the level of the graduate intake, perhaps because many of these people have moved away from home to attend university and they remain mobile. At this level, a national market position begins to develop. The level at which the market becomes international is less clear, and is more job related. International companies expect their best managers to spend time working overseas from an early stage, initially on an expatriate terms basis. The full international market-place develops around these internationally mobile people.

Assessment of the external market is essential before recruitment is begun, as the skills we require may not be freely available. It may show that we shall need to recruit people who will require training to meet our requirements, which will require sufficient lead time. Knowledge of the present and probable future of the employment market is essential because, if the market is very tight and requirements cannot easily be met by recruitment, we may need to reconsider the achievability of some basic commercial objectives.

Knowledge of the availability of various categories of individuals or skills is therefore important, together with assessments of the way availability is likely to change. The first part can be provided with some accuracy by most recruitment staff who acquire an excellent feel of the current market-place. The second is more difficult. The analysis needs to be as specific as possible on questions of when, where, and why change may occur, and the likely impact on the calibre and price of future candidates. For example, good managers may be available from another industry but they will need some retraining before becoming fully effective. However, this will be a temporary situation. Finally, the market-place is yet another element of an environment which is continually changing.

The market now, and forward trends The manpower supply plan needs to contain a comprehensive summary of the market situation and the way it is likely to develop. One aspect of the supply and demand equation is that values may escalate and the company will need to follow this trend if it wishes to retain people. This, in turn, may make some parts of the business less profitable.

If a company has any immediate requirements in a short supply sector, there is no time to address the problem. This means that it may prove to be impractical to exploit an unexpected opportunity as it will be impossible to resource. However, identifying future shortages is not always easy. Some will be obvious, but most are not. The best approach seems to be to examine influences which may change levels of demand or supply, and to evaluate how serious these may become.

The most serious general change through the first half of the 1990s will be the demographic change, which has already had an impact on the output of school leavers and graduates, and has further to bite. Other significant influences over the same period will be: the impact of technological development, particularly on information management; a variety of facets of social attitudes to work and supervision; and international, as distinct from local, demands.

In parallel with these shortage-creating influences, we are likely to see continuing reductions in the demand for lower skilled people and the resulting oversupply will not be absorbed in lower grade service work. Various authorities note the trend to increased brainwork, which will make up perhaps 80 per cent available jobs by the end of the decade, with half of that total requiring graduates. The excess supply of people of less ability, or with less education and training, will be both a limitation on national potential and a drain on social services. Given the parallel ageing of the population, we have to find means of educating, training and using a higher proportion of the population in total to generate sufficient wealth to cover the costs of the remainder.

Supply options The demographic changes have encouraged some organizations to take a fresh look at the manning of areas traditionally filled by school leavers and graduates. The use of early retirees in many supermarkets to man the tills has proved effective, with greater reliability as a bonus. So far, the logical step of extending the working age for those who wish to work, and treating age discrimination in the same way as we respond to racial discrimination, has not been accepted in the UK.

Another area of response is to women returners, more of whom are taking fresh qualifications on their way back, and provide an additional source of graduate entrants. However, many companies remain confused by these candidates because they cannot see how to process the salaries or careers of people who are not about 22 years old. Certainly they need to be handled differently, because they are older and bring a different combination of maturity, experience and skills to the table, and many will have different career ambitions. But they are a valuable alternative source.

An alternative approach to a serious skill shortage is to restructure work to optimize the utilization of scarce skills. If the skilled individual utilizes his special skills for a very high proportion of his time, with less skilled workers providing back-up and follow-through, there may be considerable benefits; many skilled individuals may actually apply these special skills for 20 per cent or less of their total time. In practice, this approach is limited because the people concerned may actually enjoy the aspects of their work which are unrelated to the key skills; the reduction of job satisfaction involved in withdrawing those activities may demotivate the individual and have a negative effect.

The most usual situations for the application of this approach are to be found in research and development departments, where design or software skills may be vital; in aspects of industrial engineering and automation, where individuals may have an extraordinary grasp of technology application; in information management, where a few senior people are able to comprehend the total system and provide guidance to others on the 'fit' of their segments; etc.

5 Flexibility in the specification

Faced with potential difficulty in locating and attracting the ideal candidate, it is as well to know how much flexibility can be tolerated in the specification. For example, tight age preferences can usually be relaxed, unless the company is wanting to fill a senior position for a fixed period until a designated internal rising star can fill the post, when a precise age restriction may be essential. Normally, age, qualifications, ideal target companies and the experience specification should all be open to some variation, as should the remuneration package.

Actions to acquire vital skills If planning can identify future skill requirements in time, plans can be developed to acquire those skills early. This is of great importance if the corporate vision defines a track which requires, for success, skills which are currently either absent or very rare in the company. These may become identified as corporate core competences for the future, and will be of the utmost importance to the achievement of the corporate vision.

The skills required may be so rare that the chances of recruiting a full team are minimal. But, if the right people do exist, it is possible to search for and locate them. If recruitment still appears unlikely, then one option is to establish a technical or commercial alliance with the company presently employing them. Sometimes this is done with the acceptance that a shared and harmonious relationship is desired, but some alliance partners' sole objective is to acquire the required expertise. Depending on the relative size of the partners, outright acquisition may be the preferred course of action, which draws the expertise and its environment firmly into the control of the ambitious acquirer. However, individuals can leave an employer and this important fact must be taken into account.

A further alternative option, is to assemble a group of people with the most closely related skills available and give them a crash course in training by a dedicated team to try to catch up and pass competitors. Coming from behind is never easy, but if the group is selected from high ability fast learners, and is linked to university or commercial services which facilitate learning, the initial catching up may be achieved very quickly. Then the requirement is for creative initiatives and fast running with the concepts to get ahead.

Revise business objectives If the skill demand is related to a perceived opportunity with a narrow time window, it may prove impossible to respond effectively within the available time and the apportunity is lost. Analysis of how the opportunity arose with minimal warning, and of the prospect for further, similar opportunities, should be investigated so that some better response can be achieved in future.

It is a fact that not every opportunity will be visible early, or will be identifiable in sufficient time for an effective response to be mounted, but the more that probable opportunities can be sighted and contingency plans drafted, the greater will be the preparedness in future.

6 External sourcing – initiating recruitment action

The basic recruitment processes appropriate to various levels and types of employee are well and outside the scope of this book, but there are some essential points to be covered. For example, there are numerous options to be considered when recruiting senior managers, but no perfect answers: whether it is better in a particular case to advertise or use consultants or search people depends on several factors. A common reason for using consultants is less for their skill than to buy their time handling a great deal of the detail of recruitment.

When do we search? If the target population is quite small and it is possible to identify the places where the individuals are likely to be, then a search is the most precise way of getting the message to most of that population. Beyond that, the search process places you in a selling situation and you will need an attractive job and an equally attractive package to land the person you seek. If the population is larger, or more dispersed, or cannot be so easily located, then a search is less effective than a large, well presented advertisement in the right media. If you can attract the interest of your potential target and give him an independent to talk to first, this is as effective as a search.

The briefing of a consultant will have to be extremely thorough, and you will want to feel absolutely confident that you will be properly represented. I prefer it if search consultants accept some penalty if the assignment is not completed because they cannot satisfy the client, although this is contrary to their normal fee structure. Whenever external people are briefed to handle a recruitment or search assignment, it is advisable to get them to provide a detailed written statement of your requirement, so that you can assess whether or not the precise message has been received and understood.

7 Applicants

Where an external organization is handling an assignment up to the short list stage, much of the initial grind is avoided. If all applications are direct to the company, systematic handling is essential. For example, applicants deserve a courteous response, even if it is only a brief 'regret' letter to a non-conforming hopeful.

Most advertisements (and requests to agencies) are likely to produce substantial numbers of applicants, so a booking-in list to check off subsequent action is valuable. An extracted list of those of interest after the initial sort can follow. The initial selection involves reading all of the applications to weed out those which do not conform to the specification, that is, most, but not all, non-conforming replies. It is invariably worth looking twice at good candidates who do not fit the age or qualification ideals, and considering the implications of selecting them. For example, there are always excellent technical managers who have come up the sales and marketing route to general management and possess the intellect to absorb and utilize an immense amount of technical knowledge despite having no relevant degree qualification. And there are frequently experienced older-than-ideal candidates who retain their drive and creativity as a supplement to experience, and are in the market following an acquisition or similar upheaval.

For most companies or groups, graduates are attracted by advertising, by distributing brochures through campus careers officies, by milk round visits and various graduate fairs. The milk round is preferrable to fairs because fairs rarely provide adequate opportunities to talk to good candidates and also attract numerous first year students on shopping trips.

Few companies are really well known at university level as good developers of young graduates. Those that are attract large numbers of applications and can therefore be extremely selective. Further, they do not have to offer high starting salaries if the norm of fast career and salary progress is established. Other organizations seeking the very best, but lacking attractiveness to graduates, may offer premium salaries (50 per cent or more over the normal rates) to attract candidates, who can expect to be discarded after a year or two if they fail to perform.

Actions being taken to improve the flow of candidates include:

- increased use of high potential young graduates to front recruitment in the field – particularly as campus managers at the universities they came from;
- increased use of career success stories in literature;
- more selective targeting of universities, plus the development of closer links with the careers staff at the universities;

- increased use of carefully selected top managers to talk to graduates in the field, as well as when they come in for interviews;
- increased attention on mainland continental (and Irish) sources; and
- attention to MBA sources, and the offer of some MBA scholarships.

Once the candidate flow is adequate, the priority is to select and then appoint. The selection process is very much a two-way process because, while the company is sorting out the individuals who match its requirements, the candidates are selecting the organizations in which they will feel most at ease and which appear to offer the most attractive career opportunities.

Initial internal interviews or short-listing externally, produce the short lists or people who fit the requirement reasonably well.

Women into management The trend towards increased numbers of women managers is already well established, but still has far to go. While the lower levels of management have many established women, the middle levels have only a small population of woman and ver few have achieved top management positions. However, there will be a wave effect, with those already established at lower levels flowing up through the system as part of the existing flows. This should be closely monitored as part of flow analyses.

This change seems to have two main spurs. There is a change in social acceptance of women in management, which will develop further, and the trend is supported by the demographic situation which means that the requirement for managers simply cannot be met without an influx of women. Apart from the shift in attitudes, employers are increasingly aware that half of their graduate intake are females, and that it makes no sense at all to restrict the source of future management by halving the available pool. So, demand is driving this trend as well as attitude change.

The battle is not totally won; some of the arguments about women in management continue. These relate to commitment and amounts of absence, although these factors clearly vary between individuals, and only become really critical where they apply to a key individual for whom there is little cover.

A problem for companies with rather rigid career structures is that some women want extended breaks, sometimes up to 10 years or more, in which to bring up children. It is up to employers to find opportunities for women who seek dual career phases, and to recognize the positive aspects of this course. This does seem to be happening as, with the progressive increase in the numbers of women managers, there is concern to retain the skills of those who become mothers. Also, there is greater concern to encourage the re-entry of women, and to recognize the maturity acquired during a non-commercial phase of a career.

A further, and potentially very important factor, arises from the psychological differences between the sexes, which may tend to make women the preferred managers during the decade. As the summary of these influences, and their impact on manager specifications, evolve, the general specification is softer than the more traditional patterns, with greater emphasis on interpersonal skills and sensitivity to working relationships. However, it is unwise to generalize about the profiles of male and female managers, and there will not be a dramatic swing.

Employment contracts As discussed earlier, efficient operation will require tight staffing standards and full utilization of people. This will result in some changes in employment practice so that a company will have a core of essential people including some specialists and consultants with high levels of knowledge who are not required all the time and are employed on a retainer basis. Additionally, there may be variable numbers of temporary and part-time people. The specialist advisers will be tied to the company – and perhaps two or these other companies which are not competitors – or they may operate within consultancy teams.

The 1980s saw pioneering efforts by several large organizations to develop home-working for a wider range of personnel, particularly through providing home-based work-stations which connect to a central computer. Less well publicized are the many individual cases where some pioneering organizations have taken steps to retain the services of valuable senior staff who have acquired family commitments or moved away from the company's base. One company keeps a valued specialist, who moved from the centre of things to a remote Scottish farm, fully employed on project analyses. These are transmitted to her company personal computer overnight. The technology is available to make these arrangements work if the will is there.

Additionally, there are service organizations which have built up their businesses using home-based women for commercial software development, and which have a strong interest in the continued training and development of their employees to meet the requirements of their customers. So far, most of these home-workers are women and, because they are fully up to date, they can move easily back into office work if they wish. In practice, it is likely that the trend to home-working will develop much further, and there will be less incentive to make daily treks to a remote office when the time and expense can be used more profitably.

8 Selection

As the final selection process begins, it is essential to be clear on the process to be used, who is to be involved, and who is to decide to make the appointment. For example, who will interview candidates and is the appointment decision to be made by the immediate boss, or is he recommending an appointment which will be decided by his boss?

The selection process will generally involve interviewing, and most managers require training in interviewing skills at some stage. The five-point system designed by Munro Fraser, which still holds good, asks interviewers to assess:

1 Impact on others – physical make-up, appearance, speech and manner.
2 Acquired qualifications – education, vocational training, work experience.
3 Innate abilities – natural quickness of comprehension and aptitude for learning.
4 Motivation – the kind of goals set by the individual, his consistency and determination in following them up, his success in achieving them.
5 Adjustment – emotional stability, ability to stand up to stress and ability to get on with people.

The art of interviewing involves structuring and controlling the use of interview time, establishing rapport with the candidate, steering the direction of the conversation to precise questions, and listening very carefully. At senior levels, listening includes grasping what is not said, and probing the reasons why, to establish a full picture of the candidate. While the most effective interviews (by a good interviewer) are on a one-to-one basis, group or panel interviews are still widely used. These need to be managed to be effective. The interviewers must agree who will take various initiatives to avoid conflicts of interest developing.

Some group selection situations may be developed along the lines of an assessment centre, particularly in selecting graduate entrants whose interpersonal skills are an important factor in their selection, or to cover aspects of work which can be observed in role-play situations. These group sessions may also be supplemented by use of psychometric tests.

For managerial appointments, the use of an external psychometric assessment can provide an invaluable cross-check on all other data, and influence the ultimate decision. For example, it is not unknown, even today, for individuals to claim they have qualifications which they do not and tests may indicate that the claimed first class honours degree is unlikely, or that the claimed track record would be difficult to achieve, given the candidate's vulnerability to stress.

The test battery, selected using an informed understanding of the position concerned and the qualities needed, will take a reading of the overall intellectual strength of a senior candidate, which can be vital given the range and complexity of the decisions he may have to take. The battery may also give an indication of stress tolerance. A reasonable level of stress may be expected in most senior management jobs so that tolerance may be taken as proven, but a few individuals do manage to build up an excellent record through a series of low stress appointments and they are extremely vulnerable if they encounter a high stress situation.

Of course, test material is available to psychology graduates, but this does not imply a competence in using and interpreting the results meaningfully. Also, some psychologists will admit that management psychology is at much the same stage of its ultimate development as medicine in the middle ages, but there are a few gurus around who can work miracles.

Once the selection is made, it should be confirmed by making a formal offer, subject to medical and reference checks, which should be cleared quickly. Many employers leave negotiation of the package to this late stage and, particularly where a search is involved, this can lead to expensive solutions. The package on offer should be presented early and resolved early, so that there is a clear agreement on that key issue before the talking begins.

Speed is important. The company which shows it can make up its mind and not get bogged down in administration – which can make the offer on the spot and hand over the formal offer before the candidate leaves the premises – is saying something powerful about themselves as an employer. Most graduates are impressed by the employer's overall image and the career opportunities offered.

Quality The balance between internal and external candidates should be evident enough for an enterprise to have a clear view of the forward career opportunities for recruited staff. With few exceptions, the demand should be for individuals who have the ability to progress beyond the initial post, and most applicants of stature are likely to seek placements which offer scope for further advancement.

One task faced by most companies is improving the quality of their total graduate intake, with particular attention to the flow of high ability candidates for the fast progression cadre. Attracting and then holding people of the quality required involves attention to a range of manpower planning issues, including:

- clarifying future requirements – numbers, quality, profiles, etc.;
- analysing demographic factors, internationally, and anticipating wider competition for graduates;
- improving the flow of able candidates to the company and the attractiveness of opportunities;
- improving the quality and suitability of those selected;
- achieving full utilization, and optimizing development during the early years, with frequent objective reviews of ability and development;
- personalizing individual development;
- progressively identifying those who appear to have the ability for fast-track progress followed by in-depth assessments of potential after about five years;
- offering additional opportunities, such as MBA course scholarships for the very best, as part of the process of rapid broadening, and attractions such as financial assistance with relocation and house purchase to supplement competitive salaries; and
- minimizing losses of people the company wants to retain.

A high percentage of future managers are likely to come from the intake of graduates and young professional staff. They may join directly from university, or after a few years' experience elsewhere, or they may be people who achieve university entrance standards and then elect to go directly into professional or vocational training. This intake should contain people able to make an early contribution; who have the personality, ability and drive to progress into managerial positions in their middle to late 20s. Graduate recruitment specifications should stress the requirement for people who match the profile forecast for future managers, although there may be other qualities required more immediately. Attracting a proportion of the very best graduates is important, so we should seek some measure of the relative quality of those we recruit.

Demographic Change

The decline in the birthrate in the UK during the late 1960s which lasted through to the mid-1970s will result in a 33 per cent reduction in the numbers reaching employment and univerity entrance age between the mid-1980s and mid-1990s. This decline is not peculiar to the UK. It applies to much of the northern half of the EC, but is less marked in strongly catholic countries and, in general, did not affect the higher birthrates common within immigrant groups.

The results have been presented as a demographic time bomb, and the lower birthrate is already having a substantial impact on the availability of school leavers and graduates as well as altering the staffing patterns of some large users. For example, it is extremely unlikely that the required intake to the nursing profession will be met in the mid-1990s without a modification of the entry specification to encourage older entrants, and alternative staffing arrangements are being examined to improve the utilization of fully trained nurses by allocating the lower skilled elements of their work to auxilliary grades. This pattern will be reflected in the manpower supply plans for many other occupations.

The impact on university entrance and, therefore, on future managers and specialists, will be significant. This will be offset partly by an increase in the proportion of school leavers progressing to further education, although this may mean some reduction in entry criteria. The numbers will be made up, in part, by increases in the numbers of older students, including, particularly, women returners.

Many companies now rely almost wholly on graduate recruitment as their source of potential future managers, and most have tidy intake and early career progression arrangements which assume a very compact age profile of around 22 for their recruits. Some of these companies are finding some difficulty adjusting their established systems and career flow patterns to handle older graduates with pre-university experience, different levels of maturity and varied ambitions. Yet these mature graduates should be seen as a valuable source of future managers, although they will require different development and career plans to bring out their full potential.

A further change in graduate recruitment will be the change in sourcing, to include mainland continental universities and, in some cases, more distant sources. Language will not be as much of a problem as the differences in graduate age, qualifications and maturity, (for example, German engineers graduate between the ages of 27 and 30), and the great differences in national salary standards.

At the other end of the age range, we have a shift towards a common official retirement age for men and women, but also towards a much greater variation in actual retirement ages. There is distinct probability that Europe will adopt the American pattern of treating age as a discrimination issue which must be ignored to give equal opportunity of employment.

Then, if the supply of future managers at the bottom end is tight during the mid-1990s, it should be possible to offset this by utilizing many experienced people beyond their normal retirement ages, subject only to competence and health. This is most likely to affect those to managers and specialists who have kept their knowledge and expertise up to date and are able to adapt to the faster moving, knowledge-based, participative organizations of the future. Retention of top front line jobs may be considered an unreasonable strain, but the value of the experience which these people have acquired over the years can be retained by utilizing them in senior specialist or counselling roles within the cluster structure. However, there will be fewer opportunities for the older middle managers, particularly those from administrative activities.

Summary

Resourcing strategy must fit the requirements of the business and should be adequately detailed. The priority should be to advance internally developed staff wherever these people match the specifications required: Every vacancy should be used as a career development opportunity.

Recruitment strategy must be similarly defined, as it provides the source material for all internal development and resourcing in the long term. For example, it is likely to emphasize the intake of graduates and other young people of a similar calibre in sufficient numbers to meet most of the future requirements for managers and senior specialists. Not all of these needs will be met from internal development sources, so specifications for recruits at a later stage should be individual and based on the anticipated forward requirements and supply as well as the immediate need.

Recruitment should follow a logical series of steps. To recruit without establishing the need clearly, or without checking the availability of internal candidates, can be potentially damaging to morale, while considered action to attract, process and select from good candidates should ensure optimum recruitment results and supplement the corporate manpower inventory. The selection process should make use of all aids available to ensure a good decision is made, recognize the limitations of interviewing by many managers, and use psychometric aids where practicable. This will be in the long-term interests of both the candidate and the employer.

12
Manpower Planning and Development

Manpower planning and development are mutually supportive. While manpower planners want development and training activities to help upgrade the manpower inventory, the development and training function is striving to improve the efficiency of individual and corporate performance, and to prepare individuals for further roles and for the future. As already noted, the more you can meet your future needs by growing your own, the better the flows through the organization, and there are positive motivational side effects.

It is this role of development which should ensure its integration into the business, for it contributes strongly to the task of supplying people with required skills and abilities. If developing the inventory is the surest and least expensive route to providing the supply, then planning specific individual development to match needs has to be seen as a key management responsibility.

It follows that the inventory is our primary source of supply for many manpower categories. But the inventory is not likely to stay static in quality and value for long. There will always be a tendency for the less saleable or usable parts of any inventory to age and deteriorate. With our human resource inventory, there is also progressive ageing, but it is a slow process, and much effort is generally devoted to improving its quality and utilization, supported by planned development and training. Inputting additional and relevant skills will, as one example, enhance quality, but the primary means of improving the value of existing stock will be by planned deployments and assignments which expand practical experience.

The human resources of any company represent its most critical resource, particularly its managers and future managers. They alone have the capacity to inhibit or enhance business development. The continuity of the enterprise and its continued growth and prosperity are assured only through them. As I emphasized at the beginning, our human resources provide our only real competitive advantage. Planned development ensures that we encourage our people to achieve and use their full potential; that they are prepared for the responsibilities they may have in the future, and are able to achieve optimum efficiency in the present; and that the best of them develop that edge which improves the company's competitive advantage.

The whole development process progressively focuses on the development of individuals. As the process is demanding and time consuming, the return on investment needs to be clear. Managers should ensure that, through their efforts, they add value to their subordinates and that they lead them well.

The Development Process: How People Grow

People grow in a number of ways. Their level of knowledge develops through a variety of learning situations, ranging from reading or watching, and various forms of education and training, to work experience doing a permanent job or part- or full-time assignments or projects. In addition to the acquisition of knowledge, some of these activities build self-confidence and competence, and encourage the development of personality, visible through improved social skills. The ability to make good decisions based on inadequate information while under pressure may be one of the abilities which a young manager develops from an operational assignment. Only by doing can he get a real appreciation of the demands and complexity of higher level work.

People develop far more from doing, from exposure and response to changing opportunities, than by any other means, although the use of training to supplement experience and prepare for further assignments is also important. A planned sequence of jobs, selected to fit developing abilities and personal preferences, and preferably under development-conscious managers, will produce the fastest growth towards ultimate potential.

The process of personal development should be designed to maximize the pace of relevant learning and personal growth by planning appropriate deployments, identifying the stage at which learning opportunities will be exhausted, and acknowledging the need to initiate fresh assignments to maintain intellectual stimula- (for example, German engineers graduate between the ages of 27 individuals to progress rapidly to high levels while ensuring that they acquire the necessary breadth of experience and vision in the process.

The designing and planning of development must be emphasized, for it rarely happens casually. Development assignments have been likened to moving plants from the greenhouse to the garden. The ground needs to be prepared and the seedlings must be brought to readiness; then they will need some protection, particularly in the early stages, and need to be watched initially in case they become battered by the environment. It is the development opportunity, far more than anything else, which enables people to grow.

The elements of development

There are numerous actions or elements in an individual development plan, including:

- Planned work experience, which should be challenging and followed by reassignment when learning opportunities in a job are exhausted, and project work and secondments, either internal or external, full- or part-time.
- Training, to provide the knowledge and skills required in current and possible future jobs, and to bring technical knowledge up to date.
- Further education towards professional qualifications, or to develop language skills, etc. Also, other self-learning and professional reading.
- Coaching, mentoring and counselling.

Most of this list is straightforward, but it is worth commenting that multifunctional project teams provide particularly good developmental experience of other functions and of the workings of the business.

Mentors

To facilitate optimum growth, the use of a high level tutor (not the direct line manager) to oversee the progress of each high potential individual, to talk with him periodically and influence the direction of his development, can be invaluable and should be encouraged. The mentor can stimulate and guide the developing individual, and also irritate the company to ensure timely action is taken to prepare the next deployment or relevant training of his charge. With more time to devote to development issues than a direct line boss, and more clout than an adviser from human resources, the mentor can more effectively ensure that the right things are done. In this respect, they provide invaluable support.

In addition to mentors, some direct line managers are exceptionally effective as developers and motivators of their subordinates. These managers need to be identified and utilized as a critically important resource. They deserve to be allocated the best candidates for they are likely to guide the growth of these people through any difficulties and to produce the best developed subordinates.

Development jobs

One of the best ways of developing experience is by assignment to carefully selected jobs. Many companies believe that some jobs are especially valuable for this purpose, and designate them as development jobs. These are reserved exclusively for the higher ability young managers as definitive steps in their personal growth. Such posts include, for example, the general managership of smaller businesses where an individual can get to grips with a full business for the first time and take responsibility for profits.

In practice, I find that development requirements are so diverse that only a small proportion of needs are adequately met by the designated development slots. Only when the total range of jobs is covered in developmental assignments can needs be met fully.

A simple exchange of positions for a set period can be valuable. It allows a manager who is progressing slowly to be returned to his old post after a two year stint elsewhere, while the faster moving manager is assigned to his next career challenge. Alternatively, the manager whose position is borrowed may undertake a project assignment for his own further development.

Although it is advisable not to shuffle managers too frequently, it is equally as important to make sure that no-one stagnates. Development planning should create real pressure for change whenever this appears to be happening.

Individual Development Plans

A management development system needs to cover every individual with any real potential for personal development. An individual development plan (IDP) should exist, however simple in format, for all of these people, from graduate intake level up to, and including, board members. Based on all available objective information about each individual (including known preferences, etc.), plus future organization and management requirement data, the IDP should record how we expect the individual to develop over the next several years, including alternative options where appropriate, and detail development plans, training requirements and anticipated appointments.

These are working documents, continually added to and annotated as plans or moves are actioned, and monitored to ensure plans are implemented. They sit with the line manager as a reminder of his commitment to planned actions, but management development staff should monitor progress. The quality of the evaluation is critically important to the future, both for the individuals and for the company, because it allows any limitations in the process to be identified and corrected.

Ready to move

Within the development process, it is vital to identify those individuals who are ready for fresh assignments and further stretching so that action to move them on to their next assignments can be taken early. Their further growth is essential and must be followed through, however valuable they may be in their present roles. To slow or block the growth of an individual is likely to lead to him leaving the company.

Periodic reviews of the abilities and readiness to move of all career staff are essential, and every vacancy provides a development opportunity. Ideal next assignments should be determined, together with provisional timing, so that moves can be planned ahead to ensure continuity. Where no local opportunity exists for an able individual who is becoming ready for a move, wider opportunities should be sought within the group. The current state of readiness to move for each individual should be evident on his IDP and is part of the overall management inventory.

Individual development plan content

An IDP is a brief summary of key information related to the individual's forward career plan. The form of an IDP can vary enormously, from blank sheets to complex forms. However, it is likely to contain:

Identification:	Name.
	Job title, company, location, grade.
	Date of birth/age.
Summary of career/	Qualifications/major training courses attended.
experience:	Dates/companies/positions/major achievements.
Strengths:	Summary of major strengths relevant to future job possibilities.
Limitations:	Notes on any factors which may restrict the scope or direction of his future development, or which need to be overcome by experience or training.
Personal preferences:	Mobility.
	Job type.
	Extent of ambition.
Development action plans:	
Job:	Ready for move, when?
	Next job/options/timing.
	Specific appointment planned.
Other factors:	Training plans to meet agreed needs.
	Actions to overcome critical limitations.
	Experience needs to be met.

(Note: If assessment centre or current psychometric data are available, this should be indicated and any key information recorded.)

Preparing an IDP is the easy part. It is implementation which causes the headaches. As with any other plan, it represents the best effort at the time the plan is made, but the business situation and environment change endlessly, as do the pace of individual development, personal preferences and mobility, and the availability of opportunities, so reviews must take place regularly.

Any plan needs to be kept close at hand so that progress can be monitored. Concern only arises when the plans agreed in an overall review begin to drift off course and are not revised. Ideally, managers should audit the progress of development plans within their own area, with some overview by the next managerial level. There should be sound business justification for changes, and evidence that the plan has been rethought and individual actions rescheduled. If this is not happening, it may be legitimate to ask why expensive management time is being wasted developing plans it is not intending to implement.

Career Paths

For many lower level jobs, training and preparation are targeted on one job or a limited range of options, with little expectation that the great majority of incumbents will show any potential for further advancement. A small number will progress into supervisory posts, largely in the same area, and a few may show some ability to progess in other ways.

It is in the area of professional and managerial staff that career paths with organized flows are relevant. Career paths are designed to encourage systematic development of numbers of similar individuals, such as the graduate or professional staff intake, to ensure that each has the opportunity to participate in the full range of training and to gain experience in a planned range of relevant activities, and then to progress logically along the most suitable career development route.

These routes can be relatively simple for most people, for the bulk of the future manager intake will enter through a chosen function, and concentrate initially on developing their knowledge and skills within that chosen area. Most will seek a variety of experience to cover all aspects of that function before concentrating on more specific operating roles within it, or a specialist aspect.

The bulk of career progression probably takes place within single functions, with only a relatively small proportion of people deliberately or casually moving between career streams. The company is likely to want a small core of high ability people to gain multi-functional experience as a foundation to general management or to top functional posts, but it would see little advantage from more widespread interchange. Similarly, for employees generally, their market values represent the sum of their knowledge and experience, and their ability to apply it, so any move to a fresh function not subsidized by management would involve a drop in value and this is rarely acceptable.

If early development is within one function, it is logical to define stages and to encourage some systematic progression through them. Normal rates of flow should evolve so that requirements could be forecast, and the core training relevant to each stage should be clear. However, the rate of individual progress should vary with performance, and appraisals will show how quickly an individual gets on top of the demands at each level, and assessments of potential show ability to cope with higher and wider ranging assignments.

Where career development expands to include more than one

career path, the pattern may develop with criss-crossing between the line and functional roles within one function, or between primary functions and assignments in other major functions, or by progressive appointments alternating between general and functional management.

There must be purpose behind individual career progressions of this type. The longer term intention might involve developing a high ability individual towards a much more senior post, with a series of hurdles to be overcome in the process. Such a career path has a distinctly higher than normal level of risk, although it may have a similarly high level of potential reward. The responsibility for the risk element should be accepted by the company in that it is the company that is taking the critical decisions to appoint the individual and it will have assessed the form and extent of the risk in advance and judged that it can be overcome. If there is a failure, and there will be some, it must be handled sympathetically as a learning experience, so that career damage is minimized for the individual, who continues to be a valuable corporate resource. Indeed, the reason for failure may be an unexpected change in the business environment which an inexperienced man could not be expected to handle.

Future organizations appear to require greater degrees of specialization, combined with a wider appreciation of where each function's contribution fits into the overall business, plus an understanding of the overall business operation. This will develop in part by the increasing use of project teams, which provide extensive cross-functional experience, and also through management training modules designed to set individual specialist areas in the context of the broader business.

Self-Development

Most employees are acutely interested and active in progressing their own development. The days are long gone when an individual accepted that his development and career would be taken care of by the company and that he would do the jobs to which he was assigned and go where he was sent. Today, individuals not only expect to be involved in the direction of their career development, but are likely to express strong views on their preferences and take initiatives to achieve their career objectives. Ideally, development becomes a partnership, with the company pursuing its needs in open discussion with its staff.

Self-awareness

Self-development is logically preceeded by self-awareness. Some organizations now run short seminars or development centres for groups of bright younger managers, which are designed to increase self-knowledge or self-awareness and to help clarify the soundness and achievability of personal career objectives and development plans.

These sessions draw out information on a range of aspects. They provide insights into personality and how other people see the individual. For example, a degree of introversion and poor relationship building might be highlighted, which may not have been understood previously and can restrict career development. The process should also explore how individuals learn and their style of learning, and may explore and challenge the personal philosophies of the participants.

Career development options

It is unlikely that the forward view will take the form of a clear single career line. Invariably there will be options but, to some extent, the options which are taken will be heavily influenced by the timing of opportunities becoming available. The chance to take a promotion is difficult to turn down if the preferred alternative is less immediate and less certain.

The task facing each individual is to identify a range of options which seem achievable from the starting point, and then to add some desirable but less realistic possibilities, with notes of the actions which would be required to make them achievable. For example, the individual trained as an accountant is likely to identify a range of straightforward options associated with progression from his initial functional training, but if he wants to progress to general management, there will be a range of additional criteria to meet.

Each individual needs to assess the options available from where he is now, weighed against his preferences, ambitions, mobility and what he seeks from life, and then determine the strength of preference for a particular track.

Career development is a partnership, owned jointly by the

manager and his manager, but in which neither has total freedom of action and each has different objectives. The boss knows that he must plan to meet the manpower needs of his organization, based on business objectives and environment. In parallel, he will want to deploy his manpower inventory as efficiently as possible while optimizing development opportunities for all individuals, some of whom may have career objectives not available within the company.

Managers who develop subordinates well

In every organization there are some managers who seem to have a golden touch with the development of their subordinates. People in their areas are encouraged and guided to develop rapidly and, subsequently, feature strongly in the lists of promoted individuals. In contrast, there are other managers who appear to place a dead hand on the careers of their subordinates. Inevitably, there is competition amongst the better younger managers to join one of the forcing houses, and great concern to avoid getting trapped in a dead end.

Observations of the development environment enable an individual to decide whether the company will be supportive in helping him to develop his career along the lines he has in mind. However, while this support is invaluable, the main drive and effort must come from himself.

Preferences, Ambitions and Mobility

Career development is strongly related to abilities but individual preferences, ambitions and mobility have a substantial influence and are liable to change. Knowledge of these influences is an essential ingredient in assembling and agreeing realistic development plans which set out the intended or most likely career paths for individuals.

There is a joint responsibility on the part of manager and subordinate to ensure that the company has sufficient awareness of each employee's view of his future, which should be on the agenda at most counselling sessions.

Career preferences

During the early years of career development, there are generally several avenues open for the next move and many individuals have clear preferences which influence the vacancies they choose to go after. One key consideration will be around the degree of specialization preferred. Those who aspire to top management may seek to broaden their experience through a number of diverse assignments to develop a generalist c.v., while others may find their career satisfaction comes from growing in a specialist function.

Selection of preferred activities may be influenced by ultimate career ambition, but other factors are present. Preferred life-style is increasingly influencing willingness to work in some of the more demanding workaholic organizations which attract some individuals who are willing to make such a commitment, but repel others. In this way, the culture of an organization, as perceived from outside, has a significant impact on employment image and its ability to attract able candidates from outside.

We have to learn to live with the views and career preferences of our people, but if we believe that the capabilities of an individual fall short of his ambitions, the disagreement may be serious. Participation in a self-awareness seminar with strong feedback from a group of peers may lead an individual to reassess his objectives and achieve greater realism.

Mobility

When the opportunity arises for an attractive appointment involving a significant geographic move, at least one third of the immediate acceptances seem to get reversed after the partner or family become involved. In most of those cases, the partner may have given a casual agreement to the concept of mobility, but react differently when faced with a reality. For the planning of potential overseas postings, the discussion has to be blunt and specific from an early stage to ensure commitment.

Career progression in some large organizations has been linked traditionally to mobility. Development required that an individual did not spend too long in one place, and was rarely promoted without a transfer. The banks and the church were good examples; large multinationals provide another. This policy is changing, and large organizations appear to be seeking new and acceptable rules. Acceptability is recognized because individual attitudes to mobility are far less permissive than a couple of decades back. Company attitudes have been influenced also by the high costs of transfers and the difficulties arising from enormous regional variations in house prices. Associated flow patterns need monitoring.

Career mobility is still expected from high ability, intensely ambitious individuals, who are clearly heading for high positions where some variation in experience and working environments is seen as essential. These committed individuals are likely to accept the opportunities to advance which are offered, and the employer is likely to have strong views on the experience it requires in its top people. The cost factor is irrelevant where the number of people is small and their future vital to the organization.

Mobility seems particularly relevant in large multinationals where those individuals who aspire to senior positions will find themselves managing and doing business across cultural boundaries. It is essential for these people to gain first-hand experience in more than one situation. In these companies, the evolving pattern requires the high performing stream to undertake foreign assignments from an early stage, in the knowledge that there are career bars for those who lack international experience.

People following functional careers in categories where organizations employ relatively small numbers (such as legal, personnel and perhaps finance) also need to be mobile to progress. There may be only limited opportunity for internal career advancement, so individuals are faced with developing their careers by changing employment or accepting slower advancement as they wait for convenient opportunities to arise. Career planning is likely to assume and encourage mobility within the function and across the corporation, so knowledge of the real extent of individual mobility is important.

Development of High Potential

The most important resource in the care of any board of directors is the select cadre of high potential younger managers, which will provide the primary source of candidates for senior management and board positions in ten to 20 years' time. The career development of this elite group is increasing under the hand of the CEO personally.

Four ages of potential

There is a great deal of difference between our view of the potential of a newly recruited graduate and our view of further potential in an established senior manager. Although significant potential can exist at all levels and age should not be a bar, younger managers do learn and develop fastest.

Mid-20s Up through the mid-20s, there is not likely to be any substantial track record to demonstrate evidence of potential. Judgements made will be based on intellectual strength, personality and perhaps the degree of maturity evident. The first years of post-academic achievements are visible, indicating the ability to adapt to a fresh situation and make things happen. The embryonic track record is likely to look good and early career plans have begun to test and stretch capability. This has been described as the exploratory stage of a career. At this age, the apparent fliers tend to be those who appear more mature, are always quite certain of what they are going to do, and are working hard to get there.

Age 28–32 This period seems to provide the critical decision taking stage in which most employers assess potential. It is at this point that track records seem to be showing clear indications about which individuals learn fast, cope with new situations, and show a grasp of broader business essentials. All of the available information is assembled to determine what is really indicated about future potential as distinct from past performance. The quality of career plans to test and stretch abilities now shows through, for those considered to have above average potential should have been placed in appointments and assignments which tested capabilities beyond their present levels.

At this stage, many companies supplement their data by making use of assessment centres which provide more detailed information on the extent and form of potential, and then talk out detailed IDPs which take into account apparent potential, individual preferences, and future opportunities.

The 30s These years provide a period of great testing and stretching as individuals climb their chosen paths at varying speeds. Some will continue to show an astonishing ability to grasp the complexities of new situations quickly and make real contributions while, for others, the pace is simply slower, or a ceiling is reached.

The 40s In the 40s, the high potential stream has thinned out considerably, and now contains only the small number of highly placed individuals who are thought to retain the potential for significant further advance. The testing and evaluation of this group to determine their suitability for the highest offices will be ongoing.

There are many individuals who will be assessed as having potential for further advancement well beyond their 40s and no cut-off point is implied here. In fact, most managers have some further potential at all stages of their careers, but high potential implies the ability to achieve significant further advance in a short period of time, and that does become progressively more rare.

Organizations which actively manage the process of development gain a significant competitive advantage. Research in the US has shown a correlation between success in top management and the breadth of experience, showing that slightly less successful top managers in the same enterprise had rather less breadth of experience.

Test and stretch

One problem in managing development effectively is that the timing of readiness for advancement is most difficult to predict. The individuals' proven abilities and their needs must be comprehensively understood, and assignments found for them in which they are challenged to the limit and must strive hard to cope. That can be a critical time if any unexpected development occurs, but the next level of management should be on the alert to provide support if necessary. In the process these individuals grow rapidly, but all too quickly they complete or get on top of the task and, once again, begin to show readiness for the next. It is, of course, essential that the next challenge be provided, even if this means giving priority to young high potential managers when more proven ability is available.

Inevitably, not every challenge is tackled smoothly. There can be errors of assignment, or the business may conspire to produce an unplanned set of environmental changes. If failure occurs, there must be a commitment to support any individual placed in a test and stretch position. If blame must be allocated for a failure, it falls largely on those who approved the appointment. The main objective in such a situation must be to recover the confidence and upward movement of the candidate by placing him or her quickly in a fresh assignment with a high probability of success, and not recording a black mark. As one CEO noted: 'When they stumble, they should be counselled in a way that shows them how to succeed rather than be shoved off the list of hot prospects.'

People management skills

One group of skills more than any other is gaining importance as a critical characteristic of future senior managers. The role of a manager involves getting things done through other people. He is responsible for some of these people whereas others will be his equals or superiors, or his customers and suppliers. His effectiveness as a manager and his ultimate performance will depend on personal relationships and his ability to get things done. As each manager exists within an enterprise, the task is to manage through the system and structure; to get things done through people within the organization, systems and cultures in which they all exist.

In observing subordinate managers of high potential, the way in which they manage their staff (and other personal relationships) should be watched closely to see whether staff follow their leadership. They should be seen to encourage open communication, be sensitive to others and handle people firmly yet compassionately, handle older subordinates well and gain their respect, and develop their subordinates. If these things are going well, it provides another positive element in the growing track record.

Monitor progress

Feedback of progress on development assignments should be recorded on IDPs so that a comprehensive track record accumulates. If career limiting factors are identified, they must be recorded and action planned to overcome them if possible. They do not disappear if they are ignored (as some people hope) and are liable to occur more severely and cause career difficulties if not tackled. Some may limit career prospects, but identification should restrict damage and ensure that evident potential is directed to a career not threatened by the limitation.

The optimum career path for a high potential candidate should be outlined for a five- to 10-year period, with ideal postings noted and selected to provide the mix of experience sought. If one of those positions is filled by a long-term incumbent, and it is considered essential to provide experience in that specific slot, then priority may need to be given to the longer term development of the high potential candidate and a fresh assignment found for the blocking individual. If this seems ruthless, one might also consider the positive aspects of a fresh assignment for a manager who has been stuck, possibly for too long, in a previous position.

Ultimately, further progress becomes more competitive as the numbers of jobs at each level decreases. Even when people reach board level it remains essential to seek indicators of further potential, and continuing growth towards the highest position should be encouraged and tested.

Future specialists

The dual track or triple track concept of switching between the general management, functional management and specialist streams – in each of which there are equivalent career streams providing comparable status and pay opportunities – has gained favour over the years in quite a number of large companies. In part, it promotes proper understanding of the complexities of the organizational balance but, also, it recognizes that some individuals can make outstanding contributions without having to manage operations. In fact many of the fundamental elements in the development of a business are determined by staff people, not by making the line decisions, but by identifying opportunities and developing strategies, and then influencing busy line executives.

The human resource area is an excellent example of where this should occur; senior specialists have the expertise and the time to to influence behaviour and systems, and to make things happen. Much of what is in this book makes complete sense to line managers but also presents them with problems of implementation. It is for the business planning and human resource specialists to quietly guide and assist their collegues in achieving the desired end results.

Increasing specialization is one of the major themes to emerge from predicted future organizations. Hence, specialists are likely to become a more significant element in the organization structures and manpower plans which develop through the 1990s. Specialists will find strong roles in the project management culture, where roles and objectives will be clear and require minimal supervision.

Career development for specialists will change form rather than become more limited. They will be able to move up within their own specialism, but movement between specialisms will be difficult or impossible. They will have great awareness of other specialisms through working in task forces, but few will become true generalists. Generalists are likely to evolve from task force leaders, although leadership will be informal as specialists work together in task forces on equal terms. Compensation potential will be as great for specialists as for generalists. Large consulting and law practices provide parallels already.

The conclusion reached by a research team at Ashridge Management College was that management development which concentrates on the doing aspects of management and the pumping in of specific skills and knowledge will be addressing only one part of future management challenges and needs. They suggest that the being elements of a person – the inherent presonal qualities and perspective of an individual – will be at least as important. These will not respond to training, but only to organizational environment and culture.

Summary

The purpose of development is to optimize the growth and use of the manpower resources of the enterprise, both currently and into the future. Where orderly internal career advancement is visible, able people are encouraged to remain in the business and company knowledge is retained. Employees tend to be motivated to perform well by the prospect of reward by advancement, and morale is high. Avoidable recruitment costs are also minimized.

Development does not just happen. It requires careful planning and discussions at several levels to balance individual and company requirements and preferences. As self-development gains greater recognition, joint ownership of careers and increasingly open career discussion increase in parallel.

There are a number of elements in development which need to be balanced. The most effective learning comes from doing, from taking responsibility and learning by experience. Selection of the right mix and sequence of job assignments and projects enables the individual to grow quickly, his development being supplemented by relevant education and training, and guided by a supportive mentor.

Individual development plans appear to be important elements in the development process because they turn loose generalized intentions into recorded specifics. The format for recording is unimportant; it is the act of recording which is vital, enabling each manager to follow up the plans for his people. This is an essential discipline if development is to be taken seriously.

13
Manpower Planning and Training Needs

Training is one aspect of development, but it is also crucial in manpower planning when a significant change is identified in a business and in the skills required.

A good example is that referred to in example 9.3, where technology change produced a radical shift in demand for both the numbers of people and the skills required over a period of some five years. Generating a substantial flow of the people employed as service engineers into the new skills area by retraining enabled the demand to be met and established employees to be retained. Although this was a major and expensive exercise, with much individual full-time training exceeding one year, the costs were offset by the avoidance of high redundancy payments for many long serving people, and escaping the expense and difficulty of recruiting a relatively scarce resource. Further, the morale and productivity resulting from this strategy both remained high.

Training Needs

Development is about total growth of the knowledge, experience and abilities of an individual, the development of the whole person as he progresses towards his ultimate potential. Development is long term and future orientated; it provides new perspectives and encourages strategic vision. In contrast, training tends to be narrower and shorter term, and is concerned with helping people to do their jobs better or preparing them for future positions. Training is one part of the development process, to which it contributes by providing supplementary opportunities to acquire knowledge, skills and attitudes largely off-the-job and to help achieve desired performance levels.

A broad business justification for training might be that it ensures all employees are provided with the necessary knowledge and skills to enable them to operate most effectively in the achievement of business objectives. Additionally, and as an investment, training should provide able employees with the knowledge and skills they will require in future assignments.

Beyond this, attitudes to training diverge. At one extreme is a commitment to encouraging the total development of the individual as a whole person, with open access to training and knowledge-expanding sessions, including self-development interests, some of which may not be relevant to present or future jobs anticipated by the employer. (Ford runs an outstanding scheme of this type). At the other extreme is the view that training should be focused narrowly on business performance improvement and have an early impact on the bottom line. This might be achieved, for example, by putting a training-cum-business consultant into a project team to improve project performance, but with no general concern for developing people. A good middle-of-the-road objective is that all training actions should be in response to legitimate, business-related training needs. As one consultant put it, 'If you think training is expensive, try ignorance.'

The role of training in personal development

The greatest part of a manager's personal development will take place on the job, learning from the boss and learning from doing, as he is progressively exposed to an increasing variety and complexity of assignments and new levels of responsibility. However, formal training is part of the management development process and, if it is carefully planned to complement each step of a manager's development, it can make a significant contribution to improving his current job performance and preparing him for further stages in his career.

All training must have a clear purpose and value. It should be designed to meet defined individual and company needs. The design should be both time- and cost-effective and should take into account individual learning abilities. We must:

• Ensure that training adds value, and has a direct influence on business performance.

- Re-establish training needs at regular intervals.
- Design, or review and update, the content and form of all training programmes to maintain high standards of quality, and to meet training needs in the most cost-effective way.
- Endeavour to measure the effectiveness of training in relation to the required impact on performance.

Training needs arise from the requirements of the individual within the business, or from the business itself. The individual will identify training needs: to help him improve his performance in his present post and to assist in his preparation for a different or higher level position. The company initiates training in response to changing environmental factors which alter the objectives of a company and its managerial jobs, and the knowledge and skills required by its managers, and to respond to changing technologies or environmental changes which affect the ways in which managers will do their jobs.

At least once each year, a comprehensive updating and analysis of training needs should take place.

Individual training needs

A range of activities provides sources of data on the training needs of individuals. Most of these data are assembled on IDPs, where it is integrated into career plans such that the requirement is properly defined, the urgency established and provisional timing set. Most of the more urgent requirements will be scheduled for action in the immediate 12 months, while some longer term training related to future assignments may be scheduled for subsequent years. This great range of precisely identified needs will have to be summarized before a corporate training plan can be assembled.

An important contribution to IDPs, particularly regarding actions which may improve performance in the present job, comes from the performance appraisal process. This should provide a clear analysis of the individual's ability to do his job at the performance standards required. It should identify shortcomings in performance and what can be done to overcome them, and include agreement on specific training actions. Further, the appraisal discussions should cover the training felt to be necessary by the individual as well as his manager.

The other major contributor to IDPs will be the conclusions of the assessment centre and any other tests of potential. As part of the assessment of the ability to do other or higher level jobs, it is essential to identify gaps in knowledge, experience and competences, and to evaluate the extent to which training can fill these in. Actions which can be taken should be incorporated into IDPs, even if the appropriate timing is two to three years ahead.

As a supplement to the training needs identified to meet company performance and deployment requirements, individual growth objectives are likely to generate some further requirements. For example, there is an increase in the number of young people who want to obtain an MBA, and a parallel increase of external full- and part-time courses, many with company sponsorship. Most employers are willing to provide some support, even where the MBA is not seen as relevant to the individual's present work, because the enhancement of overall knowledge is attractive and increases the value of the inventory.

Corporate training needs

An organization capability audit based on business plan objectives and the changes expected in the environment is quite likely to identify factors which are expected to alter the operating environment and lead to a demand for new or different knowledge or skills, and which will require serious attention. The ways in which the necessary skills are to be acquired may involve a combination of external recruitment plus internal training, possibly in a relatively short time-scale. One issue where the training contribution will be critically important may be recognition that the company needs a rapid advance in its use of IT and that this is likely to alter the jobs of many middle managers.

Training needs analysis and priorities

The mass of detail on the training needs of individuals, plus the blocks of training required to meet corporate needs have to be analysed and summarized to produce an overall statement of the company's training needs and priorities. This will provide the justification for modifications to established company or corporate training programmes, the specifications for new programmes, and the numbers and levels to be covered, and will also provide the basis for booking individual training commitments in the immediate future (i.e. at least one year ahead).

A typical response on completion of an analysis of current (one year) training needs is that the company will need two to three years to get through it all. Sorting out priorities should not prove too difficult, but may involve going back to source material and judging the urgency of each element. Some of the larger requirements will stand out as essential and urgent while others will clearly be less so.

Any tendency to postpone or put aside training in identified requirements for aspects of man-management skills should be resisted. Many managers seem curiously reluctant to participate in training to improve their skills in counselling and interviewing, although these may be critically important to their effectiveness. Some of the largest and best-managed companies expect more than half of their total management training effort to be spent improving man-management skills.

The completed analysis provides the detail to be turned into training actions for the next cycle of 12 months, and is a critical element in the planned development of the manpower inventory.

Training Actions

Training is concerned with creating a rapid learning environment for identified groups of individuals with similar needs to increase their knowledge, skills and experience of predetermined activities, functions or behaviours. As people learn continuously from daily events, training should encourage more directed and intensive learning in specific areas, to bring knowledge up to a desired level, or performance up to a required standard, and should also enhance the individuals' learning abilities.

Training is work or activity related. Academic training or education has its emphasis on systematic intellectual teaching, the provision of a base of theory. There is no boundary between education and training – only a difference of emphasis – and some sections of training require an introduction to, or reinforcement of, basic theory. Once the needs are identified, summarized, and priorities determined, a programme of training actions can be developed.

Meeting the needs – how people learn

As the purpose of training is to impart knowledge or skills to those being trained, for training to be effective, some understanding of how people learn, or can be motivated to learn, is necessary. Training and learning are two different things. To quote the old proverb, 'you can lead a horse to water, but you cannot make him drink'. In the same way, you can put someone through a training course, but you cannot make them learn.

If we want people to learn, we may need to provide encouragement and support for self-development. It may also be appropriate to assess their suitability for learning. For example, entry to an academic course is likely to have an entry gate of successful completion of a preparatory or lower level course, which indicates an ability to comprehend the subject matter at the level required; an intellectual standard. Some training courses have (or should have) comparable entry gates in the form of an assessment of individual ability to cope with the training programme. There is no point in placing people on courses which are at too advanced a level, and others may have intellectual limitations or some form of learning difficulty which may place them at a disadvantage.

The approach to teaching is of vital importance. It has been suggested that formal education systems tend to immunize adult students against learning; that much of what we learn as adults is picked up in less formal settings, or even by accident. This provides an initial pointer to the sort of learning environment and structure of training required to optimize learning by adults.

A situation where the trainer sees himself as the giver and the trainees as receivers in a junior school sense is evidently not going to be effective, particularly with high ability people. The adult learner does not like to feel dependent and seems to want to take both responsibility for his efforts and full credit for achievements. He is likely to have strong views on his own training needs and how these may be met, based on past learning experiences. Ideally, he will want to be involved in determining the duration and content of learning and to be an active participant rather than passive recipient. He is likely to seek some measure of the effect or effectiveness of the training experience and will be influenced in his judgement by his degree of enjoyment of the process.

Action learning

The most effective form of learning from training at senior levels is likely to be some form of action learning. This can move much of the activity outside the training centre, although some theoretical input or grounding may be needed but this will generally be accepted if it is well presented with active, participatory discussion. The main learning is generated from questioning and problem solving, using case studies which are live and therefore very real and detailed. Action learning requires participants to work in small groups, and to clarify learning by questioning their individual learning objectives as a preliminary to team-working on these live projects. Learning is primarily by doing and from each other and, where possible, the team should be encouraged to carry the project through to implementation rather than present a conclusion and walk away. Learning from each other has several facets, from sharing experiences constructively, through interactions with team members, involving both criticism and advice, to reviewing with each other the lessons learnt from the agreed actions.

Involvement in real-life problems which require a solution and action alters the perspective enormously. By mixing training with reality, the learning process is enhanced. Realization that there is rarely enough information in complex real-time decision taking may be one of the key lessons. These real problems move training into the realm of development, because one of the best development situations is an assignment in a lively project team. The distinctive flavour of this training comes when participating managers are teamed with specially selected training staff, who operate as business consultants, to address real problems, and where the consultants support and steer the learning from within the project.

Learning in these situations is from demanding and practical experience, following which the students reflect on their observations and construct their own patterns of concepts or generalizations. The end result is a learning experience which may visibly pass through to the bottom line.

A learning culture

Ultimately, individuals will learn if they choose to. No matter how much effort is put into the design of training situations, if there is resistance to learning, the training will not be effective.

Resistance may stem from management attitudes and a voiced consensus that training is a waste of time. That sort of cultural resistance is not unusual and very difficult to dislodge, but it can be done. In a large construction group, I identified a range of current operational problems which were clearly hitting the bottom line, and assembled a management training package to show in practical terms how some of these could be tackled. To fit the macho image of the senior managers, the course was designed to run for three 14-hour days, beginning on Sunday evening. The trial group duly arrived for what they described as their holiday – they dropped this phrase two hours into Monday morning. The involvement in new approaches to real problems caught their interest and we had to fight off demand for places on the programme until the top 200 managers (including all directors) had been through. And it really did have an impact on the bottom line.

In more enlightened organizations, the recognition of the value of learning is high. I emphasize learning, not necessarily training, because training is no more than one opportunity to learn.

A learning culture encourages learning by everyone in the organization, and does so by providing many opportunities to learn but, more importantly, it encourages a way of thinking where everyone wants to learn and takes positive steps to do so which go well beyond any normal job related requirements. If there is a new development in the business, everyone wants to know about it, about the implications, and about the opportunities it may create elsewhere in the business. Expert help is brought in to run evening seminars, and everyone participates, in their own time.

This is the same attitude found in groups of high ability individuals who are dissatisfied with their present situation and are convinced that improvement is possible. It fits into a culture of openness and total encouragement for development, one that selects people who want to grow and then does more than just give them responsibility by creating an environment which maximizes their growth and development.

Of course, you cannot just go out and create this in any ordinary company because it would terrify many of the residents but, as a vision to work towards, it is something for many human resource staff to savour and some to achieve.

Meeting the needs – structure of training programmes

Once training needs have been identified and priorities established, the means of addressing the requirements can be planned. The bulk of training in any large organization should be internal and local, possibly supplemented by corporate and external activities, depending on the degree of specialization and any one-off requirements.

The core of internal training will be essential preparation for the work to be done by the students at every level and preparation for advancement level by level, plus a range of functional, technical and man-management courses associated with the needs of the overall business and the broadening of its managers. It will also instil an understanding of basic corporate values. Core programmes are likely to have an individuality related to industry and culture and the corporate approach to development and training.

The purpose of the core training programmes is to ensure that individuals are properly prepared for the work they will do and for each major step forward in their careers and, where appropriate, to ensure that they acquire a common understanding of corporate culture and systems. Definitions of the basic knowledge and skills or competences which are essential for smooth transition to each new level provide the basis for the core training modules, from entry level through to middle management. There may be variations in core knowledge needed in different streams; the core knowledge for all graduate entrants will be different to that for all finance staff, or all people with supervisory responsibilities. Figure 13.1 shows a typical corporate training structure.

At basic school leaver level, youngsters may enter a company or Government sponsored training scheme in preparation for work.

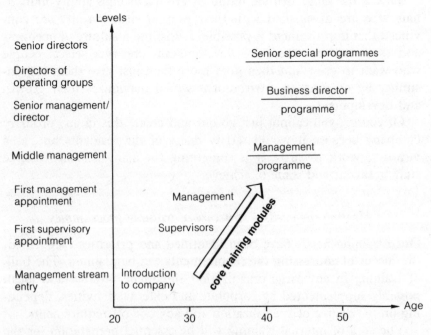

Figure 13.1 Management training structure

Some of these courses may last several years, with a mix of further education and work experience, but may then lead into jobs which need the acquired skills but which have little or no promotion prospects.

At this intake level, there is likely to be some general induction covering the company structure, philosopy and general administration, followed by more specific training covering the industry, product familiarization, basic financial management and human relations skills, and company operating systems, depending on entry level. The pattern of training following entry is likely to be streamed by intake levels and function, concentrating on the development of specialized knowledge.

Company requirements for career staff will require training in a further range of grounding skills, covering company systems, man-management skills and the basics of how to write a report, make a presentation and read quickly. There may also be finance for non-finance people, marketing appreciation for all, and relevant technical briefings. Company culture is likely to come through strongly in these programmes, with particular emphasis on any new thinking, attitudes or behaviour felt to be critical.

As individual careers develop, the first supervisory appointment should be preceded by a deliberate core of preparation, covering the continuing development of relevant functional skills and knowledge of financial systems, but with an emphasis on the development of man-management and leadership skills and also on the integration of learning modules into a comprehensive understanding of how the business works. This will fit into the manpower plans' requirements for the relevant categories.

Later, the first managerial appointment should be preceded by a similar, but more advanced programme, with a further programme before the individual begins to manage other managers. At senior level, many organizations will look for development programmes outside their own boundaries, perhaps to group headquarters if they are part of a very large organization, or to the major business schools and management training establishments.

The detailed structure of each module throughout this range of training programmes needs to be built up from the identified needs and a knowledge of the targeted participants and how they are expected to learn. The form of modules should be variable. Provided that they meet the needs of the participants, the variation in the ways the needs they can be designed in an enormous variety of ways, being influenced particularly by corporate culture and both management and training staff preferences.

The introduction of any new corporate system, or a programme of culture change, is frequently backed up by training programmes which are more exercises in communication. Training can be thought of as communication with a specific purpose, and the use of training resources and techniques to present and sell new practices does create a learning situation which is legitimate. For example, the launch of an updated appraisal programme should be presented with strong training support. To be effective, these special programmes must be seen to have been started at the top, and to cascade down level by level, with all managers seen to participate, giving everyone a common understanding and language.

Nominations for training

The selection of individuals at every level to attend any course must be evaluated carefully. Attendance must be linked to their agreed training needs and to their planned career development, corporate development and corporate manpower requirements. Further, the individual must be capable of understanding the training and benefiting from it. But, most important of all, is that the individuals must have a personal commitment to participate enthusiastically and to complete the intensive and demanding self-development opportunity which any training course provides.

Where appropriate, the nomination of a delegate to any programme should be timed to coincide with an anticipated job change or promotion, or some reorganization that will affect his duties and responsibilities. It is essential that participants should understand and support the objective. Attendance is normally sponsored by the immediate boss who has a responsibility to brief the attender fully and clarify the expectations. Attendance should never be a company requirement. There has to be choice for the participant and he must be committed.

The sponsor (and his boss) have a further responsibility; to ensure that their nominees do attend courses as booked, and are not distracted or withdrawn. Programmes are expensive to organize and run. Apart from the fact that the full costs should be charged when withdrawal occurs at a late stage, the opportunity to use that place for another individual may be lost.

On return from a training programme, the sponsor should debrief the participant to ensure the purpose has been achieved. The participant should be encouraged to do most of the talking. I find it useful to request a written report, giving a full assessment of the course and the learning obtained, and to follow this up after, say, three months, with the question, 'What have you done differently in the last three months as a direct result of attending the course?'.

Record of training

If we are serious about the objectives of training, and the purpose of each course, it is important to record participation so it counts in inventory analysis. For example, a number of companies will not promote an individual to the next significant level until their preparation – including participation in appropriate training courses – has been completed. Such organizations keep a note of individuals who are fully prepared for such promotional opportunities.

Completion of various specialist training prepares individuals for assignments which come up occasionally and for which a records search will be used to identify candidates.

A further application of training records is in the monitoring of the subsequent progress of groups, such as the class of '84, as this may provide pointers to the value and effectiveness of a sequence of regular programmes. For example, one company found that it retained virtually no-one from its main future managers courses after five years and discovered that, because the expectations raised were rarely met, participants saw the course as valuable preparation for job hunting and subsequently found themselves highly prized elsewhere in the industry.

Effectiveness

Training effectiveness is not easy to measure, but deliberate effort to evaluate training might lead to an evaluation of the following points:

Trainees' initial reactions: However carefully any course or seminar is designed and run, individual reactions vary widely, but the discipline of writing a short immediate comment on each session will enable any common reponses to influence subsequent programmes.

Learning: Where the subject matter is clear, such as for specific inputs of functional knowledge, it is possible to get some measure of before and after proficiency. However, for most management courses the knowledge areas and levels are not definable with sufficient precision to use in this way, and one has to look at the use of knowledge and at behaviour.

Behaviour: Changes in job related behaviour may be evident, as in the construction industry case mentioned earlier. So too may the influence of training on particular competences. While these are evident in individuals, the use of newly acquired skills may be inhibited unless the surrounding managers possess and are using these same skills.

Organization behaviour: Where large groups of people attend the same or similar programmes, the reinforcement provided by many people trying out the same new ideas can lead to acceptance and consolidation. Measurement may still be difficult, but it is universally evident that certain changes have occurred. On a smaller scale, any team which has worked through a competitive live project will have been stimulated sufficiently to carry on with the project and use the skills they have acquired. If, when split up or returned to their original environments, they find their learning cannot be successfully communicated and absorbed, they will tend to revert to previous attitudes.

Evaluation can be attempted as people leave the training centre, but measures of effectiveness really need to be based on permanent changes in behaviour back on the job. The effect of the corporate culture on the use of acquired skills, and the influence of a wide variety of other factors, make it progressively more difficult to be specific about the impact of training. Ultimately, one looks at progressive improvement in corporate performance, and can attempt some judgement of the influences which have contributed to change, which will include training.

Apart from the effectiveness of the training itself, we should also analyse time. Many training courses are longer than necessary. (Some are designed that way to justify the price being charged.) With in-house training, there is no justification for padding and, because the training is designed to meet the specified needs of a known population, the content and format can be tailored to concentrate on essential material, to stretch the participants and to minimize the time required. Time is a critical cost element, as training costs should really include the total remuneration costs of participants while away from their jobs. Almost any factor which will reduce training duration (but not reduce training effectiveness) will provide cost improvement.

14

Managing Manpower Losses and Excess Inventory

Excessive loss of employees is of great concern to the manpower planner and to the business. There is no point in expending great effort to attract, develop and train people who will not stay with the organization. This is especially true for people with key skills of critical importance to achieving business objectives, for it is likely to place those objectives at risk.

Analysis of manpower turnover

Losses are important to the company in that each individual who leaves takes with him a knowledge of the company and of his job which can rarely be replaced from outside. The impact of turnover is a reduction in efficiency, even when a new appointment is made immediately.

It is important to the company to know and understand its manpower turnover situation. To begin to do this, it must understand the character and mix of its workforce for any overall 'turnover index' to be useful. It is essential to go into detail, to be aware of the rates of loss for each type and category of staff, and to assess those figures in relation to the current population in each category. For example, a high proportion of recent recruits is likely to reflect a higher than average turnover.

The formula most generally used to express turnover is:

$$\text{Annual manpower turnover} = \frac{\text{Leavers over 12 months} \times 100}{\text{Average manpower over same period}}\%$$

In making calculations of likely future loss rates, normal retirements may be treated separately as they are, of course, certainties.

Statistically calculated loss rates for all other employees can be built up gradually, together with trend lines, and become progressively more meaningful and useful. From these analyses, we can make forecasts of expected loss rates with increasing accuracy, given sufficient detail of existing employees in the categories of interest.

Manpower turnover seems to follow reasonably clear patterns, although these do fluctuate with changes in supply and demand. This makes it possible to forecast probable future loss rates for most categories. In general, most categories of lower grade employees have high early loss rates. People decide very quickly whether or not they like the work, the company or their supervisor and leave almost immediately if they are dissatisfied. If they have come into a training programme, the drop-out rate may be very high in the first days and weeks. The first few days, then, are critical. If the individuals can be encouraged to settle immediately, they may stay for life. If not, they will look elsewhere immediately. Statistical analysis produces a picture showing the heavy loss rate during the initial period, and then a reduction until it reaches a plateau of steady loss.

A very similar pattern is found in the losses of new graduates, although the peak occurs about 18 months after recruitment, around the time when first assignments come to an end. It seems that many graduates believe that they should collect several companies on their c.v.s at an early stage, and that a good time to move is between assignments. Companies which make the effort to involve graduates in the choice of their next assignment at an early stage can reduce this loss rate considerably. The same thing applies at the three-year stage, when they have completed their second assignments.

Once a pattern is established as the norm for a category, it can be applied directly to forecasting future loss rates for that category and taken into account in recruiting programmes. But be careful if you ease up on recruitment because, shortly afterwards, the loss rate of employees from the category will also ease up since there will be fewer very short-service employees.

Of course, statistics do not need to be on an annual basis. As appropriate, rates can be worked out on data for a month or a quarter, but these may suffer from short-term fluctuations. Weekly or monthly updates which provide a running average based on the latest quarter will quickly highlight changes in a trend or norm if you are keeping a close watch on leavers. Remember that, in most categories, data for employees with short service are likely to produce different figures from data covering long-service employees.

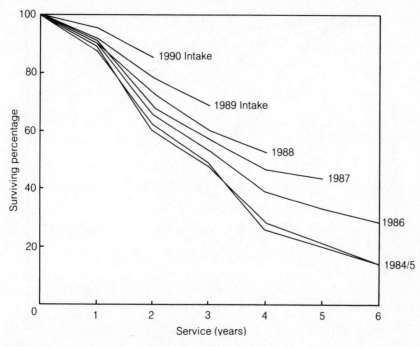

Figure 14.1   Retention of graduate intake cohorts

Another valuable way of presenting manpower losses is to change the emphasis from the negative view of who has gone to the positive look at who has stayed. Survival rates have to be based on intake cohorts – groups of similar employees who joined the organization at roughly the same time and in the same category. Figure 14.1 shows the steadily improving retention of the cohorts of graduates recruited over a number of years, while figure 14.2 reflects increasing competition for young accountants, the cohorts again consisting of annual intakes.

No turnover analyses have much to contribute to our knowledge of retention when focused on a single position, but bring in fifty trainee assemblers a quarter, on a regular basis, and efforts to improve the survival rate by better selection and training can be clearly demonstrated. One calculation used in association with this approach is to measure the half-life of the category: for how long do we manage to retain at least 50 per cent of the intake? If that period is too short and can be extended as a result of retention actions, the effort can be financially significant.

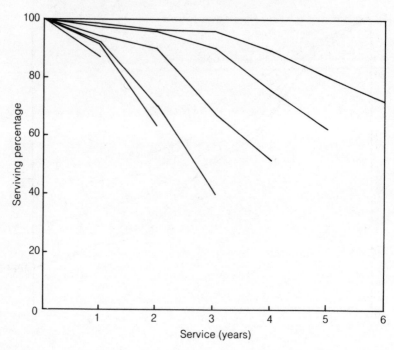

Figure 14.2 Deteriorating retention of cohorts of young accountants

Age may be a factor in loss rates for some categories. Older recruits may tend to be more stable. A simple age/service scattergraph of the category under review will highlight this quickly, and may point to a desirable improvement in the recruitment specification. I have seen this occur within a group of semi-skilled assemblers, where the loss rate of women under 30 was nearly three times that for older women. By encouraging intake from the older group, the losses were minimized.

An analysis of the age versus grade distribution of losses, when compared with the total company age versus grade picture may show, for example, that a high proportion of the younger men in the higher grades are leaving. Such a finding would suggest important losses of high calibre people and clearly should lead to a closer study. A straightforward age/salary comparison of leavers against the total population may be used to check this same point, where the overlay of leavers can be seen to be excessively from the high end of the salary distribution at younger ages.

Parallel analyses may show proportionately heavy losses from various groups, some of which are likely to be known but others may have been unsuspected. Identification is the first step towards attacking the problem.

Termination patterns vary substantially for different categories of employee, and also with variations in the economic climate. Taking job category first, as we move from manual workers through into technical and then managerial categories, losses of very short-service groups become increasingly rare. Senior individuals do not like to have very quick changes in their personal histories. However, after 18 months to two and a half years' service there can be a reasonable claim to have completed a job well and be seeking new opportunities not available internally. Careful analysis may show up a second, lower peak at about three to four years, coinciding with completion of a second job. After this, the varying length of job cycles gradually smooths out into a progressively lower loss rate. This pattern is most pronounced at the graduate intake levels, but is recognizable up through the executive levels of the company. Benefits gradually lock in longer serving managers and moves become fewer.

Why people leave

People leave jobs for many reasons. The most commonly quoted is still leaving for more money, but that is rarely the trigger which leads an individual to search for another job. It is well worth making an analysis of reasons for leaving. Identifying the factors that influence turnover through carefully run interviews with those about to leave, provides a basis for estimating future trends and taking action to alter those trends. Depending on the findings, these actions may include changing company salary levels and benefits or altering supervisory or company style to make the working environment more attractive. However, the quality of interviewing is critical, as leavers tend to be rather reticent about their real reasons for looking outside.

A study made of two neighbouring and near-identical plants showed the one with the higher pay levels having the highest turnover levels. Investigation revealed substantial differences in supervistory style, with heavy handed, authoritarian supervisors in the higher paying unit virtually driving good employees out of the door and blaming low wage levels for their plight.

Almost the only significant reason for seeking other employment is dissatisfaction in some form with the existing job. While this will occasionally be money related, it is more usual to find that it is dissatisfaction with the job itself, or with the way it is supervised or required to be done, or with the perceived absence of prospects of advancing to higher level posts.

If the work is below the capacity of the job holder, he is likely to become bored and uninterested, perform poorly and seek other employment. A surprising number of jobs are over specified, by which I mean that the recruiting specification is set at too high a level so that appointees tend to be qualified to handle higher level work. This is acceptable only where a company is using a particular post as an entry or induction level, with rapid subsequent progress to a higher level. Good examples of these are graduate entry positions. If individuals get stuck in entry posts, they will leave quickly. Graduate losses usually tend to reach a peak around 18 months after recruitment, as individuals complete first assignments and cannot see early and attractive moves ahead.

Another particularly important influence on turnover is corporate culture – the way we do things around here – and the fit of employee attitudes to that culture. If people are at ease with the way things are done, gain satisfaction from their personal efforts, and have some confidence that their ambitions can be met in the company, it is less likely that they will feel the need to seek other employment.

If culture inhibits someone from doing a job in the way he thinks it can be done best, and where he sees his performance limited by silly regulations or outdated traditions, he may choose to go and work elsewhere. This is likely to become a stronger trend as younger managers and professional staff – and indeed, employees generally – become steadily more concerned with life-style and personal respect. Managers will need to lead and motivate subordinates more positively through the 1990s to minimize avoidable losses.

An extraordinarily damaging change occurs when graduate recruitment is stopped for a year or two. In the event of a turndown in business and some redundancies, it may appear sensible to trim recruitment. However, the graduate intake is a key element in a very important flow. If there is no intake to take over the jobs of the graduates who are completing their first year, they cannot be released for the second year jobs, and so on through the early parts of the flow.

The impact of this is immediate frustration and a hunt for alternative jobs in which the individuals can advance. They have become ready to progress and the absence of opportunity in one company will not stop them, thus seriously damaging the internal flows in the company they leave. Proper management of this situation requires ongoing graduate recruitment combined with some deliberate weeding out throughout all levels of the structure to control the selection of leavers.

Unfortunately, we do not want to retain all employees with equal determination, and there will be some categories in which steady wastage is required, such as where people have skills which are becoming obsolete. Such people tend to hold on tightly if there is little alternative work available and, if retraining or redeployment are not options, possible they may need to be encouraged to leave.

Control means that you must look critically at individuals who are becoming less effective and are not responding to encouragement. A vulnerable category is middle management, a level which is being greatly affected by changing organization and management skills. If individuals do get stuck in the middle levels, it may be because they lack the potential to adjust to changing needs, or because there are no openings.

In a large manufacturing organization, generations of super-intendents and managers were appointed during their early 30s and were high performers, but the way ahead was blocked for ten years. Almost all of them stayed in one post for that period, but their growth was stunted and none made a successful transition to the next level once the way forward began to clear. Somehow, some means of opening higher level positions should have been found to enable the best of them to continue their advance. There cannot be absolute rights to ownership of any job, especially when there are strong competing candidates and the overall management quality of the organization is placed at risk.

A similar problem occurs with air stewardesses' jobs, which are seen by many airlines as young persons' jobs. There has to be a career transfer point which is clearly communicated at the time of appointment and properly operated, to provide other work opportunities, thereby maintaining the outflow.

Ready to move

Of all our employees, the ones most likely to be lost are those who are on top of their present jobs and are beginning to look for a new challenge. If there is no indication of that new assignment developing internally, they will be interested in external opportunites and are vulnerable to an attractive offer. As these individuals are likely to be amongst the best of our people, losing them by simple neglect is foolish, or worse.

Any retention policy needs to identify the people you can least afford to lose. This list would include your key top people, those identified as able to suceed them, and all other individuals of high potential. It would overlap with a listing of people with essential corporate competences or skills.

Human resource strategies should spotlight these people, and any reasons for their possible disenchantment need immediate attention. While pay is the most visible cause of dissatisfaction, it is almost certain that the real concerns for this group will focus on career development opportunities, the interest being shown in their growth, the existence and implementation of agreed personal development, and involvement in discussing possible next assignments, especially as readiness increases. This discussion and involvement indicate company flexibility in selecting attractive opportunities in good time, and is inclined to ensure that all but the most exceptional external approaches are shrugged off with cool indifference.

As a personnel director, one essential piece of paper on top of my desk was the list of key people approaching readiness to move. It might as well have had an action-this-day stamp on it, because it attracted attention daily. Inevitably, there is the occasional loss from the list and each justifies an open-minded investigation. I have been astonished over the years at how many times the highly regarded key (but departing) figure has changed overnight into someone the company is relieved to see go. While this may conceal embarrassment, it does little to sound a warning of what may be a serious problem.

Managing Excess Inventory

In an era of 'downsizing' or 'rightsizing', many organizations are facing situations where they have more employees than they need or will need. Some of this results from a general tightening of manning standards and removal of excess layers, some is being generated by office automation and some by business changes.

The 1970s and 1980s saw major changes in manning associated with production automation; the 1990s will see office automation bite deeply. Many companies which feel that they have already been through that phase will find that they have taken only the first small step – like the major insurance group which is half-way through a three-year programme to install its next generation of information processing systems but now realizes that it must take out in excess of 20 per cent of its total staff as a result, despite considerable business growth and a tight control of recruitment.

Perhaps the advantage this group has is that it has recognized the implications and has planned to handle it. Many managements think solely in terms of the installation of equipment and systems, and put aside the staffing issues until later. This sometimes happens even where questions about resultant savings are answered with clear statements which justify the capital expenditure by resulting manpower savings.

In practice, it is always possible to build up a set of assumptions and to see the form and scale of manpower change in situations like this. Apart from the overall numbers, which may not be precise, the plan will identify the changes in skill requirements and changes in physical location involved, which may require extensive planning to implement, and without which, the millions spent on equipment and systems cannot be utilized. As is inevitably the case, it will be the people who make it possible to achieve the goals.

This particular example is not rare or unique. Very many of the technology changes which reduce the required manpower levels have a reasonable lead time which enable a full range of options to be considered. Redundancy is not the only answer and the next section is concerned with the range of options open to manpower planners.

First and foremost, we want to continue to employ all or most of the existing workforce if this is practicable. These people know the company and have expertise, much of which we may prefer not to lose. Certainly they have advantages over new employees who have to get used to the company from scratch. So we should examine seriously the possibilities of retraining and redeployment and only consider redundancy as an expensive last resort, though sometimes unavoidable.

Retraining and redeployment

Redeployment – employment of existing manpower on alternative work – may be possible without retraining but, usually, some form of preparation for new work will be necessary.

Straightforward redeployment opportunities occur when a different part of the organization has an immediate need for exactly the skills which are becoming available. Within a large group, central co-ordination of all vacancies at times of cut-back may delay the filling of some positions marginally, but it enables all available internl candidates to be given first consideration and this can be very important if there is a threat of redundancy.

A more normal situation is that the people being released are from jobs that cease to exist due to product or technology change and there is no identical work within the organization. In this case we need a breakdown of the skills used in the old jobs for comparison with analyses of the skills required in other jobs for which there is an ongoing demand. The objective is to match the required skills or skill types as closely as possible, to establish job opportunities for which retraining is a practical and acceptable course.

For example, one company found a close match between the skills used by fitters and tool-makers, whose work was in decline, and the skill requirements for other positions such as some categories of computer programmer. They took an experimental batch of potentially redundant tool-makers and put them through an intensive two-week conversion course which identified that more than half would be fully able to cope with the more extended retraining course, and allowed the others to drop back into their old jobs. In this way, the company gradually reduced the manning levels in the declining areas on a controlled basis and provided a supply of good, trainable people to feed into the new technology areas. The enthusiasm of the people making the conversation was a major factor in the success of the programme, although none had previously considered careers in the areas to which they transferred.

It was the careful use of skills analysis which opened up this retraining avenue. Significantly, it was not an expected or natural career route and the secret was, undoubtedly, in adopting an open-minded, experimental approach, which paid off handsomely.

Another example is less dramatic, but socially significant. The company was running down its heavier mechanical work and developing far more light engineering subassembly work. The former was traditionally men's work; the latter, women's work. Offered the alternatives of redundancy, or similarly graded and paid subassembly work, numbers of men began to accept the traditionally female jobs and, after some initial unease expressed by both sexes, quickly settled in as competent performers.

A lot of retraining involves updating or adapting existing skills to new ideas or technological advance. While individuals have a responsibility to themselves for keeping up to date, this is not always possible, and the company must create both the environment and the opportunity to keep knowledge and experience in line with the developing needs of the company.

There is one further option to consider under this heading. It is possible, as an extreme measure to avoid redundancy in some situations, to find a means of utilizing people who are not ideal. This may involve restructuring some jobs into a non-ideal form to enable work to be done by non-ideal people, e.g. partial deskilling of jobs to enable lesser skilled people to be employed. While this may be workable, it must be recognized that it may have employee relations implications, may prove more expensive, and cannot be recommended as a normal action. However, I have seen this approach used to overcome an identified skill shortage, with the full co-operation of employee representatives.

Redundancy

Once redundancy becomes inevitable, a clear strategy is essential, to give as much choice to those affected as possible. Of course, there is little scope for flexibility if a total closure is involved but, even then, it is worth involving all of the people in a review of the situation and the possible options to convince them of the logic and inevitability of the closure before getting on to the nuts and bolts of how it will be handled.

Where a proportion of the employees must be lost, encouragement for older people to take early retirement, and financial packages which encourage others to leave, can help in minimizing enforcement. This may be accompanied by quiet encouragement for some individuals to stay and others to leave, as the manpower planner should have identified the required new mix and level of skills and management will be endeavouring to achieve the required balance while retaining the more effective people.

Redundancy is no longer considered socially unacceptable. It will almost invariably be uncomfortable, both for the employee made redundant and the manager responsible for communicating the decision. For some, it will involve extended periods of hardship since, in a world of rapid technological and other change, some skills have simply become obsolete. Other individuals, with few skills or abilities, have difficulty fitting into a world of more thinking jobs and progressively fewer unskilled positions. Service industries are increasing, but service jobs require customer orientated service attitudes which are not easily developed in middle life. This leaves some redundant people inadequate, frustrated and, perhaps, not retrainable for available work within their categories.

However, there are some people who look back on their redundancy with a sense of relief. They could, for example, have been retained in lower grades and less satisfying jobs, and become very dissatisfied. The decision to make them redundant jolted them out of their complacent acceptance and set them off on an aggressive and successful search for a job more in line with their abilities, which they now enjoy.

I once had to counsel a man whose original job has disappeared and who, out of compassion, had been retained by the company without a proper job. Although his security was guaranteed, he had suffered a nervous breakdown, thinking he would never have a worthwhile role in the future. We agreed a basis for parting company and got down jointly to the task of seeking a new job outside the group. The immediate impact was a restoration of self-respect and, remarkably soon, a suitable external appointment.

From that time, I have not been frightened by redundancy situations. Two things are essential, though: fair, even generous, financial treatment of those who must be affected, with the option to volunteer if there can be any choice; and absolute commitment to help and guide redundant employees to seek out, apply for and hopefully get offers of other jobs. This direct assistance, through to the point where they can take up new appointments, should be accepted as an essential part of the releasing company's manpower policy and practice which, in my view, cannot be wholly subcontracted to an outplacement agency.

Redundancy terms fall outside the scope of this book. In any case, I cannot deal adequately with them here as they vary too much for generalization. The basis of the package will probably need to be influenced by company requirements. If extended notice is being given (and the longest reasonable warning should be given), bonus payments for staying on until the company's work requirements are met should be considered, to guarantee that the required workforce is available and assist in planning run-down phasings. In other situations, bonuses may be paid to encourage immediate or speedy departure, but these situations should be rare because they indicate inadequate planning.

Some redundancies will be enforced because a plant is closing down, but other instances can arise from cut-back in manpower levels and leave a degree of choice open to employees. In these siutations, encouragement of volunteers can reduce or even remove the pressure. The opportunity to retire early, on a pension, or to collect a sizeable sum with which to launch a small business can be highly attractive to some employees. In practice you may find an excess of volunteers and a need to be selective about who you release.

The need for careful counselling is as important among this group of volunteers as with enforced leavers. We need to be sure that volunteers are absolutely clear about their intentions and subsequent rights. Advice on the problems of a new small business should not be excluded from the service.

For enforced redundancies, and particularly plant closures, generous and sympathetic guidance and help are essential. Once closure is accepted, the objective is to open the way to alternative work opportunities. We need to advise people on local work opportunities, or lack of them, together with other options. We need to open an employment office on our premises, and get other company recruiting staff to use that facility. We may need to provide guidance on alternative careers, on retraining opportunities, including adult training and other full-time courses. We need to give guidance on being interviewed to long-service people. In summary, we need to provide a full range of personal services for the people affected, run, if the numbers are significant, by a project manager committed solely to that task.

Core and Temporary Employment Contracts

In planning our future manning structures, it is likely that the concept of essential core staff plus a range of other categories will become normal, and defining the requirements in each category will be a necessary part of the manpower plan. As the concept gains acceptance, we shall identify a central core of employees as the permanent workforce required to cover the essential base work-load. Permanent will not necessarily mean on the payroll, because another aspect of future employment contracts will be that numbers of specialists will be employed on a retainer-on-call basis, being brought in as and when their particular skills are required. The way legal and some human resource specialists are used is a good example of this.

All other activity will be covered by a variable number of temporary employees. Temporary may be the wrong word for many of these people because they may develop long service, but there will be differences between their employment contracts and those of core staff. The purpose of the temporary category will be to provide the flexibility required in manning levels, particularly in businesses where rapid change may result in much sharper fluctuations in the demand for products or services. Employment contracts will need to define this fact and the terms applicable to short-time work or lay-off.

This approach is not popular with employees as it offers less security, but it does reflect the commercial realities where work volumes are likely to become more variable. The practice is likely to become more common in those industries most open to rapid technological or product design change. It is also an option where a decline in the required workforce is foreseen but additional people are required in the short term. Then the established workforce can be safeguarded and is likely to support the strategy of utilizing temporary help.

Allocation to categories will be more complex than is implied by core and temporary, because we are already seeing a pattern where a rising proportion of essential services is subcontracted to specialist suppliers, and where many high level functional specialists are moving into professional groups comparable with finance and legal partnerships to provide services as though they were in-house team members or employees. Questions of turnover in these groups may present fresh questions for manpower management.

15

Management Continuity: Changing Management Specifications

Managerial activity, after having been relatively static in content and style historically, has begun to change dramatically in recent years and the pace of that change is increasing. A number of influences are transforming the activities and specification of the effective manager. By the end of the 1990s, managers who have failed to respond to these influences will find themselves being swept away by a new breed of manager which understands fully that manpower resources play a vital role in providing competitive advantage and that to utilize them best demands inspired leadership rather than the traditional 'I command, you obey' approach.

The term, manager, here refers to all positions with titles, from chairman, director or manager through to supervisor. I also deliberately include those specialist individuals who may not manage people directly, but manage a function or functional activity or specialist area, and are part of the management process of an organization. As organizations evolve, these specialists will become increasingly important in managing the business.

It is now essential for companies to evaluate the effect of these influences and begin to update their management resourcing strategies, adjusting graduate and other recruitment specifications and the emphasis in management development and training to ensure that their managers are prepared for the future.

Few companies are focusing clearly on these changes as yet. There is a widespread feeling of impending change, which has prompted many human resource people to initiate reviews of the competences which they need. Regrettably, much of this analysis has concentrated on idealistic competency structures. Other companies have focused on the future, but have involved large cross-sections of line management in the reviews. In general, these studies have produced views with an 18-month horizon related to concrete changes which are firmly in next year's budgets, and which are ultra conservative about longer-term changes in managerial roles.

There is no effective short cut. It is necessary to use visionary individuals from within an organization to develop a realistic scenario of longer term changes, perhaps with some outside help. This scenario has then to be sold to the more open-minded senior opinion formers in the organization as a preliminary to generating positive discussion of the aspects of potential change.

The scale of this potential change is so great that some managers can be expected to close their minds and reject it on the basis that nothing like it has happened before.

Impending change

There is an enormous volume of change in the world, some of which will have an impact on what a manager is, what he will do, and how he will do it. Think-tank sessions have produced extensive lists of expected changes which could influence managerial practice. These are described in detail in chapter 1 but can be summarized as follows:

- Business environment changes will demand managers with much wider knowledge of overall business operations.
- Product/manufacturing technology developments will call for managers to be more technologically aware.
- *Knowledge* is expanding exponentially, presenting managers with the task of being more selective, while ensuring that key data are not overlooked.
- The IT revolution will take away one of the main justifications for hierarchical management structures.
- Social change is a strong factor in the move towards more open and participative management styles and organisation.
- *Organization* structures are becoming much flatter with broad spans of control, and some have progressed further into cellular structures.
- Corporate core competences will become more overtly linked to achieving the corporate vision and competitive advantage.

Profiles of Future Managers

It is the accumulation of these various influences which produces the profile of the future manager. Any one of the influences would have a dramatic effect, but the coming together of this entire range within a short period of time will generate a radical change.

Many human resource people are becoming aware of some of these developing influences and have put great effort into identifying the competences required now. They have become embroiled in the difficulties of terminology and of defining and structuring generic competences. In doing so, they have generally overlooked the key issue of trends to the future – the essential first stage – and finish with, at best, an incomplete picture with a short-term horizon.

What a manager does, the way he does it and the way he fits into the organizational relationships, as well as the skills and qualities he needs to be effective in the particular situation, can be determined. While the range of these competences may be quite complex, it is possible to define the person specification or profile required for an existing or proposed management position without great difficulty.

The process of defining the requirements of future managerial jobs would be straightforward if the enterprise had a clear picture of the business environment, business objectives, organization shape, systems and operating style within which the future positions will exist. In reality, the pace of change of virtually all the influences which will shape each job make that projection difficult. However, the top management of the enterprise should have a clear vision of its future objectives and likely evolution within the developing business environment, and, if the full range of potential influences on the requirements from future managerial jobs is understood, then the best available scenario can be assembled. From this, a picture of future managers in that situation can be determined. The quality of this process is aided by the extent to which most influences have already developed in some situations, so that the emerging picture is based more on realities than on theory.

The vision required from a manager

Japanese companies frequently have visions which look 20 years or more ahead, and well beyond the potential of current resources. The purpose of the vision is to indicate the broad direction, against which all opportunties can be assessed as they occur. A clear understanding of the vision must, therefore, have been communicated to all managers likely to take longer term decisions, so that the pattern of decisions conforms to the vision.

Within a corporate vision, it is a key part of every manager's job to visualize the future of his own activities. We expect him, as a minimum, to produce a detailed budget for the coming year and contribute to the corporate five-year plan, but hope for a more creative and wider ranging participation.

Analysis of the implementation of five-year plans suggests that there is generally a reasonable degree of accuracy in the projections for the first 18 to 24 months, when much of the change is already built into firm commitments and the manager has something concrete on which to base his planning. It is evident that beyond the 18-month horizon, the level of certainty drops sharply, and many forecasts of the extent of change become far more conservative. Only the exceptional line managers will have a deeper understanding of emerging influences, and it is up to them to develop a wider scenario and to examine the potential impact. This can be used to develop a more general understanding of the future business.

The vision required from a manager cannot be restricted to those business factors currently having an impact. It must also relate to possible future changes in every aspect of his environment which may affect the work he does and the way he manages.

Competences of the new species

Profiles of future managers will vary between companies and countries, between different types of jobs and between different levels. For this reason, no universal profile can be produced. However, there will be some common threads in the pattern, and the three factors which my research suggests will most significantly increase in importance are interpersonal and leadership skills, intellect and computer literacy.

Interpersonal and leadership skills The arrival of the new species will see the final demise of those traditional managers who have been able to command only on the basis of their position in the hierarchy, their official rank or status. They have not been respected by their staff, and may have lacked the essential knowledge, interpersonal skills or general ability to handle their responsibilities competently. In all probability they have reinforced their power over subordinates by withholding information. Adopting a remote and superior stance, they have managed in the classic 'I command, you obey' mode, and faithfully served those above them who managed in the same manner.

As command/obedience becomes obsolete and largely disappears, very few of these managers will adapt and survive. Entrepreneurs building their own small companies may provide a residual base for survivors.

The combined influence of changing social attitudes and developments in information management on organizations and on management style will switch selection of managers almost to election by subordinates. A manager will need to be accepted and respected by his work group if he is to lead effectively, and their judgements will be based on a combination of his professional competence and his skills with people.

The vital importance of interpersonal skills has long been recognized by leading companies. Organizations such as IBM expect their managers to spend one week every year training to enhance these skills. The virtual absence of training in interpersonal skills in other companies says something specific about their cultures and valuation of their human resources.

The future manager's skill in dealing with people will need to be of a high order because he will have little hierarchical authority and must depend on his abilities to lead and inspire. He will need to develop skills which enable him to lead able people acceptably, to communicate fully and openly, to motivate and bring out the best contributions from people. These qualities will be essential to effective managerial performance in a non-authoritarian style.

Existing managers will have to learn that, to remain effective, they must gain acceptance from those they lead rather than just exercise their authority.

Intellect   In general, the intellectual level of managers is well above the average for the population at large, but there is a substantial variation between those managers.

It is evident that the intellectual demands on managers are increasing, which may mean that the intellectual cut-off point for really effective managers will rise to a higher level. This is due to the increasing volume of knowledge and business data, plus specialist inputs, flooding in to them, which they must assess and act on. In turn, this will make greater demands on analytical and decision-making skills. Inability to handle and assess this volume will limit the individual's career prospects.

Reliable judgements of the intellectual capacity of potential managers will need to be based on psychometric tests because it is already evident today that a proportion of highly articulate managers have acquired contemporary jargon and persuasive manners, yet, under probing, reveal a lack of real comprehension of many issues and an inability to arrive at logical decisions.

The volume and complexity of new knowledge available to managers will increase enormously. They must be able to select relevant information, understand and interpret it in relation to the total business. This will demand a highly developed intellect and may highlight the limitations of the less able existing managers.

All managers will need to understand the detailed workings of the total business, the contributions made by the various functions, and the workings of the environment in which the business exists. For generalists, understanding the potential of contributions from each function, and the ability to comprehend the business significance of their inputs, will be vital.

For functional or specialist managers, the ability to grasp the value of inputs from other specialisms, so that one's own input is logical and balanced, will be vital. In the end, the differences in the knowledge and ability requirements for general and specialist (line and staff) managers will not be notably different, and each will be intellectually demanding.

Computer literacy All managers will need to acquire keyboard skills and be at ease with the manipulation of large volumes of data through personal work-stations.

Most managers under 35 acquired keyboard skills at schools and universities; their elders should be able to acquire keyboard skills and operate increasingly user-friendly terminals without too much difficulty. They must come to understand the volume and form of material in the expanding corporate database, and in other sources, and how to access and manipulate these data to provide the comprehensive analyses required as a basis for decision making. So, computer literate will mean being able to access and utilize the database, in the way that literacy means being able to access and utilize written material.

Other factors Clearly, this is not a complete list of future competences, it is just a selection of three which will become far more significant. It seems evident that managerial competences will not suffer a sudden catastrophic change, but they have been evolving steadily for some time and the emphasis on several of them will change rather more rapidly over this decade.

The extent of these changes will vary widely between companies. The broad influences listed provide guidance on the issues to be evaluated within an organization, so that the scale of applicable change can be determined in each situation.

Recruitment and Career Development

Growing and developing future managers has always been a demanding task, requiring thought, planning and dedicated guidance over extended periods. This complex activity has not previously had to cope with a change in its end product on the scale currently faced; now, in a single decade, the way in which the vast numbers of existing managers function must be redirected. In addition to this formidable challenge, the next generation of new managers must be recruited and initiated.

Further, the whole shape of reward management, from motivational reward, through career advancement, to basic remuneration practices, will need to be adapted to fresh criteria.

In all this change, there are enormous opportunities for the evolution of human resource policies and practices which enable companies to achieve huge advantages over competitors by attracting, holding and giving free rein to the best people.

Graduate recruitment, as our major source of future managers, needs to be influenced now by the emerging profiles, in particular by recognizing the future need for the high standards of interpersonal skills.

Career development and training must place greater emphasis on the development of these skills now, and increase awareness of the changes which are emerging so that established managers have maximum warning of the adjustments which many of them will need to make over the next few years.

Remuneration

It is premature to plan changes in remuneration structures and policies, but the indications are that traditional grading structures will be discarded. Valuations of the new managers will shift to measures of the ability of individuals to contribute to the business, based on their specialist or general management knowledge, ability to relate that knowledge to business requirements or opportunities, and personal ability to articulate and argue a case.

Hierarchical factors will be as irrelevant to remuneration as they will be to organization. Differentials which have been related to levels in the corporate structure will be replaced by relative value of contributions. This will sometimes result in high individual remuneration deep in the organization, quite possibly exceeding payments to managers of clusters of specialists. It will not follow that the specialist who contributes most should be made leader of the group because this may reduce the input of his specialist abilities and thereby reduce his effective value.

Conclusion

Awareness of these developments, and assessments of the required pace of response are of vital concern to corporate managements as they plan for longer term continuity. Strategies and actions within corporate business visions and plans must also strongly influence the shaping of management development programmes in all organizations.

16

Management Continuity: Planning Management Succession

Above a certain organizational level, manpower planning ceases to be concerned with questions of numbers by category, and becomes concerned with individual positions and individual incumbents. There may be some associated numbers for the purposes of the business plan but for real planning we need to put aside those numbers and get down to the detail. And as the detail directly involves all top managers in the organization at a personal level, this is inevitably a different type of exercise and some parts are highly confidential.

Succession planning is covered in some detail in my book *Practical Management Development* and I do not propose to cover the same ground here. However, it is relevant to describe the general approach to planning management succession, and to comment on how succession may be handled with flexibility in a business environment involving rapid changes.

Future Requirements

As explained earlier, it is important to have a clear view of where the company is heading and what its objectives are, to ensure that the envisaged future organization and management staffing are relevant to that future. The previous chapter reinforced this requirement by examining some of the influences for change in the structure and content of managerial jobs which will have an impact during the 1990s, and examined some of the ways in which those influences will alter the mix of competences required from our future managers. These changes may appear marginal until they are examined carefully within your own business. Then, you will find the need to begin to alter recruitment specifications now against the requirements you anticipate later.

In the same way, it is appropriate to give thought to the likely shape of your organization, and the associated corporate culture, which will be relevant through the final years of this century. Your developing organization is likely to be quite different from the one you used through the 1980s.

Further, you will need to consider the extent to which you might progress towards establishing a core staff, making greater use of retained external specialists, and using temporary or part-time people, or home-workers, to handle the rest. Interesting manpower planning questions arise at every level, but top-level manning remains the most complex and demanding.

Management Succession: The Classic Approach

Management continuity planning focuses most strongly on the top levels of the enterprise, where succession to the top management group itself is particularly important, but this slice represents no more than the tip of the iceberg. Continuity and effective resourcing are important at every level of the organization, but management succession is concerned with individual positions and people throughout the management structure. Succession is to do with the passing of responsibilities from one generation to the next, ensuring that every management position is filled with a competent individual at all times and that suitably prepared heirs and spares are available when a planned requirement is scheduled, and having cover in emergencies.

Management continuity or succession planning is a major concern in the manpower supply planning process. I described this review process as the master programme within resourcing and development activities because it is concerned both with short-term management deployment and with the longer term (three to five and five to ten year) projections, integrating organization development and manpower deployment with business development in the changing environment. In addition, it is concerned with ensuring effective resourcing and continuity of management and provides an occasion to assess the effectiveness of management development policies and strategies.

Succession planning, then, is essentially part of the wider ranging and ongoing manpower planning process. In this process, the corporate vision of the future, the business objectives, the scenario of changing environment, corporate systems and culture are 'translated' into required organization structures and management specifications, at a series of points in time, and into supporting human resource strategies. The review brings together these requirements and the inventory of individual managers – their diverse abilities and degrees of effectiveness, rates of growth, career preferences, and so on – to match the supply of people with the requirements or demand. The periodic succession plan report records this process (as a snapshot of current thinking at one point in time) and provides a basis for a subsequent audit of progress.

Succession plans aim to ensure the continuity and depth of high level competence in management throughout the organization. They indicate the required structure and manning options over the time-scale of the plan, but these options remain open until appointment decision points are reached to allow the forecasts of management requirements and the track records and suitability of possible successors to be reviewed before the final selection is made.

Present organization and appointments provide the starting point for discussion and review of the plan. These are often set out in stratified organization charts which summarize the information available on each position and person. Figure 16.1 shows an example of such a succession planning chart. When discussions take place, the relevant individual development plans and more detailed personnel data should be readily available. Subsequent stages of the plan should also be set out in chart form where possible, as the pictorical representation highlights the changing organization shape.

The Management Continuity Report

The management continuity report is either a summary of deliberations which have taken place over several months, or a snapshot at a single point in time of the current stage in a continuous process. Its evolution should follow the sequence detailed in chapter 9 on manpower supply planning, so that the top level plan represents the top slice of extensive activity down through the organization. In the plan, there may be some current manning problems, but the main emphasis will be on the longer term and the adequacy of the

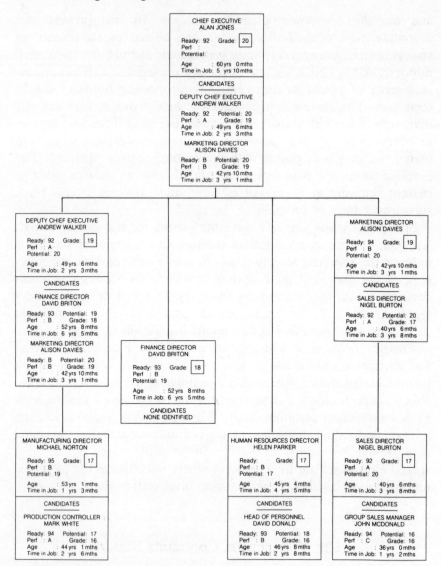

CHIEF EXECUTIVE
ALAN JONES

Ready: 92   Grade: 20
Perf   :
Potential:

Age   : 60 yrs 0 mths
Time in Job: 5 yrs 10 mths

CANDIDATES

DEPUTY CHIEF EXECUTIVE
ANDREW WALKER

Ready: 92   Potential: 20
Perf : A   Grade: 19
Age   : 49 yrs 6 mths
Time in Job: 2 yrs 3 mths

MARKETING DIRECTOR
ALISON DAVIES

Ready: B   Potential: 20
Perf : B   Grade: 19
Age   : 42 yrs 10 mths
Time in Job: 3 yrs 1 mths

DEPUTY CHIEF EXECUTIVE
ANDREW WALKER

Ready: 92   Grade: 19
Perf : A
Potential: 20

Age   : 49 yrs 6 mths
Time in Job: 2 yrs 3 mths

CANDIDATES

FINANCE DIRECTOR
DAVID BRITON

Ready: 93   Potential: 19
Perf : B   Grade: 18
Age   : 52 yrs 8 mths
Time in Job: 6 yrs 5 mths

MARKETING DIRECTOR
ALISON DAVIES

Ready: B   Potential: 20
Perf : B   Grade: 19
Age   : 42 yrs 10 mths
Time in Job: 3 yrs 1 mths

MARKETING DIRECTOR
ALISON DAVIES

Ready: 94   Grade: 19
Perf : B
Potential: 20

Age   : 42 yrs 10 mths
Time in Job: 3 yrs 1 mths

CANDIDATES

SALES DIRECTOR
NIGEL BURTON

Ready: 92   Potential: 20
Perf : A   Grade: 17
Age   : 40 yrs 6 mths
Time in Job: 3 yrs 8 mths

FINANCE DIRECTOR
DAVID BRITON

Ready: 93   Grade: 18
Perf : B
Potential: 19

Age   : 52 yrs 8 mths
Time in Job: 6 yrs 5 mths

CANDIDATES
NONE IDENTIFIED

MANUFACTURING DIRECTOR
MICHAEL NORTON

Ready: 95   Grade: 17
Perf : B
Potential: 19

Age   : 53 yrs 1 mths
Time in Job: 1 yrs 3 mths

CANDIDATES

PRODUCTION CONTROLLER
MARK WHITE

Ready: 94   Potential: 17
Perf : A   Grade: 16
Age   : 44 yrs 1 mths
Time in Job: 2 yrs 6 mths

HUMAN RESOURCES DIRECTOR
HELEN PARKER

Ready: Grade: 17
Perf : B
Potential: 17

Age   : 45 yrs 4 mths
Time in Job: 4 yrs 5 mths

CANDIDATES

HEAD OF PERSONNEL
DAVID DONALD

Ready: 93   Potential: 18
Perf : B   Grade: 16
Age   : 46 yrs 8 mths
Time in Job: 2 yrs 8 mths

SALES DIRECTOR
NIGEL BURTON

Ready: 92   Grade: 17
Perf : A
Potential: 20

Age   : 40 yrs 6 mths
Time in Job: 3 yrs 8 mths

CANDIDATES

GROUP SALES MANAGER
JOHN MCDONALD

Ready: 94   Potential: 16
Perf : C   Grade: 16
Age   : 36 yrs 0 mths
Time in Job: 1 yrs 2 mths

Figure 16.1   Stratified succession chart

managers currently being developed through the system to meet the requirements anticipated in three to ten years' time.

The most serious fault in most succession planning is that it gets oversimplified. Managers begin to find problems with the complexity and uncertainty of assessing how they expect individuals to develop through the coming months and years and find difficulty in matching individuals with possible vacancies. They balk at adding further uncertainty in the form of changing organization and competency requirements and prefer to assume that the status quo will remain unchanged. One large company, about to introduce some radical organization change, still carried out its annual succession planning with a written assumption that no organization change would happen for ten years, believing that the succession planning task would have become impossible otherwise. At best, this approach will outline current strengths and emergency cover, and identify individuals thought capable of advancement, which provides no more than some sort of inventory, but it is of no help in determining what action is necessary to prepare people for the future or for future positions. Also, it will not give any indication of the company's ability to provide sufficient suitable people to resource a new business opportunity.

Continuity planning is virtually meaningless unless it is carried out against the best available projections of the organization's shape and management requirements in the future. The business is not going to be the same in future; the business environment is already changing and further evolution is inevitable. Because these changes are reflected in the business plan, their influence on future management requirements is visible. Many of these changes will alter the balance of skills we require in our managers, so it is essential that they are specified at the opening stage of succession planning.

In a larger corporation, the board may set out the form of the continuity report which is required from subsidiary companies as follows. It should:

1 By way of introduction, state the key management development and succession issues, noting relevant business factors and planned or likely organization changes.
2 Show succession plans for your immediate reporting line and the next level, supplemented by broad notes on planned moves for current job holders, and the preparation of individual successors. How are people to be made ready?
3 List your high potential people who do not yet appear on the top succession charts, particularly those in the 25 to 35 age group, with individual notes on your star achievers.
4 Detail the actions you have taken to improve the quality of your graduate (and other future management) intake, and to speed the progress of the most able.

To make subsequent discussions more productive, the board often asks a group management development adviser to discuss the position with the report writer and agree the key issues as the agenda for the board meeting.

It is evident from this that succession plans cannot be presented baldly and that the scene has to be set by a clear introductory statement. This introduction needs to present the ways in which the organization and management positions are expected to change during the period of the plan and demonstrate how it will resource the anticipated future requirements rather than a past structure. It has to recognize that some positions will retain the same titles, but will require drastically updated competences which may unseat incumbents. The introduction should also incorporate a statement of the anticipated future organization and, only after that, should the report get down to questions of deploying individuals.

Introduction to the continuity plan

All succession plans need to be introduced by a statement of expected changes to set the scene and lead into a clear picture of requirements at specific future points for which succession (or resourcing) must be planned. For example, the combined impact of advanced information management and changing attitudes to work and leadership will lead to flatter organization structures and alter most management jobs, independent of all other change. How will existing managers adapt to the changing demands placed on them in their present jobs? And how will the company handle individuals who will be displaced?

The introduction should give an assessment of the impact on organization and human resourcing of all business and environmental factors, and then go on to explain projected organization requirements for the next two to ten years, with forecasts of the numbers, categories and levels of managers required over that period. (Here again, the word *manager* includes all management, up to and including the chairman of the board.)

While the succession plan will be based on the business plan, with its associated scenarios and assumptions, some other options may be thought serious enough to cover with contingency plans. Possible mergers, acquisitions or disposals may also be covered, since they can have significant management implications which should be evaluated. Even a straightforward demerger can alter the management requirements significantly.

Timetable

The management development function is likely to include a review cycle along the following lines.

Month 1	Board defines issues to be given special attention.
Months 1–7	Subsidiary companies prepare draft report and briefs for review.
Months 5–7	Initial discussions between subsidiary companies and corporate management development staff to establish key issues for agenda.
Month 8	Preliminary reviews by subsidiary company board members.
Month 9–10	Final reports completed and collated for submission of succession plans to the central board.
Month 11	Board review of succession plans.
Month 12	Prepare and discuss action plans and priorities for the next cycle.

Most reviews at board level will require the succession plans from different parts of the organization to be set out concisely and in a standard format. Example 16.1 shows such a format and the associated notes for guidance are incorporated in the previous section. These forms obviously vary from company to company, largely reflecting personal preferences for layout and style.

Management Succession: Managing the Inventory

The alternative to the classic approach assumes that you can develop a scenario which defines expected change and within which you can plan the development and deployment of management resources. This approach is based on the assumptions that the classical level of detail cannot be achieved accurately enough and that, in any case, the future organization will be continually flexed such that resources are developed to the maximum degree and deployed in some optimum way at each point in time.

Although this is not truely planning, it may be necessary in rapidly developing situations, and it does seem to be an approach favoured by some companies. Both the planning and the inventory management approaches may not anticipate the requirement for a particular manpower need, and general development of the total inventory may not achieve sufficient development of some key skills

Confidential
DATE: November 1990

Organisation: Excelsior Electronics

Plans for board and management committee

Incumbent Position / In position since: (Month/Year)	(Age)	Replacement plan 1991	1992	1993	1994	1995	1996	1997	1998	1999	2000	Comments
Chairman & Chief Executive Officer Tony JONES 4/85	(61)				BOSTON (52) JONES to retire							Organised with a Chairman & Chief Executive Officer, and a President & Chief Operating Officer, the ideal structure would have one with a marketing/sales background; the other with a financial/human resources background. Boston was previously Senior VP-Marketing.
President & Chief Operating Officer Joe BOSTON 5/90	(49)				APPLEBY (56) BOSTON to Chairman							Appleby is the only internal candidate and is highly qualified for the position.
Vice-President – Finance Hank SMIT 3/83	(64)	APPLEBY (44) SMIT to retire			JENKINS (32) APPLEBY to President/COO							When Smit retires in March 1991, Appleby will become VP-Finance in preparation for his move to C.O.O.
Vice-President – Logistics Fred APPLEBY 1/88	(43)		JENKINS (35) APPLEBY to Finance		HANSON ? JENKINS to Finance							When Appleby moves to VP-Finance Jenkins will succeed him for three years, probably followed by Bill Hanson.
Vice-President – Marketing Ian MACDONALD 5/90	(43)			WILLIAMS (43) Transfer to Corporate HQ								MacDonald is one of this company's highest potential executives, and his next move is planned into corporate headquarters.
Vice-President – Human Resources Anne SLOAN 2/87	(52)											
Vice-President – Manufacturing Charles HARRISON 10/89	(56)		SCHWARTZ (49) HARRISON to retire early									Harrison should be replaced no later than mid-1992 when the current reorganisation is completed. He excels in day-to-day management but not at board level.

Example 16.1 Management succession plan

sufficiently, so both approaches have limitations. (My own preference remains with the planning approach.)

Against a particularly fluid future, a classic continuity plan based on the most favoured scenario should be backed by a comprehensive inventory of existing managers, with comments on the extent of individual flexibility. Finally, an overview should summarize the strengths and limitations of current managers and their readiness to assume anticipated forward positions against this background. This should include specific comment on the identified high potential stream which may not feature on the major succession sheets, but which represents the major source of longer term successors. Comments should cover an assessment of the possibility of bringing forward some of these individuals to meet unplanned requirements.

The review should not concentrate solely on line and functional management, since there will be an increase in the requirements for high ability specialists through the 1990s and these individuals will form an essential part of the future organization. The supply of some of these activity, rather than people, managers may prove very difficult to meet. We need to accept that some specialists in narrow functional areas will not have careers in one company, simply because their numbers within one organization are too small to provide adequate career ladders. As some leave, their replacements will be recruited. Even so, encouraging their personal development will ensure optimum contribution while they are with us.

As the continuity process operates at every level, there is a need for an adequate two-way flow of information so that managers at the lower levels can take into account the availability of people from other areas, and the probability and timing of moves to other areas for their current people, as they carry out studies for their own levels.

Minimizing uncertainties

Situations arise where the uncertainties in the forward business scene appear to be too extensive to enable an optimum scenario to be developed. Analyses of these situations tend to show that the most serious uncertainties involve timing. There may be a recognition that a range of identified business changes are coming, but that the precise form of change is still evolving and the timing of the impact remains uncertain (within a specifiable period of, perhaps, several years).

The objective should be to pin down the anticipated changes against separate aspects of the business or against separate business units, then to develop a forward view of the most likely organization and note the variable time-scales. An assessment can be made of how this future organization might be staffed against several timetables. For example, it may be possible to prepare individuals and achieve effective staffing at a later date, but there might be difficulty if the timing were to be brought forward; or alternatively there may be people ready shortly who cannot be kept on ice for delayed introduction. The business plan, of course, will require achievable solutions for every time variant.

Succession plan impossible

If it is concluded that the degree of uncertainty in the available options makes any attempt at succession planning impossible, an emergency approach is required. From a business point of view, we have to assemble the best possible assessments of the abilities of managers to fill the range of possible future organizations, and identify any managerial limitations in these possible courses of action so that contingency plans can be prepared.

Where a number of uncertainties exist, it may be possible to match the range of management requirements as they occur in different divisions or subsidiary companies with candidate readiness from a central management inventory. Of course, the preparation of candidates would need to be more general than for a single post but this in itself is healthy and, in periods of exceptional change, may become the pattern for the future in some companies.

A variation on uncertainty, as seen by one CEO, was that, 'We simply cannot see all the things we are going to have to do.' Almost all business change, even in relatively static, slow changing industries, appears to produce new or different problems and needs from those identifiable from prior experience, and unanticipated people requirements. The visibility of these new or different needs invariably occurs at a late stage as a new situation begins to bite. Only then do the information needed to manage it and the manner of managing become evident. The required competences must then be obtained by matching those already available internally, by an unplanned transfer, or by urgent external recruitment. Hopefully, the inventory database enables us to match the need internally, and to rely on there having been sufficient broadening in the overall management development process to have developed the necessary competences to a sufficient degree.

In companies facing this degree of uncertainty, the use of quarterly reviews to update and reassess the overall deployment of the management force appears to be the most effective action. By bringing together the latest view of the short-term future, full details of each member of management and flexible minds, optimum short-term deployments can be arranged to match competence to business needs.

I suspect that, in those industries coping with the most rapid developments in their business environments during the 1990s, we shall see a considerable development in the use of management inventories as the focus of management development and succession planning. The concern will be to optimize the growth and development of all managers to the fullest extent of their potential against a wider range of possible business scenarios and less than acceptable probabilities of choice. This approach must be matched by unusually wide ranging reviews of management deployment, at more frequent intervals, as events clarify the path of environmental change.

The Inventory

Managing the inventory obviously starts with ensuring that the inventory is comprehensive. (It cannot be effective if the whole approach is to cut out administration.) The inventory of what exists will need to include data on individual competences, based on experience, skills and knowledge. Interpersonal skills are also likely to be critically important, so strengths and limitations may need to be itemized. An assessment of growth potential, with supporting evidence of the likely form and direction of that growth, will be important.

In general, it will be valuable to have an understanding of each individual's capacity to develop, to acquire new knowledge, to adjust to new situations and his ability to work at a higher level.

Some of the newer databases endeavour to profile jobs and people. The primary objective is to guide individual development to improve performance in the current role, but it is inevitable that one experiments with matching the assessed profile of an individual against the profiles built against jobs. In theory, if this can be done well, it is a good way of identifying candidates for a short list.

One example utilizes the profile building up the Hay points for jobs against evaluations of individual managers using the same criteria. I think that we should accept that this type of profiling is experimental and should be run in parallel with more traditional approaches at this stage. However, the quality of some profiling will help short-list suitable candidates for vacancies in a company operating universal and non-directed development.

A difficulty which concerns me with this approach is the realism of the profiles, because it is very hard to make these precise and sufficiently meaningful. In filling a top marketing position recently, we sought practical experience of many quite specific aspects of marketing, but we also wanted a high level of theoretical comprehension of how those aspects actually worked. The best candidate on the surface turned out to have only general understanding of principles, and was rejected in favour of an individual who had spent seven years after graduating, in two of the best companies for training in FMCG marketing. The sophisticated profiling system had been unable to differentiate the critical points. Alternatively, the ideal specification might have been met by a marketing MBA, with suitable experience. I am not sure how well profiling will segregate such candidates in future as we improve our use of competency analyses, but perhaps we shoud be satisfied if they all appear on a short list for further review.

Managing the inventory will require some process similar to the classic approach to succession, with detailed reviews at regular intervals, but with the objective of achieving the optimum deployment of available management resources at that time and for the immediate future.

This approach may lead to a greater frequency of re-assignments and require greater mobility, since changes in business emphasis and priority are considered only in the immediate sense rather than anticipated and prepared for. It appears a significantly weaker approach to management resourcing and is likely to reduce the quality of continuity. For those reasons, this approach should be considered as a back-up system while classic planning is not functioning due to the scale of change becoming so great that there is little option but to react to demand until some degree of stability is restored.

Summary

Management continuity or succession planning is an ongoing task at every level of management and is concerned with the effective resourcing and continuity of management into the future. It is an integral part of management resourcing and development strategy, and top level succession planning is the most critical management level in the review process which is at the heart of that strategy. Continuity plans tend to be recorded in detail and reviewed in depth once each year, but this is a continuous, everyday activity.

Any report of the succession situation represents a snapshot which is immediately out of date, but it enables the assumptions and scenarios towards which future appointments are being prepared, and the progress, suitability and planned preparation of designated candidates, to be challenged and monitored.

A full introduction to the plan should be prepared. It is important that succession planning should be based on the best judgements of the way the business, its environment, its culture and management organization and management competency requirements will develop over the period of the plan, so that future managers are prepared for that future. We do not want to develop cavalry colonels for a nuclear age.

Continuity involves naming the preferred candidate for each future position, plus other serious contenders. This provides the basis for their ongoing development and testing against the demands of the future positions, and does not involve making any final commitment prior to the point where a successor must be named.

Finally, an examination of the quality of the high potential stream coming through, and their ability to meet the envisaged longer term requirements of the corporation, together with a review of the whole process of management development, is properly part of any management succession review.

17
Manpower Control and Audit

Planning provides the basis for control. If we think our way systematically through all the options open to us and define a set of action plans, we should not stop there, but go on to monitor our actual progress against the plans. Every facet of the plan should be monitored, starting with the basic assumptions around which the plan is built, for if these change, the whole plan must be flexed around the revised assumptions.

If we assume that our sales volume will be 100,000 units and, subsequently, orders enable us to aim for 115,000, the manpower requirements will be affected, materials intake will be affected, and the whole plan flexed around the changed needs. Usually, a range of assumptions will change in various ways and the formal plan is only the starting point for flexing.

Further, we require a steady feedback on much of the detail in the plan. For example, we need data on the actual manpower situation, including costs, against the standards built into the plan. If the plan calls for reductions in manpower which are not being achieved, the excess costs of overmanning may imply a serious threat to the unit's ability to meet its profit objectives. This review, or audit, is a basis for controlling our progress against the plan and brings reality into what could become a theoretical study rather than a practical business plan.

All company controls should have their roots in plans, and all company plans should be checked to make sure objectives are achieved. Controls should be flexible. The basic assumptions on which the plan is based should be monitored closely. As those assumptions change, the plan will be modified for the total business, not just for a single functional element. The monitoring should then ensure that planned actions are being implemented.

Manpower Controls

Manpower control is concerned with achieving agreed manning standards across the organization. These should be:

- as built into plans and budgets;
- subsequently flexed for changes in assumptions; and
- subsequently improved by better utilization, or changed systems, etc.

This sounds simple but, as we have seen, establishing appropriate manning standards is a difficult and complex operation, and the constant fluctuation in work volumes and content, available manpower, and short-term forecasts further complicate the job. The manpower controller must constantly balance out all the pressures within the business and aim to achieve the best use of manpower. The critical single objective is to optimize utilization – to achieve the best possible productivity – because the many small changes within the business occur much too quickly for manning levels to be adjusted accordingly.

A control is required on all manpower movements if any form of manpower control is to be effective. It is not enough only to control recruitment, and leave no control on internal transfers, because this could permit manpower to build up to excessive levels in some areas by internal movement. Every single appointment should be subject to the control procedure.

The procedure required will ensure that the position is properly authorized before being filled. Even in small companies, the philosophy should be the same, and may involve the managing director asking a few blunt questions. We need to be certain that the position really exists in a defined organization; that the job is clearly defined and has a full specification; that it has been built into the current budget, or flexed budget if sales and product mix have been changed; or that there is a clear supplementary budget. (We should stress here the need to monitor the business position very closely, particularly in fast changing markets.)

These routines establish that a vacancy is legitimate, but there are further requirements. Manning standards may have been used to establish the budgeted requirement, but is the standard still valid? Is there an alternative way of getting the work done? Indeed, is the work still essential? I hold the view that checking the real need is an important step in approving a vacancy. Only when it is clearly established that the post must be filled should authorization be given.

This may sound like an extended ritual, wrapped up in red tape, and no doubt it could be. However, it can be reduced to a straightforward and automatic discipline that takes very little time, and causes delay only when the thinking has lacked clarity. It can save unnecessary appointments being made. The routine in a larger company might require collecting a series of signatures on pre-appointment documents, simply confirming that specified checks have been completed by line managers. A proportion of these should be audited.

Why make every case a subject for fresh review? The first reason is because the detailed work of almost every department changes slowly, and the filling of a new position provides an opportunity to see whether manning requirements should be updated or not. Most checks are passed very quickly, but sufficient changes are highlighted to fully justify an automatic review. Without it, I would suggest that unnecessary manpower, equivalent to 5 per cent of the total, could be absorbed into the organization annually. Look around you at some of the results.

In this process of reviewing requirements, I believe that some of the best controls exist where management of a company or division has pushed the real control on manning standards and use of manpower back down to the supervisors, and at the same time encouraged them to make use of the basic data already at their fingertips to watch their manpower productivity.

A supervisor, given a moderate degree of guidance, can establish the factors of loading which influence his manpower requirements. If a supervisor is involved in determining how best to use his manpower and in determining at what point some change in the level of manning is necessary, and if his decisions and judgements are accepted, he becomes personally committed to making manning standards generally tighter than any which might be imposed. Management confidence builds up on the evidence of supervisor-controlled weekly graphs of manpower utilization, showing patterns of achieved improvements.

Control needs to cover every manpower movement; all appointments, internal and external, including all transfers and all recruitment; all temporary or agency employees; and even all job and grade changes. After all, a grade change can mean a 10 to 20 per cent increase in pay levels for people affected. Manning standards should include statements of the grade levels since one objective of a manpower control system is cost control.

Who should control manpower? The short and obvious answer is that it should be the chief executive but, in a large organization, the responsibility has to be delegated. In theory, the logical direction for delegation is to personnel, the function which deals with manpower. Sometimes this will work, but a conflict of interests is likely to develop. The personnel function has responsibilities for employees and their welfare, and for industrial relations negotiations. Close awareness and involvement in the business itself, and the manpower requirement is, curiously, seen as a conflicting interest and some personnel departments are not geared to manage an effective manpower planning and control function. However, I believe it is essential that personnel staff should be commercially involved rather than commercially naive.

Manpower Audit

Physical control against standards and plans really needs a further activity which asks 'How do we know that the system has been working as we planned, and that our plans have been properly implemented?'

We need feedback on what has actually happened, and we need to audit how it happened. Let us look at some of the possibilities.

Audit of manpower requirements   With all the care that should go into manpower control, how many appointments slip through the net, and in what circumstances? The audit should check through a selected batch of personnel records and identify the approval of each recorded change. This may reveal that some categories of transfer tend not to be covered by approvals and indicate a major hole in the control system.

A second check would be of departmental records of who is employed and what they do against personnel or payroll records. Sometimes there are differences because local managers do things to get round paperwork. A favourite form of correction is to produce wage and salary review sheets incorporating all the implemented but unofficial changes.

The third check is for agency or temporary employees, who are sometimes used to pad out manning levels without proper approvals or recognized needs. I know of a division that uncovered Bill and Ben, two agency employees who had come in 13 years earlier, and were never recognized as part of the head count until a detailed audit was carried out. Almost all audits of the use of temporary and contract staff lead to immediate savings.

Audit of manning against manning standards   When manning standards are revised, it may be appropriate to retain a few existing people who are identified as excess to the new standards. Over a period of a few months, natural wastage and transfers will remove the problem and questions of forced transfers are avoided.

Unfortunately, a few managers and supervisors are exceptionally able at maintaining their over-strength, somehow managing to get replacements even when someone does transfer or leave. It is these situations that the audit should identify. There may be a need to confirm that the standards are correct, but then positive efforts must be made to get the actual manning into line with standards, and the department or the manager should be earmarked for close control in future. Manpower controllers get to know the empire builders quickly.

Where a major cut-back is being played in low key, it may be appropriate to give up to a year for actual manning to drop to the new level without enforced wastage. However, we should expect to see some progress towards the new levels and should audit at least quarterly for evidence of intent.

Audit of manpower utilization   At any one time, there are a number of manpower categories in short supply, either locally or nationally, which affect the operation of the company. An audit is necessary to examine how well we are using our existing employees in the skill categories concerned.

I am assuming that all of the obvious things within the present structure and systems have been done, and that utilization looks – on the surface – to be good. The audit should take the form of a study to see whether some fundamental change, such as restructuring of work, is achievable, because such a move may completely relieve a skills shortage.

Although the pressure to improve utilization is particularly strong at times of shortage, audits of utilization should be encouraged wherever there is a feeling that standards fall short of what might be achievable, or where employees are leaving the company because they feel underemployed.

Audit of manning systems Where any system has been in use for a number of years, examine it to ensure that it is meeting the requirements, and that there are no unnecessary or unused statistics, tabulations, reports, or forms of any sort. The requirements from manning systems evolve continuously. Regular attention to systems can identify some activities can be discontinued or reduced in frequency, or enable fresh demands to be met.

Slippage in potential manning standards due to sloppy administration or lack of audit can provide a major loophole for rising manpower expense. The concept of a field analyst in a large company, constantly out in the subsidiaries and divisions to audit manning standards, is a good one. It is a job for a high calibre analyst and excellent for developing an appreciation of the total, detailed operation of the organization, and will probably change hands every two years.

Audit of recruitment, training and development actions One of the most critical failures of some manpower planning programmes has been due to the way that training and development programmes have been planned but not implemented. I find it astonishing that this should happen as frequently as it does.

Senior managers today are very busy people. They have to determine their priorities and allocate time to the most important issues, delegating less important work, but checking to see it is done. Too often, the implementation stages of manpower supply planning get lost in this maze, and its potential impact on the business goes unrecognized.

In general, senior managers are recognizing the critical importance of people to a much greater extent, rather than just paying lip service. The result is that planned developmental and other supply actions are higher on priority lists, are owned more by managers, and are getting done. Equally, where this is not happening, manpower problems are becoming more serious.

References and Further Reading

Bennion, M. and Casson, J. 1984: *The Manpower Planning Handbook*. McGraw-Hill.

Drucker, P. F. 1988: The Creating of the New Organization. *Harvard Business Review*, January/February.

McBeath, G. 1990: *Practical Management Development*. Oxford: Basil Blackwell.

Manzini, A. D. and Gridley, J. D. 1986: *Integrating Human Resources and Strategic Business Planning*. American Management Association.

Margulies, N. and Raia, A. 1972: *Organization Development*. New York: McGraw-Hill.

Naisbitt, J. and Aburdene, P. 1990: *Megatrends 2000*. Sidgwick and Jackson.

Patten, T. H. jr and Vaill, P. B. 1976: Organization Development. In R. L. Craig (ed.), *Training and Development Handbook*, New York: McGraw-Hill.

Quinn Mills, D. 1985: Planning with People in Mind. *Harvard Business Review*, July/August.

Revans, R. W. 1983: *ABC of Action Learning*. Bromley: Chartwell Bratt.

Richards-Carpenter, C. 1986: Manpower Models for CPIS Users. *Personnel Management*. February.

Roger, Alec 1963: *Handbook of Human Resource Planning: Practical Manpower Analysis Techniques for Human Resource Professionals*. National Institute of Industrial Psychology.

Schein, E. H. 1985: *Organization Culture and Leadership*. San Francisco: Jossey-Bass.

Sidney, E. (ed.) 1988: *Management Recruitment*. Gower.

Stemp, P. 1988: *Are You Managing?* London: The Industrial Society.

Stewart, V. and Stewart, A. 1979: *Managing the Manager's Growth*. Gower.

Vancil, R. F. 1987: *Passing the Baton: Managing the Process of CEO Succession*. Harvard Business Review Press.

Waterman, R. H. 1988: *The Renewal Factor*. Bantam Press.

Index